Introductory Papers on
DANTE

By the same author

★

DOROTHY L. SAYERS

Introductory Papers on
DANTE

with a preface by
BARBARA REYNOLDS
Lecturer in Italian in the University of Cambridge

Poiche di riguardar pasciuto fui,
tutto m'offersi pronto al suo servigio,
con l'affermar che fa credere altrui.
Purg. xxvi. 103–105.

Wipf & Stock
PUBLISHERS
Eugene, Oregon

Wipf and Stock Publishers
199 W 8th Ave, Suite 3
Eugene, OR 97401

Introductory Papers on Dante
By Sayers, Dorothy L.
Copyright©1954 The Estate of Anthony Fleming
c/o Watkins Loomis Agency acting in association with
David Higham Associates
ISBN: 1-59752-491-3
Publication date 1/1/2006
Previously published by Methuen & Co., 1954

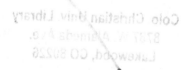

Errata

Dorothy L. Sayers, *Introductory Papers on Dante*

p. 1, para 2, last words, lines 5 and 6: "so" and "of" should be transposed

p. 6, footnote, line 1: "on" should read "in"

p. 16, lines 1, 5: "Diomede" should read "Diomed"

p. 17, line 10 from end: "COGNOSCER" should read "CONOSCER"

p.34, lines 12-13 from end: "*gaietta pella*" should read "*gaetta pelle*"

p.37, Italian quotation: "*perpetualemente*" should read "*perpetuamente*"

p.40, 10 lines from end: transpose "mother" and "father"

p.53, footnote: insert superscript "1"

p. 54, line 7: "*Seraphin*" should read "*Serafin*"

p. 56, footnote: insert superscript "4"

p. 77, footnote: "*for*" should read "*from*"

p. 82, first Italian quotation: "*si*" should read "*sì*"

p. 89, line 4: "*voluntà*" should read "*volontà*"

p. 91, Italian quotation, line 5: "*moi*" should read "*noi*"

p. 94, line 9: "bird's" should read "birds'"

p.105, 3 lines from end: "quattrocento" should read "trecento"

p.114, 9 lines from end: "redintegration" should read "reintegration"

p. 157, lines 5 – 6: "*si*" should read "*sì*"; "*fiòco*" should read "*fioco*"

p. 163, Italian quotation, line 1: "*guarder*" should read "*gaurder*"

p. 164, line 15: omit comma after "*se*"

p. 168, line 9: "*basso voglio*" should read "*bassa voglia*"

p. 169, Italian quotation, line 3: "*ti*" should read "*tu*"

p. 171, Italian quotation, line 4: "*si*" should read "*sì*"

p. 172, Latin quotation, first word: "*ecee*" should read "*ecce*"

p. 186, 3 lines from end: "*piu*" should read "*più*"

p.200, line 14: "Vedeva" should read "Vede"

p. 201, line 3: "*finefur*" should read "*fine fuor*"

p. 201, 2 lines from end: "*silogizzò*" should read "*sillogizzò*"

p. 202, 7 lines from end, Italian quotation: should read "*che 'l gran comento feo*"

p. 202, footnote: note "44" should read "144"

Series Foreword

It is now sixty years since Dorothy L. Sayers gave her first lecture on Dante. Few people were then aware of her new interest and the audience of three hundred who attended the Summer School of Italian at Jesus College, Cambridge, in August 1946 did not know what to expect. They were attracted by her fame as a detective novelist and as the author of the radio plays on the life of Christ, *The Man Born to be King*.

She had been drawn to Dante by Charles Williams, whose book *The Figure of Beatrice* appeared in 1943. A year went by before she acted on her resolve to read the *Commedia* right through and when she did the whole direction of her work was changed. At the same time, it fulfilled and completed all that she had done. I have told the story of her discovery of Dante in my book *The Passionate Intellect: Dorothy L. Sayers' Encounter with Dante*, of which a second edition has now been made available by the present publishers.

Her first lecture, entitled "The Eighth Bolgia," was a highlight. It led to a series of lectures, given mainly to subsequent summer schools. They were published in two volumes, *Introductory Papers on Dante* and *Further Papers on Dante*, and, posthumously, in *The Poetry of Search and the Poetry of Statement*, which contains lectures on several other subjects besides Dante. All three have long been out of print and in demand. It is with great pleasure that I welcome their reprint.

It should be remembered that these lectures were written during and immediately after World War II, at a time when the collapse of European civilization was imminent. Dante's message concerning sin and virtue seemed, to Dorothy Sayers, startlingly relevant to the current situation and she made it part of her war work to explain and interpret it from this point of view.

The first volume contains the most profound of her lectures. They also show the extent to which she felt she could rely on an audience to follow her argument, a situation that has changed in the ensuing sixty years. The most challenging is "The City of Dis," a lecture written for a group of mature undergraduates, recently returned to academic work after their experience of war. They knew the realities of evil and the state of the world and were a particularly responsive audience. So were the civilians who listened to her explanations of the Christian truths she perceived in Dante's allegory as well as the public who bought her translation, *Hell*, one of the early Penguin Classics.

The second volume, *Further Papers on Dante*, is more literary in quality and represents her talent as an entertainer. It contains the first lecture, "The Eighth Bolgia," on the subject of the famous canto concerning Ulysses and offers for the first time a solution to a mystery that had not been solved for six and a half centuries. The volume also contains the contribution she had previously made to *Essays Presented to Charles Williams*, in which her appreciation of Dante's talent as a storyteller is vividly presented.

The third volume, *The Poetry of Search and the Poetry of Statement*, was published after Sayers' death. It contains three lectures on Dante, one of which, "The Beatrician Vision in Dante and Other Poets," indicates the direction her work would have taken had she lived. She was convinced that Dante's vision had been shared by many poets before and after him and she was planning to write a work entitled "The Burning Bush" to show his connection with the mystic tradition.

In "The Meaning of Purgatory," one of the lectures contained in the first volume, Dorothy L. Sayers wrote:

> To appreciate Dante it is not, of course, necessary to believe what he believed, but it is, I think, necessary to *understand* what he believed, and to realise that it is a belief which a mature mind can take seriously.

The vibrant voice that first communicated these lectures has long been silent but the children, grandchildren, and great-grandchildren of the generations that first heard them now have the opportunity of reading them. They will discover that their relevance to the modern world has not diminished.

Barbara Reynolds
Cambridge 2006

To
the Organisers and Students of
the Summer Schools arranged by the
Society for Italian Studies,
who so kindly encouraged me
to talk to them about
Dante

PREFACE

THIS book on Dante by Dorothy L. Sayers makes possible a new relationship between Dante and the modern reader. With the gradual decline of interest in Italian literature which has characterised cultural life in this country during the present century, to read Dante has come more and more to be regarded as an enterprise best left to the professional scholar. The amateur reader (who reads for pleasure rather than for profit), though confident of his ability, and his right, to derive enjoyment from other, equally difficult, masterpieces of European literature, has surrendered his birth-right with regard to the *Divina Commedia*, at least as far as the whole work is concerned. Certain well-known passages, chiefly from the *Inferno*, still have the power to speak directly to him, but to venture beyond these is to court the uneasy self-consciousness that comes of trespassing on academic preserves. In order to compensate for this, the modern reader tends to create, as others have created before him, a phantasy Dante, a kind of mediaeval bogey, grotesque, of the dark ages, unprogressive, irrelevant to the world of to-day; or else a mystical, disembodied visionary, out of touch with reality, a head-in-the-clouds poet, impractical, unintelligible to ordinary men. None of this need have occurred. There has been no such surrender, for instance, of Shakespeare, Racine, Goethe or Cervantes. In respect of these and other major writers of our heritage, scholars and amateurs have found a companionable and often mutually stimulating *modus vivendi*. Yet the thing has happened: a poet who wrote for ordinary men and women has been relinquished by them to the learned, for whom he did not write. From this "seconda morte" erudition cannot resurrect him. Only other writers, with their creative powers of insight, imagination and interpretation, can now restore the lost relationship. A fortunate beginning was made some time ago by Mr. T. S. Eliot who re-discovered in Dante a poet's poet. More recently, the late Charles Williams revealed to modern mystics the still vital essence of the mystical content; and now Dr. Sayers, who is both a trained scholar and a creative artist, brings her vitalising powers to the task of reviving before our eyes the living Dante, not the

vii

biographer's Dante, but the poet alive in his writing, "vivus per ora virum".

"Dante wrote to be read by the common man and woman": this is the first and perhaps most important of the many home-truths which Miss Sayers startles us into remembering. It is of course perfectly true. Had Dante intended otherwise, he would have written in Latin. He wished particularly to reach those who had never had leisure enough to learn Latin or to attend a regular University course. This does not mean that he was a "popular" writer, but simply that he wrote for a public wider than the academic circle. His demands on his readers are high but they are not exclusively erudite demands. He assumes that they are well-read (they must certainly know their Virgil), of lively but adult mind, and actively experienced in life. Naturally, there were the intimate friends, the fellow-writers, that inner circle of elect to whom, or to whose memory, any poet secretly addresses himself and whose response he inwardly conjures as he writes. There were also those for whom the political message of the work was directly intended, the temporal and spiritual rulers of the world. Nevertheless, the main impact of the *Divina Commedia* was aimed at humanity itself. As poet, narrator, artist, delineator of character, visionary, moralist, he relied on a participation of which the majority, rather than a select minority, were capable. What concerns us now is whether the qualities of mind and soul which Dante assumed in his readers are permanent, basic qualities, still to be assumed in us, and, consequently, whether the communication which he sought to achieve can be re-established today. Because she believes that this is in fact the case, Miss Sayers has set herself to provide us with means of renewing our approach to Dante, both by her translation of the *Commedia* and by the publication of these papers.

Dante is not a "popular" writer and this is not a "popular" book about Dante; that is to say, neither Dante nor Miss Sayers deceives us into believing that difficult things are easy to understand. Anyone capable of fundamental emotions such as anger, sorrow, terror, awe, pity, love is also capable of responding to the *Commedia* in certain of its aspects; but only the reader who is able and willing to make a great deal of mental and spiritual effort can come anywhere near appreciating the work as a whole. Miss Sayers does not ignore or under-estimate the difficulties:

what she does is to remove one by one various obstacles which prevent us from confronting the difficulties as they really are. The zest with which she performs this service is so invigorating that even the most apathetic are likely to be stirred into taking some trouble on their own account. To be guided by Miss Sayers along the intricacies of simile, metaphor and allegory or to watch the tangle of literal, allegorical, moral and anagogical significance resolve under her clarifying analysis is an exciting and absorbing experience. The breadth and power of her interpretation of Dante's thought and the vividness of her appreciation of his art so enlarge and enliven the mind that the reader (and the listener, as those who were privileged to hear these papers delivered as lectures can testify) finds himself scaling height after height. In her capacity for communicating mental exhilaration Miss Sayers is unequalled.

The clarification and encouragement offered by this book are, however, subsidiary to its main purpose. Having enabled the modern reader to make a fresh start with reading the *Commedia*, Miss Sayers then challenges him to accept its message:

> The thing that the modern reader and critic find so difficult, when confronted by a great poet, is to accept him. To realise what he is saying, to believe that he means what he says, to admit that what he says matters—all this is disquieting. It is more comfortable to explain him away, with his meaning and his greatness and his power. Despite all our surface liking for toughness and violence, ours is a timid generation, wincing at decision and envious of other men's conclusions.

Like Dante, Miss Sayers does not pull her punches.

Cambridge
June 1953

CONTENTS

The City of Dis was originally written for the Confraternitas Historica, Sidney Sussex College, Cambridge.

INTRODUCTION

As for the vast literature on Dante, I cannot think of it without experiencing a kind of dizziness. One cannot open an Italian review without saying to one's self: "Another book, another article that I ought to have read before expressing my opinion on this question!"

Etienne Gilson: *Dante the Philosopher.*

Entia non sunt multiplicanda praeter necessitatem.

William of Ockham.

Ad modum loquendi, remissus est modus et humilis, quia locutio vulgaris, in quâ et mulierculae communicant.

Dante Alighieri: *Epistle to Can Grande.*

Great poets mean what they say.

J. Middleton Murry: *Keats and Shakespeare.*

THESE papers were read over a series of years to various audiences, consisting for the most part of students and other persons who were not Dante specialists. I have not attempted to remove all traces of the speaking voice, nor yet those repetitions of key-passages and basic principles which are inevitable when a lecturer has to begin each time, as it were "from scratch", with a number of new listeners. Here and there I have expanded passages which my time-limit had compelled me to compress unduly, or added footnotes to elucidate a point more fully. The papers are arranged in logical, rather than chronological order; but I have appended to each the date when it was first delivered.

Dante-scholarship has by now reached so advanced a stage of complication that M. Gilson's *cri du cœur* quoted above finds an echo in the heart of everyone who is called upon to speak or write on the subject. To ignore the work of innumerable conflicting authorities is to expose one's self to the imputation of ignorance and presumption; to take them all into account (supposing one could possibly do so) is to bury Dante and his poem under a cairn so heavy that nothing can issue from it except the faint voice of his protesting ghost. Yet Dante wrote to be read by the common man and woman, and to distribute the bread of angels among those who had no leisure to be learned.

What is needed, I think, for the ordinary reader is a few sign-posts to the obvious to guide him through this wood where the *diritta via* is so liable to be smothered by the brambles of controversy. It is the obvious which very often gets overlooked by contemporary criticism, whose hypertrophied historical sense and obsession with the psychology of the unconscious seem to compel it to thrust aside the poet's own account of himself and the avowed intention of his work, in a frenzied search for the "real" man and the "real" meaning supposed to underlie them. Almost alone among the strife of tongues, Mr. Middleton Murry, in a phrase of trumpet-like clarity, has summoned us to believe that "great poets mean what they say". And it is Dante himself who has set up the necessary sign-posts, in that *Epistle to Can Grande* which is now almost unanimously accepted as his and (oddly enough) almost unanimously ignored by his interpreters.

He says there (1) that the *Divine Comedy* is an allegory. This, in a day when the technique of writing and reading allegory have been largely lost, makes it advisable to examine the nature of allegory in general, and also Dante's characteristic use of natural symbol and imagery, in place of the conventional personified abstractions which we have come to expect.

(2) Secondly; he says that this allegory is to be interpreted throughout at four levels: literal, political, moral, and mystical. I have accordingly tried to disentangle the four strands of interpretation and to keep them distinct.

(3) He says further that the *literal* signification (only) is concerned with the state of souls after death. Since people can be interested in Dante without being instructed Catholics, a brief summary of the Catholic doctrine of Hell, Purgatory, and Paradise seemed useful for the avoidance of confusion and misunderstanding.

(4) Fourthly; Dante says that the *allegorical* (i.e. the real and important) signification is concerned throughout with the behaviour of man in *this* life, "according as by good or ill deserving in the exercise of his free will he becomes liable to punishing or rewarding justice". I have therefore tried to show how the great poem "to which heaven and earth have set hand" is relevant, not merely to fourteenth-century man, but to twentieth-century man, and indeed to man in all ages and all places.

These four principles, laid down by the poet, seem to me to be indispensable to any intelligent or enjoyable reading of the *Comedy*, and I have kept them in mind continually. Dante is a difficult poet, in the sense that he deals with a great subject which is not to be mastered without thought, but he is not a wilfully obscure poet. When once we have grasped the assumptions from which he starts and the technical vocabulary which he uses, he is for the most part lucid as the day. He uses no "private" imagery and preaches no esoteric doctrine; his poem is as public and universal as the Christian Faith itself.

One image, although not private, is a personal one, and that is the master-image of Beatrice, which he himself made public in the *Vita Nuova*. His life and work are centred in that overwhelming personal experience by which the Love that made and moves the worlds was mediated to him through the grace and beauty of an actual living woman. All attempts to deny the reality of that experience (and there have been many) plunge the interpretation of the *Comedy* into a welter of chaos and contradiction: but when that reality is accepted, everything else falls into place and the whole great Christian structure locks together in a single sacramental unity. In the light of the Beatrician vision the poem is seen for what it is; the experiential living of a faith, on every level of experience.

The bar to which the critical interpretation of a major work has to be brought is in the long run that of consistency. Any thesis is suspect if in the working-out it piles hypothesis upon hypothesis, qualification upon qualification, or if it obliges us to accuse the poet of incoherence, self-contradiction and stupidity. "Great poets mean what they say". If (like the Croceans) we dismiss the allegory as irrelevant, we disintegrate the poem into a jumble of picturesque episodes and detached discourses and seek in vain for the "poetic unity" which was rejected in the framing of our postulates. If we disregard the doctrine on which the literal meaning is based, we shall see no more in Dante than did Horace Walpole, when he called him "extravagant, absurd, disgusting, in short a Methodist parson in Bedlam". If we confuse the four levels of interpretation we shall conclude, with Professor Whitfield,[1] that Dante jettisoned his whole theme in the course of his poem and was too shallow-pated even to notice what he was doing. If we do not take seriously the universal relevance of Dante's message, we shall land ourselves, like too many critics of the "historical" school, with a dead poet and a dead poem, mere laboratory specimens for antiquarian research. And if we deny the image of the living Beatrice, we shall be off with old Gabriele Rossetti along the dreary path of numerology and cryptogram, to end up with a gnostic or atheist Dante laboriously confuting in an undecipherable code the very truths which he is openly asserting with the whole power of his poetry.

---

[1] J. H. Whitfield: *Dante and Virgil* (Blackwell, 1949).

There are, of course, periodic fashions in Dante-criticism; at any given moment, the "real" meaning which we seek to separate out from Dante's universal complex is the projection upon his work of our own immediate preoccupations. We can see the emergence of these fluctuating emphases by the history of Dante-appreciation in our own country. During the slow re-birth of awareness which took place from the eighteenth century on, we find little attention paid to anything but the literal signification of the poem and the poetic presentation of this odd "Gothic fable". Then comes the devoted pioneer spade-work of the great textual critics of the nineteenth century (Moore, Paget Toynbee and others), together with an earnest concentration upon the moral signification. The doctrinal structure of the poem is taken seriously by men like Wicksteed, Oelsner, Carroll, and Warren Vernon, the development coinciding and expanding alongside of the Tractarian and Oxford Movements, and the re-discovery of Thomist theology. Overlapping this, in the fin-de-siècle mood, is the Romantic Revival, with the Pre-Raphaelite stress laid upon the *Vita Nuova* and the Beatrician image of love. This, because it had no theological roots and opened no window upon the intellectual light of the *Commedia*,[1] evaporated into eclecticism and sterility, so that during the first half of the present century we get a lull in interest, coinciding with that critical demand for "pure poetry" to which Dante's intellectually integrated poetical structure offers so four-square a resistance. Of late, the troubles of two wars and the world-wide upheaving of social foundations have ushered in a corresponding preoccupation with Dante's philosophy of the active life and his doctrine of Empire; Bruno Nardi in Italy, Etienne Gilson in France, and, recently, Professor d'Entrèves in England concern themselves vigorously with the political signification, and attention is focused upon Virgil and "my Lady Philosophy". Latest of all, in his book *The Figure of Beatrice*, Charles Williams initiated what is likely to prove the next great movement in Dantism—an exploration of the long-neglected mystical signification.

I have seen it suggested that this new concern with the mystical is merely a return to nineteenth-century romanticism and the cult of the Blessed Damosel. That is a considerable under-statement. Williams is harking back, not sixty years but six hundred: the mystical interpretation derives not from Dante Gabriel Rossetti but from Dante Alighieri.

[1] See Nicolette Gray's pregnant little study: *Rossetti, Dante and Ourselves* (Faber, 1947).

"The fourth sense is called anagogical"—it is concerned, that is, with what the Middle Ages called "contemplation" and we call "mysticism". This level of interpretation has hitherto been left almost unexamined, and that for two chief reasons. First, the average literary critic, like the average man in the street, has only the vaguest notion of what mysticism means, usually confusing it with romantic nostalgia, mystification or cryptography. Secondly, the mystical theologians have, from the sixteenth century onwards, applied themselves almost exclusively to mapping out the Way of Negation. Indeed, those who know anything about the mystical way at all tend, both explicitly and implicitly, to identify it with the Negative Way. Dante's, however, is the Affirmative Way, and although Edmund Gardner—almost the only pre-Williams critic in this country to consider the *Commedia* at the mystical level—made a gallant effort to bring it into relationship with the traditional lay-out of the Way of Negation, the stages do not really coincide, and the result is only partially satisfactory. But until the anagogical level has been given due and full consideration, the interpretation of the *Commedia* cannot be made solid or complete.

A great work of art has vitality for us only when it speaks to our condition. When, for any reason, we step out of the scope of its relevance, it seems to retire from us like the tide, and we are left stranded amid the backwash and detritus left by the last great wave of critical enthusiasm. During such periods of ebb much valuable research can still be carried on, but the power of the work is, as it were, withdrawn, awaiting a new turn of events or a new interpretative insight. The work itself is either treated with a reactionary contempt, or accorded a mere formal recognition. Voltaire, in 1756, wrote: "Vous voulez connaître le Dante. Les Italiens l'appellent *divin*: mais c'est une divinité cachée; peu de gens entendent ses oracles: il a des commentateurs, c'est peut-être encore une raison de plus pour n'être pas compris. Sa réputation s'affirmera toujours, parce qu'on ne le lit guère." Ironically enough, the following century was to see all Europe reading Dante as it had never read him before. There is no moral, except that one should be careful how one tries to be funny.

History has her own technique for cheating the prophet and confounding the cleverness of the clever. The cultivation of the "historical sense" is, from one point of view, a defensive mechanism devised by critics to keep on the right side of history and prevent her from thus turning time's tables upon them. A sense of history is, of course, an asset, so long as it shows us men of like passions with ourselves, situated in a particular environment, and ordering their behaviour by certain conventions and assumptions. It is fatal to both understanding and enjoyment if it shows us men wholly alien to ourselves, the mere creatures and puppets of an environment. Strictly speaking, no one has any business to write about the Middle Ages unless he can, without strain, without sense of incongruity, and without book, think in the mediaeval idiom and interpret his own daily behaviour in mediaeval terms. In other words, the critic must establish with his subject an I-Thou, rather than a We-They relationship. This is perhaps a counsel of perfection, although thinking in the idiom of another age is in fact not much harder to learn than thinking in a foreign language. Both disciplines do, however, call for an elementary acquaintance with the grammar. That is why, in these introductory papers, so much space is given to the consideration of mediaeval allegory, philosophy, and theology, as distinct from the appreciation of Dante's poetry as such. When all is said and done, Dante is not primarily a theologian, politician, or philosopher; he is a poet. But it is difficult to surrender our wills to the poetry, if all the time our minds are worrying over problems of interpretation, or shying at theological bogeys which have no real existence. The clearing away of a few hurdles which time and change have interposed between us and the true aim and meaning of the *Commedia* is not the same thing as critical appreciation and enjoyment—it only opens up the way to delight and makes appreciation possible.

The thing that the modern reader and critic find so difficult, when confronted by a great poet, is to accept him. To realise what he is saying, to believe that he means what he says, to admit that what he says matters—all this is disquieting. It is more comfortable to explain him away, with his meaning and his greatness and his power. Despite all our surface liking for toughness and violence, ours is a timid generation, wincing at decision and envious of other men's conclusions.

> *Ed egli a mei, come persona accorta:*
> *"Qui si convien lasciare ogni sospetto;*
> *ogni viltà convien che qui sia morta.*
>
> *Noi siam venuti al luogo ov'io t'ho detto*
> *che tu vedrai le genti dolorose,*
> *ch'hanno perduto il ben dell'intelletto."*

E poichè la sua mano alla mia pose,
con lieto volto, ond'io mi confortai,
mi mise dentro alle segrete cose.[1]

---

[1] And like a man of quick discernment: "Here
Lay down all thy distrust," said he, "reject
Dead from within thee every coward fear;

We've reached the place I told thee to expect,
Where thou shouldst see the miserable race,
Those who have lost the good of intellect."

He laid his hand on mine, and with a face
So joyous that it comforted my quailing,
Into the hidden things he led my ways.
Inf. iii. 13–21.

DANTE'S IMAGERY: I. SYMBOLIC

THE poetic image, says Mr. Cecil Day Lewis, is "in its simplest terms
. . . a picture made out of words".[1] Much of Dante's imagery can be
discussed in terms just as simple as that. For a great part of his poetic
strength lies in his power of using words to make a visual picture, so
that it is as though we had seen with our eyes the things he describes—
things, it may be, familiar as a snail on the garden path, but which,
until he painted them for us, we had "passed perhaps a hundred times
nor cared to see"; or, it may be, things that no mortal eye has ever
seen—the "baked" skin of the sinners running under the fiery rain
on the burning sand of Hell: the reedy shores about Mount Purgatory
with the sea shimmering in the dawnlight and the ship of souls glowing
towards us from the far horizon, "like Mars through thick vapour":
or the mystic rose of Paradise, shining up, rank over rank of the blessed,
in that strange light which is the glory of God reflected from the surface
of the Primum Mobile.

But my present purpose is to essay the more complex task of examin-
ing the symbols in the imagery—the meaning and content of the
pictures. And here, perhaps, the twentieth-century reader experiences
a certain difficulty. He is apt to shy a little at the words "meaning" and
"content". For we have fallen into a habit of distrusting any work so
art whose foundation is consciously intellectual. As in the making, of
also in the reading of a modern poem, the pictures that come floating
up out of the dark sea of the unconscious link themselves together into
an associative pattern, until gradually, some kind of significance seems
to emerge. But to strip off the imagery and present the naked intellectual content is next door to impossible, for the images *are* the content,
and the significance scarcely exists apart from them.

Now, when we turn back to the mediaeval allegorists, we shall be
disappointed if we begin by expecting their poetry to be of this kind.
Dante, when writing the *Vita Nuova*, said explicitly: "Deep shame it
were to him who should rhyme under cover of a figure or of a rhetorical
colour—*sotto veste di figura o di colore rettorico*—and, afterwards,
being asked, knew not how to strip such vesture from his words, in

---

[1] C. Day Lewis: *The Poetic Image* (Cape, 1947), p. 18.

I

such wise that they should have a real meaning." For him, the conscious and intellectual significance exists in its own right, and is the function for which the imagery exists. But to the modern reader, accustomed to the new kind of poetry with its rich tangle of associative images, suggesting far more than can be consciously defined, this kind of poetry in which the imagery is only a handmaid to, or adornment of, what one might call the dogmatic content, is apt to appear thin, impoverished and artificial: and it is because of this, I think, that the first impression left by the *Commedia* is often one of dryness, bareness, abruptness and perhaps of a cold didacticism.

In dealing briefly with this matter I have, of course, simplified and exaggerated. There is plenty of modern poetry which is consciously didactic in the ancient or classical manner; and (since no poet ever really works to the poetic theory he lays down, but writes as his imagination leads him and concocts the theory afterwards) there is also plenty of ancient poetry in which modern critical methods can clearly trace the subconscious association of images. But, roughly speaking, there is this difference of emphasis between the two kinds of poetry. It is very well brought out and illustrated in Mr. Day Lewis's book which I have already quoted—*The Poetic Image*.

Now, it is a great obstacle in the way of appreciating the poetry of another age or "mental climate" if we approach it with our minds full of pre-suppositions about what we think it ought to be like. This assumption that our own habits of thinking and speaking are the only right and satisfactory ones is responsible for a great deal of the foolish and "debunking" criticism of great writers from which we have been suffering of late years.

I cannot say too often or too strongly how necessary it is to find out what a poet actually said, if we are to enjoy his work and understand it: and we can never find out what he said if our minds are cluttered up with ideas about what we think we should have put into the poem if we had written it ourselves. We shall be looking for things that are not there; and, failing to find them, we shall conclude that the poem is empty. The things that are there, we shall never see at all, because the mental eye has a sad tendency to see only what it is looking for.

We may perhaps illustrate this from the difference between the mediaeval attitude and our own to that mysterious realm of interior chaos which we call the Unconscious. Recent psychological research, together with a number of other contributory factors, has influenced us to emphasise—possibly to over-emphasise—the importance of the unconscious in determining our actions and opinions. Our confidence in such faculties as will and judgment has been undermined, and in collapsing has taken with it a good deal of our interest in ourselves as responsible individuals. We tend to see ourselves as kaleidoscopic patterns shaken together by the play of unconscious impulses, much as the pattern of modern poetry is formed out of the association of unconscious imagery; and that is the reason why that kind of poetry expresses us to ourselves. Now, mediaeval people knew about the unconscious all right—they were not so stupid or so unobservant as not to be aware of its existence. But they were not greatly interested to explore it. They were, of course, greatly interested in some of its manifestations —dreams, for example; but their method of interpreting dreams was, to our minds, faulty and unscientific. Their attention was not turned to the unconscious: it was almost wholly occupied by their absorbed interest in something different: and, as Dante truly points out, when your whole attention is focused on one thing, you become deaf and blind to everything else.[1]

Let us look at Virgil's great discourse on Love in the 18th canto of the *Purgatorio*. He speaks there of those "first cognitions"—the *prime notizie*—and the "inclination to the prime objects of appetite—*de' primi appetibili l'affetto*"—which are, he says, in every creature that is conjoined with material substance, "even as the instinct in bees to make honey". These instinctive awarenesses and impulses, making up what he calls the "prime will"—the *prima voglia*—are morally neutral, neither good nor bad in themselves. They simply are; nobody knows where they come from; the plants and beasts, he implies, are governed by them, meriting neither praise nor blame. But man, he thinks, has something else:

"In order that to this will every other may be related"—in order, that is, that the conscious mind may co-ordinate its desires and keep them natural and innocent—"innate with *you* is the virtue which gives counsel, and ought to guard the threshold of assent"—"*la virtù che consiglia, e dell' assenso de' tener la soglia*". "The threshold of assent" and the "guardian of the threshold"—these seem rather familiar terms. Possibly we thought that the censor and the threshold were discovered or invented by nineteenth-century psychologists; but we see they were not. This, then, is the point at which the mediaeval psychologist really sits up and takes notice. He is interested, not so much in what comes up out of the unconscious as in the crossing of the threshold—in what

[1] *Purgatorio* iv. 1–12.

happens to that undifferentiated "prime will", which is common to plants and animals and men, when it meets the guardian and is either rejected or else translated into action by the assent of the will.

Personally, I am inclined to agree that this is still a question of absorbing interest, practically as well as theoretically, and I sometimes wonder whether, in our anxious plumbing of the unconscious, we are not a little apt to lose sight of this exciting drama which plays itself out on the threshold. I remember, years ago, being engaged in correspondence with a young man who was extremely enthusiastic about the psychology of the unconscious, and who insisted that the urge which issued in the writing of a story about a murder and the urge which issued in the committing of a murder were one and the same urge, with no difference between them. I was writing murder-stories at the time and may have been prejudiced, but I objected that it did seem to me as though there must be a slight difference of some kind somewhere, since the results were so different. I added that society in general must be aware of the difference, since it rewarded the one result with royalties and the other with the gallows.

It is precisely on this difference—on the point at which conscious choice is exercised upon the undifferentiated subliminal urges—that the attention of the mediaeval thinker was riveted. The *Divine Comedy* is an allegory about that choice. The whole poem is one gigantic composite image in which this drama of the threshold is presented to us by means of a series of word-pictures which, locking together, make up the pattern of the soul's choice.

We will now look for a moment at that word "allegory". Allegory is a literary form which has been out of favour for so long that we have almost forgotten how to write or read it: but in the fourteenth century it was so natural for writers to cast their ideas into this kind of pictorial shape that allegory was the "dominant form", as the realistic novel was yesterday, or as the romantic drama was in Shakespeare's time. Whether it was a scientific argument, or a philosophical theory, or merely a love-story that the mediaeval writer wanted to write about, the thing always tended to come out as an allegorical poem; and his readers were so well accustomed to this style of writing that they had little difficulty in interpreting it. As the other Lewis—Dr. C. S. Lewis—has pointed out in his excellent book *The Allegory of Love*, allegory was not, for mediaeval people, a long-winded, indirect way of saying something that might have been more plainly put: it was the quickest, most direct and most vivid way of writing at a time when the technical vocabulary of psychology and of the physical sciences had not yet been perfected and popularised. And one might perhaps claim that it still is.

An allegory is a dramatised metaphor. A metaphor is a compressed simile. A simile is the perception of likeness in unlike things, presented in such a way that the understanding of the one helps to understand the other. For example:

"The leading of a Christian life is sometimes attended with spiritual difficulties inducing sensations of alarm and despondency." That is as dull and abstract a statement as I can manage to produce on this exciting topic. Let us enliven it by a simile: "It is as though a man were fighting against a powerful enemy." Let us now compress the thing into a metaphor: "The Christian soul is often the arena of a hard battle against alarm and despondency." That is more vivid; "alarm and despondency" have ceased to be abstractions: they are already half-personified, and the "Christian life" is developing a kind of landscape of its own—there is a territory of undefined extent called "the soul", with a battleground in the middle of it and people fighting there. Now let us take the final step, and fully personify both the Christianity and the enemy: "Then Apollyon straddled quite over the whole breadth of the way, and said, I am void of fear in this matter; prepare thyself to die: for I swear by my infernal den thou shalt go no further: here will I spill thy soul." [1]

That is allegory; and we may perhaps admit that we are more likely to attend to and remember it than the sentence about the "spiritual difficulties". Instead of the plain statement we have here an image: and although we could, if we liked, strip off the *veste di figura* and reduce the thing once more to abstract terms, we should feel that in doing so we had lost, not merely the dramatic excitement but also some of the depth and scope of the signification. That phrase, "Apollyon straddled *quite over the whole breadth of the way*" not only calls up a whole series of associated ideas about the "strait and narrow way", the *cammin di nostra vita*—it also conveys more powerfully than a hundred arguments the colossal size and strength of the evil will within the soul, and the terrifying sensation of being hopelessly caged and cooped in so that all progress is impossible. The image, that is, is none the less powerful and rich in associative suggestion because it has a definable intellectual content.

The drawback, of course, which everybody has noticed about the

[1] John Bunyan: *The Pilgrim's Progress.*

allegorical method is that, however we may embellish the story with dramatic and pictorial detail, it is not always easy to feel any close human sympathy with personified abstractions, and that their conversation, if confined strictly to what might reasonably be said by a being whose nature is composed of *nothing but* Anger, Envy, Chastity, Prudence, or what-not, is apt to be rather limited and repetitive. Great allegorists all have their special methods of getting over this difficulty. Spenser delights us with romantic incident and enchanting description: he does, however, tend at times to ramble and to lose hold of the main thread of the allegory. Bunyan, sticking much closer to his intellectual content, has an extraordinary knack of making theological argument exciting, and is incomparable in giving his abstractions human form and colour. If we carefully analyse the work of these two allegorists, we shall see that there is in both of them a very subtle and ingenious slipping to and fro over the boundaries between allegory and straight narrative; we cannot always be quite sure whether a character is simply an abstraction—a "quality in a substance" as Dante calls it—or another complete human character. Demas, for instance, and Giant Despair are quite certainly abstractions: but Bunyan's Ignorance is a *person* who crosses the river at the end, like the other pilgrims, and then finds the back door into Hell. Spenser says: "I labour to portrait, in Arthur, before he was king, the image of a brave knight, perfected in the twelve private moral virtues." The heroes of the twelve books, then, with the other characters, are abstractions—qualities in Arthur. But what of the episode in which Arthur himself enters the story to rescue the Red-Cross Knight? How exactly does a man come to the rescue of his own holiness? In cases like this, nobody can say for certain whether the landscape of *The Faerie Queene* or of *The Pilgrim's Progress* [1] is a state within the individual soul or a place in the world of society. The ambiguity does not matter greatly: it has probably never troubled anyone reading and enjoying those books for the first time, or prevented him from getting the meaning out of them.

But Dante's method is different—so different that it has led some people to say that "his method is not wholly allegorical". That is quite wrong. He is as consistently allegorical as Guillaume de Lorris, who wrote the first part of the *Roman de la Rose*. Where Dante departs from standard allegorical practice is in the kind of characters he uses

[1] *The Holy War*, on the other hand, is pure allegory, on which the setting is the human soul, and all the characters (except, of course, Emmanuel) qualities within that soul.

to people his poem. Guillaume's characters (apart from the figure of the lover himself) are *all* personified abstractions, qualities in the substance of the lady who is his heroine, and whose mind provides the whole mise-en-scène of the poem, and who never appears in her own person. But, except in a few isolated episodes of a rather special kind, Dante does not use personified abstractions at all: he uses historical personages, who are *symbolic images* of the qualities they represent. We may see the difference at once if we compare Dante with Spenser. In *The Faerie Queene*, we find a personified Chastity called Belphoebe, who allegorically represents (among other things) Queen Elizabeth: if Dante had written the poem, we should have met, wandering about that enchanted woodland, Queen Elizabeth herself, allegorically representing Chastity.

One practical advantage of Dante's method is at once obvious: since the images in the poem are actual human beings, their interests and their conversation need not be, and are not, restricted to the sins or virtues they symbolically represent. Virgil, who in this convenient and elastic scheme represents a good many things, such as Human Wisdom, the Imperial idea, Poetry, and Natural Virtue not illuminated by Christian Grace, may talk not only about philosophy, empire, the *Aeneid*, and humanist ethics, but also about Mantua. Guido da Montefeltro, besides telling the story of how he fell into the sin of counselling fraud, may express a human and touching interest in the state of Romagna. Count Cacciaguida, in the Heaven of Mars, does not merely typify patriotism and family affection—he can gossip delightfully and at length about the manners and customs of ancient Florence. Francesca da Rimini can wring our hearts as no personification of Lust could ever do. Arnaut Daniel, dropping into his own Provençal on the high, fire-swept, last ledge of Purgatory, touches and amuses us by this double compliment to his native country and to Dante's linguistic accomplishment. It is charming and faintly absurd in its frank humanity nor does it in any way invalidate the imagery by which Arnaut is, to Dante and to us, the eager repentance of a poet—perhaps too of a poetry—which in celebrating the beauty of the flesh has soiled the flesh.

But much more than this kind of literary flexibility is involved in the use of these symbolic images. And let me here quickly explain the sense in which I am using the word "symbol". I do not mean the *conventional symbol*, by which a sign, arbitrarily chosen, "stands for" some thing with which it has little or nothing in common and which might just as well be represented by some other sign. In arithmetic, a squiggle like a cottage loaf stands for the number eight: in heraldry, three gold lions on a red background stand for England: in the popular language of flowers, pansies stand for thoughts: at the end of Tommy Atkins's letter a row of X's stand for kisses. By general agreement and long tradition we are content to accept these symbols for what they represent; but any connection there is between the symbol and the thing symbolised is arbitrary and accidental. A squiggle of ink *is* not in any real sense the number 8: lions *are* not England—indeed they are not even English, and any hopeful connection we may make between the valour of lions and of Englishmen rather breaks down when we remember that, properly speaking, the lions should be called leopards: pansies *are* not thoughts—it is only that the name *pensées* was fancifully given to them at some time by the French: the letter X *is* not a kiss, and nobody who had never experienced being kissed would derive any knowledge about the sensation from contemplating the symbol.

But there is another kind of symbol, very different from this, which is called the *natural symbol*. It is most important not to confuse the two kinds, otherwise we shall always be falling into misconceptions, especially when we are exploring the borderland between religion and the arts. A natural symbol is *a thing really existing, which by its own nature represents some greater thing of which it is itself an instance*. Thus, the arch, maintaining itself as it does by the mutual thrust and pressure of all its parts, is at once an instance and a natural symbol of that great dynamic principle of stability in tension by which the physical universe is sustained. Beatrice, a real and beloved woman, is, in the eyes of Dante, an instance and a symbol of all creation glorified by love. The Incarnate life of God on earth, because it is a historic fact, is at once the supreme instance and the unique natural symbol of the whole history of man, and the whole nature of God, and the relations between them. I lay stress on this last example, because it illustrates the comparison between the two uses of the word "symbol". When certain people say that the story of the Incarnation is "merely symbolic", they usually mean that it is not a historic fact. But if it is not historic, then it is either not symbolical at all, or else "merely" a conventional symbol. If, on the contrary, it is a historic fact, then it is a natural symbol, and by contemplating it we can really learn something about God and Man. Because that, precisely, is the distinctive mark of the natural symbol; it is itself an instance of what it symbolises: and therefore, by simply being what it is, it tells us something about the true nature of that greater thing for which it stands.

Now in the *Divine Comedy* we do, of course, encounter many instances of that conventional symbolism which serves as so convenient a shorthand to convey our ideas. Such, on the small scale, are the conventional colours of red, white and green worn by the three theological graces in the pageant of Beatrice and repeated in her own dress. Such, on the large scale, is the whole conventional topography of Hell, Heaven, and, to a less extent, of Purgatory. Dante was too good a theologian to suppose that Hell was a hole in the ground, or that Heaven was a physical place, located beyond the fixed stars. But to depart from the conventional symbolism by which we "rise up" to Heaven and "sink down" to Hell—a symbolism endeared by long centuries of tradition, and not without its appropriateness—would have been sheer waste of the accreted associations gathered about those images. He uses them, therefore—not without an explicit warning against a too literal interpretation. His Purgatory is more original; earlier theology, both popular and official, had tended to place Purgatory among the purlieus of Hell, or even to combine the two localities into one—the difference being only that for the redeemed there was an end to torment, and for the unrepentant, none. For all that, the figuring of Repentance and Purgation as a mountain to be climbed may be fairly classed as conventional symbolism, however individual may be the conception of Dante's Purgatorial landscape.[1]

Essentially, however, in its grand architecture, Dante's poem is built up out of *natural symbols*. Here we must remind ourselves of what he said of it himself in that *Epistle to Can Gronde della Scala* which accompanied the first ten cantos of the *Paradiso*; "The subject of the whole work, then, taken in the literal sense only, is 'the state of souls after death', without qualification, for the whole progress of the work hinges on and about that. Whereas, if the work be taken allegorically, the subject is: 'Man, as by good or ill deserts, in the exercise of the freedom of his choice, he becomes liable to rewarding or punishing justice'."

Note, by the way, that when Dante speaks of the *subject in the literal sense*, he does not say: "The subject is the story of how the author went on a journey through Hell, in the bowels of the earth, emerged at the Antipodes and climbed the mountain of Purgatory, and thence proceeded up through the seven spheres to the Empyrean." This *story* is not what he means by the "literal subject". That is only the fictional

[1] The question of Dante's possible debt to Arabian literature in this connection is the subject of much discussion, which need not concern us here.

dress in which that subject is presented. The literal subject is "the state of souls after death"—of individual souls, or of souls in general. The *allegorical* subject—that is, the real and important subject—is Man, the being endowed with free-will, in his whole relation with the God who is righteousness. We observe that this allegorical subject is much wider than the literal subject, *and includes it.* What happens to you and me after death is both an instance, and a natural symbol, of the permanent relationship between Man and God, between free-will and justice, whether in this life or in the next, whether seen in the individual soul or in the soul of society, whether in the religious or in the secular sphere, or in any section or department of those spheres.

For it is characteristic of natural symbolism that because—merely by being what it is—it exhibits a universal pattern, it can be interpreted at many levels, and remains a true figure at every level. It is like the rings in a tree-trunk which show the pattern of its growth; at whatever level you saw through the wood, the rings tell the same story. Hear again what Dante says himself about levels of interpretation. He takes a verse from the 114th Psalm: "When Israel came out of Egypt and the house of Jacob from among a strange people, Judah was His sanctuary and Israel His dominion"; and he shows how it may be understood in four ways: "For," he says, "if we inspect *the letter alone,* the departure of the children of Israel in the time of Moses is presented to us." That is the *literal subject*—a historic fact—an instance and a natural symbol of deliverance. He goes on: "If the *allegory,* our redemption wrought by Christ" (that is, Moses is a type of Christ and the Exodus a type of the deliverance wrought by the Incarnation): "if the *moral* sense, the conversion of the soul from the grief and misery of sin to the state of grace" (that is the same symbol interpreted at the level of the individual soul in *this* world): "if the *anagogical*" (or we may say, the mystical) "the departure of the holy soul from the slavery of this corruption to the liberty of eternal glory" (that is, again, the same symbol interpreted at the level where the world of time and the world of eternity meet, in the life of prayer and contemplation).

It is after this manner—nothing narrower or more exclusive than this—that we have to interpret Dante's *Comedy.* He says so, and he ought to know what he intended. It is the story of the way of the soul at all times. It is, for example, the way of the individual soul in *this* life. At that level of interpretation, the whole landscape (so to call it) of Hell, Purgatory and Heaven, is within the soul. The vision of Hell—the profound and hideous pit narrowing from the weak compliance of a mutual indulgence, through abyss after abyss of ever-deepening corruption to that frozen horror of treachery in which every last vestige of truth and mutuality is paralysed and atrophied—is the vision, deeper than the psycho-analyst's plummet ever sounded, of the possibilities of corruption in you and in me, of the will to death and chaos, of the lie in the self. The figures of Francesca and Farinata, of Thaïs and Ciampolo, of Master Adam and Ugolino and Judas are the figures of our own weaknesses and pride and greed and falsehood and treachery: their state is the state to which we may bring ourselves—in which it is possible for our free choice to rivet and fix itself, if, having lost Beatrice, who is Grace, we lose also Virgil, who is Humanity, Art, Accuracy, Decency—whatever it is of light and sanity that remains with us in our worst moments.

Or we may take the *Inferno* at another level, indicated by Dante's many images of the City and the Empire, and see in it the slow decay of a degenerate society. Or again, we may watch, mirrored in these images, the way of Romantic Love, when it corrupts itself and turns to hate and treachery: or the way of the artist whose art becomes prostituted and false: or the corruption even of the religious instinct itself. And so with the images of repentance and redemption: so also with the ecstatic flight from circle to circle of the mystic dance which is the joy and freedom of the spirit in the willed surrender of its own self-will. At every level of experience, the image exhibits the same universal pattern.

A detailed examination of Dante's symbolic imagery would demand many volumes. But once one is in possession of the key to unlock this particular kind of symbolism, the interpretations present themselves, unforced, as one reads and remembers the poem. The important thing is to remember how vast and universal is the pattern that the symbolic imagery reveals, so that one does not fall into the error of restricting the allegorical meaning of the poem to a single level of interpretation. To see in the *Comedy*, as old Gabriele Rossetti saw, "nothing but" a political tract aimed against the Papacy, is rather like saying that the Queen's coronation is "nothing but" an elaborate excuse for the letting-off of surreptitious fireworks—it is not so much that it is untrue as that it is grotesquely inadequate. (Incidentally, the words "nothing but" are always a danger-signal in criticism. Whenever we come across them we may be pretty sure that the mind of the critic is dangerously limited.) In much the same way, when we begin to read the first canto of the *Inferno*, we shall very likely find a footnote by the editor, saying that the Three Beasts—the Leopard, the Lion and the Wolf—"stand for" Florence, France and the Papacy, respectively. So, in a sense, they may; but to my mind this is to put the thing the wrong way round. It would be truer to the spirit of Dante's symbolic imagery to say that, at one level, Florence, France and the Papacy "stand for" that which is more generally typified in the Leopard, the Lion and the Wolf: they are local and limited manifestations of a pattern of sin which is displayed in the Dark Wood by the Beasts: in Hell by the three main divisions of Incontinence, Violence, and Fraud: in the individual heart by the master-passions of Lust, Wrath and Avarice: in the pattern of human growth by the special temptations incident to Youth, Manhood and Age.

Having got so far, we need not, I hope, linger upon that peculiarly vicious system of interpretation which represents the *Comedy* as a kind of compensation-fantasy, by which Dante revenged himself for a disastrous political career of frustrated hopes and prolonged exile by putting his enemies in Hell and his friends in Heaven. For one thing, the accusation is quite untrue; many of the people he "put" in Hell were his friends and very few of the inhabitants of Hell can be proved to be his personal enemies. But he saw—as indeed we all see in certain public figures—the images of sin and salvation: of tendencies which he recognised in himself and in society, and which he knew to be damnable, and of virtues which he knew to be heavenly: and he used these figures to show what vice and virtue were. He may have been quite wrong about what happened to those people in the after-life—and if so, he himself will no doubt have been the first (as he says of Pope Gregory the Great) to "smile at his own error". But he saw in a simoniac pope or in a notorious traitor the image of something damnable walking the world, as we might see it in a Julius Streicher: he saw in a Buonconte or a Forese Donati, something that, with all its faults, still clung, tardily and feebly it might be, but tenaciously, to the hem of God's garment, as we might see it in a thousand people whose lives, from some points of view, are no better than they should be: he saw alike in a Piccarda and a St. Francis a divine radiance which communicated to him the eternal joy of God, as we also may see it, whether in a personal friend or in the life of a canonised saint. And in Beatrice he saw that vision of the eternal glory which is sometimes communicated to us in a personal—or it may be even an impersonal—relationship, and which fills us at once with an immense conviction of beatitude and with a crushing sense of our own unworthiness. These things he sets before us as types and images, which, merely by being what they are, display to us the universal pattern of loss or salvation, at whatever level we interpret them.

I have repeated several times, perhaps tediously often, those words: "merely by being what they are". I insist upon them because they help us to understand the interesting and at first rather puzzling way in which Dante often handles his imagery. Sometimes he talks *about* the particular sin or virtue which is being punished or rewarded in the particular circle, cornice, or sphere to which he has introduced us. Sometimes he simply shows us the image and lets it produce its own effect without explanation. Thus, in the *Purgatorio*, on the cornice where Wrath is expiated, nothing is said about the nature of wrath at all. Dante only meets one soul there, and spends his time discussing with him the problem of free-will. All that he has to say about wrath is conveyed by the image of its appropriate expiation—the envelopment in a black and pungent smoke which chokes the breath, shuts out the light of the sun and hides each soul from its neighbour. That is what anger *is*—that blinding, stinging smother which comes rolling upon one, so that one cannot see straight or breathe freely or realise what one is doing. *That* is the thing that has to be purged away—to be realised first as a thing external to the self, and so patiently endured as its own punishment until one is quite sure that no taint of inward assent to it remains within the soul. For we shall remember that in the *Purgatorio* the duration of the soul's detention upon any cornice is not imposed from without. The soul is its own judge; so soon as it *feels* itself free from stain it *is* free, and arises of its own volition to "go up higher".

So, too, with the rewards of Hell, which are the permanent realisation and possession of that which one has desired, and to which one impenitently clings for ever. Thus in the second circle Dante shows us the double image—the sin as it seemed at the time to Paolo and Francesca; the sin seen *sub specie aeternitatis* for what it really is. "He so manages the description," says Charles Williams, "he so heightens the excuse, that the excuse reveals itself as precisely the sin. . . . It is *lussuria*, luxury, indulgence, self-yielding which is the sin, and the opening-out of hell. The persistent parleying with the occasion of sin, the sweet prolonged laziness of love." [1] That is Dante's first image, and a hundred painters have painted it; the two handsome heads over the one book, the high romantic tale of Lancelot, the careless innocence of

[1] Charles Williams: *The Figure of Beatrice* (Faber, 1943), p. 118.

3

it all—"*soli eravamo e senza alcun sospetto*—we were alone and quite without fear". (This does not mean, I am sure, as some commentators say, "without fear of being surprised"; they have not reached that point; Francesca is telling the story of how she and Paolo first came to know the power of love. No, but without fear of themselves, of each other, of love, "the lord of terrible aspect": they "thought no harm", they were not *thinking* at all.) Then the blushes, the exchange of deliciously troubled glances, the sudden trembling, the kiss, the first abandonment—"*quel giorno più non vi leggemmo avanti*—we read no more that day". That is the image of the sin as it seemed; the image of the sin as it *is*, is the helpless drifting on the black wind which "*di qua, di là, di giù, di su li mena*—up and down, hither and thither it bears them", the playthings of a passion which, because once they would not, they now cannot control. In the next circle—that of Gluttony— Dante does not give the first image. After all, we know Gluttony— rather a warm, cheerful, convivial kind of sin, is it not? That, says Dante in effect, is what you think. Look at it as it is; a cold sensuality, a filthy wallowing in the mire under drenching rain, each soul blind to its neighbours: a brute appetite tears them and howls over the feast. You have seen it? Very well. Now you know all about Gluttony and we need not discuss it further: you have only to look at the image.

Let us pursue this use of the image further—into the very technique of the poetry. The mention of Francesca may serve to remind us that much of Dante's symbolism is conveyed to us by an elaborate series of parallel images—some of them as obvious as the contrasted examples of vice and virtue presented to us on each cornice of the *Purgatorio*, some more recondite, whose significance only strikes us when we have soaked ourselves for a long time in the poem and are beginning to notice things which at first escaped us in the swift succession of events. A whole lecture—indeed a whole book—could be devoted to those significances which are a matter, not so much of the images themselves as of the *placing* of the images. It is a thing which may be compared to the composition of a picture; the subtlety by which a number of objects, more or less significant in themselves, gain an added significance from the relations of balance and perspective in which they stand to one another. Let us take only one example which may stand for all in its peculiar subtlety and—when once we have seen it—its appalling power.

I suppose that of the whole *Comedy*, the two most famous episodes are those of Paolo and Francesca and of Ugolino and Ruggieri.

Thousands of people who have never read another line of the *Comedy* know those two stories, at any rate by reputation. The Francesca image is placed very near the top of the Abyss—it shows "the first surrender of the soul to Hell—small but certain".[1] The sin it figures is that of carnal passion—a sin whose venom and excuse at once is mutuality. Lust is not (at this point) merely self-indulgence: it is mutual indulgence. It may put on a specious appearance of generosity, even of self-sacrifice. It is an exchange in love, even if it is an exchange of deadly poison. The gradual and inevitable steps by which the perverted mutuality declines into selfish appetite, into mutual grudging, into resentment and sullen hatred: thence into violence and sterility and despair: and so into the long and melancholy series of frauds and falsehoods by which human beings exploit one another,—those are the steps by which we painfully clamber down the hideous descent from Acheron to Malebolge.[2] Then, deep down under the feet of the giants —the primitive mass-emotions and mass-stupidities which remain when the bonds of natural love are loosed—we come to the lowest deep of all, where treachery feeds on treachery in the cold and darkness of the frozen heart. Mutuality here makes its last appearance— Ugolino the traitor, locked immovably in the ice with Ruggieri the traitor, "so close that the one head seemed a cap to the other", and gnawing his scalp with an unappeasable appetite of hatred. "He that may never more from me be parted," says Francesca, tenderly, of Paolo: "thou shalt know why I am such a neighbour to him," says Ugolino, grimly, of Ruggieri. This, then, is the end of mutuality— mutual love has perverted itself into mutual hate. If Dante and Beatrice had not, by the grace of God, been preserved to be themselves, they might have begun like Paolo and Francesca and ended like Ugolino and Ruggieri. We know that such perversions can occur. But does Dante, in fact, say this? Not in so many words. He only shows us these two pairs of images; in each case he lays stress on the fact that the sinners are *together* to all eternity; in each case there is a temporary pause in the torment—a lull in the wind, a pause in the gnawing— while Dante interviews them: in each case only one of the pair speaks, and in each case tells his or her story. Paolo and Francesca were partners in the guilt, and Francesca excuses Paolo along with herself: Ugolino and Ruggieri shared the same guilt in antagonism, and Ugolino excuses himself at Ruggieri's expense—there is a contrast in the parallelism. And in case we should think this accidental, we may

[1] Charles Williams: *op. cit., loc. cit.*   [2] Cf. *The City of Dis*, pp. 132 *sqq.*

compare both with the intermediate pair—Ulysses and Diomede in the 8th Bolgia; they too "share the punishment as they shared the guilt" and are pent together in one flame for ever: here again, the one speaks and tells his story and the other is silent. Here, however, mutuality is lost but not yet turned to hatred; Ulysses neither excuses Diomede nor excuses himself at his expense—he merely ignores him.

These symmetries might be enough of themselves to declare Dante's intention: but he has not left it at that. He has linked Francesca at the top with Ugolino at the bottom by the very structure of the speech and rhythm of the verse. Here is how Francesca begins her story:

> *Ed ella a me: "Nessun maggior dolore*
> *che ricordarsi del tempo felice*
> *nella miseria; e ciò sa il tuo dottore.*
>
> *Ma se a conoscer la prima radice*
> *del nostro amor tu hai cotanto affetto,*
> *farò come colui che piange e dice.*

> (Then she to me: "The bitterest woe of woes
> Is to remember in our wretchedness
> Old happy days—as well thy doctor knows;
>
> Yet, if so dear desire thy heart possess
> To know that root of love which wrought our fall,
> I'll be as those who weep and who confess.")

And here is Ugolino:

> *Poi cominciò: "Tu vuoi ch'io rinnovelli*
> *disperato dolor che il cor mi preme,*
> *già pur pensando, pria ch'io ne favelli.*
>
> *Ma se le mie parole esser dien seme,*
> *che frutti infamia al traditor ch'io rodo,*
> *parlare e lagrimar vedrai insieme.*

> (Then he began: "Thou bid'st me to renew
> A grief so desperate that the thought alone,
> Before I voice it, cracks my heart in two.
>
> Yet, if indeed my words, like seedlings sown,
> Shall fruit, to shame this traitor whom I tear,
> Then shalt thou see me speak and weep in one.")

Nobody can very well miss the structural and rhythmical symmetry there; in each case there are two terzains, the first opening with four introductory syllables: "*Ed ella a me*"—"*Poi cominciò*", followed by an expostulation at being required to tell a story which renews the misery: the second beginning in each case "*Ma se*", and giving a reason for complying, and ending, in each case, with an almost identical phrase about "weeping and speaking together". But even that is not all. When we examine them closely, we shall see that *both* passages are derived from one and the same classical source; the speech of Aeneas to Dido in the 2nd book of the *Aeneid*, the actual quotations from that speech being almost equally divided between the two passages, and the juxtaposition of "speaking and weeping", which is a conflation of two lines in the Latin, being common to both.

(Since it would be difficult to disentangle this extraordinary verbal jig-saw merely by reading the passages, I have desired the printer to print all three passages in such a way as to make their relations quite plain.)

CORRESPONDENCES in *Inf.* v. 121–6 and *Inf.* xxxiii. 4–9, showing the common derivation from *Aen.* ii. 3–13.

Passages common to *Aeneid* and *Francesca* printed in capitals
   „ „ „ *Aeneid* and *Ugolino* „ „ small capitals
   „ „ „ *Aeneid, Francesca*
          and *Ugolino* „ „ italic capitals

Aeneid ii. 3 sqq.

INFANDUM, regina, JUBES RENOVARE DOLOREM ...
    ... quis *TALIA FANDO* ...   ⎫
temperet a *LACRIMIS* ...?   ⎬Protest
SED SI TANTUS AMOR CASUS COGNOSCERE ⎭
 NOSTROS ...
QUAMQUAM ANIMUS MEMINISSE HORRET luctuque refugit, ⎫Consent
incipiam.   ⎭

Inferno v. 121 sqq.

Ed ella a me: Nessun maggior dolore   ⎫
 che ricordarsi del tempo felice   ⎬Protest
 nella miseria: e ciò sa il tuo dottore.   ⎭
MA SE A COGNOSCER la prima radice   ⎫
 del nostro amor TU HAI COTANTO AFFETTO, ⎬Consent
 farò come colui che *PIANGE E DICE.*   ⎭

Inferno xxxiii. 4 sqq.

Poi cominciò: TU VUOI CH'IO RINNOVELLI ⎫
 DISPERATO DOLOR CHE IL COR MI PREME ⎬Protest
 GIÀ PUR PENSANDO, pria ch'io ne favelli. ⎭
MA SE le mie parole esser dien seme,   ⎫
 che frutti infamia al traditor ch'io rodo,   ⎬Consent
 PARLARE E LAGRIMAR vedrai insieme. ⎭

One could not, I think, find a much more vivid illustration of Dante's whole method of setting his images—whether verbal or pictorial—squarely in the reader's eye and allowing them to do their own work. Whether Dante deliberately set himself from the start to hammer home his point by this ingenious use of the *Aeneid* speech: or whether, when he came to his second pair, the *Aeneid* speech boiled up spontaneously out of his unconscious memory, I do not of course know, nor does anyone. That the finished result is perfectly conscious and deliberate I feel sure; a pattern so subtle, ingenious and sustained is the work of the whole poet, and not of detached portions of his personality.

At this point we may, perhaps, add something to what we said earlier about the universality of the images. It is customary nowadays to hunt through a poet's ostensible meaning, in order to discover hidden images of sex. No doubt if we are ingenious enough we shall be able to discover a cryptosexual symbolism in Dante. But we shall fall into the great modern error of overlooking the obvious if we do not realise that, in the *Comedy*, the overtly sexual image is, like other images, chiefly used as a natural symbol of something greater than itself, which includes sex. In the 2nd circle, the *image* is sexual: but the sin of mutual indulgence is found in relationships other than sexual; in the reciprocal doting of parents and children, for example, at one level, or, at another, in peace-at-any-price policies, whether in the Church or in the State: and we ought to interpret it so. Vice versa, in the 3rd circle, the *image* is not sexual; but there may be, in sex as in other things, a selfish gormandising appetite which is not excluded from the condemnation of the Gluttonous, and is only too well symbolised by the cold filth and the rending talons. This exchange among the images is exemplified almost startlingly by the Francesca-Ugolini parallel; one image is sexual, the other not, but both are equally images of perverted mutuality: and that this is so, Dante has taken especial pains to make clear to us.

I have tried to show that Dante's allegorical imagery, being based on natural symbolism and purporting to display a universal pattern, is susceptible of being interpreted in very many ways and at many different levels. I think perhaps I should add a word or two on the subject of what may be called "reading-in". We are continually being warned against "reading into" a poet meanings which may not, or could not, have been in his mind at the time. This warning is valuable in so far as it prevents us from claiming, for example, that, because Dante speaks of "the centre upon which all weights down-weigh", he therefore "anticipates" the Newtonian theory of the mutual attraction of bodies; or that, because he demanded certain very definite measures of Church reform, he was "a Protestant before his time"; or that, because he was aware of the existence of the threshold and the censor, he was quite capable of writing all the works of Freud, Jung and Adler rolled into one. In his factual knowledge and intellectual background a poet or prophet is of his own time: his poetry is all the better for that, and so is his prophecy. It does him no honour to try and turn him into a kind of crystal-gazer or professional tipster. But when it comes to the interpretation of symbolic imagery, then we must not allow ourselves to be abashed by the historic school of criticism into emptying a poem of its universal content. If an image displays the universal pattern, it will display it at all levels and in all circumstances, whether the poet was or could have been conscious of these possible applications or not. It has happened even to me in writing a novel, to resolve a problem of human relationships in a manner which was recognised by a priest of my acquaintance as symbolising the right and proper resolution of a relationship between the soul and God. I protested that I had had no such ambitious idea in mind: but, when once the significance of what I had written was pointed out to me, I had to recognise that what the priest said was true. While dealing, so far as I was aware, simply and solely with a specific human situation, I had unwittingly stumbled upon a universal image. The meaning that another person had "read into" that image was the real meaning: and as soon as I was shown it, I accepted it, and found that, incidentally, it illuminated the connection between that and a number of other passages in my own books which had previously seemed unrelated. Compared with Dante, I am infinitely little, as he is infinitely great: but I mention this because, as compared with him, I have the dubious advantage of being alive and available for reference. I am here to admit that I did not see the full meaning of what I was writing: I am here to admit that, when the full meaning was "read into" it, I was ready to accept and acknowledge that meaning for the real meaning. I am convinced, then, that we need never be afraid to read into the great images of Dante all the fullness of significance which they can be made to contain—so long, of course, as our interpretation does not involve a degradation of the image and is not incongruous with the general purpose of his allegory. A great poem is not the perquisite of scholars and critics and historians: it is yours and mine—our freehold and our possession; and what it truly means to us is a real part of its true and eternal meaning. Let me conclude with the words of a seventeenth-century writer,[1] which sum up almost all that there is to say about the natural symbolic image:

All truth is shadow except the last truth. But all truth is substance in its own place, though it be but shadow in another place. And the shadow is a true shadow, as the substance is a true substance.

[1] Isaac Penington.

(1947)

DANTE'S IMAGERY: II. PICTORIAL

PER correr miglior acqua . . .

Our journey through the dark labyrinths of allegory and symbolism has been, if not precisely a hellish grind, at least a journey over a somewhat steep and laborious road. We now emerge into a lighter air, and may with a clear conscience shake out our sails for a pleasure-trip on smoother waters. The only difficulty is to know which route to take and what to look at; the Pictorial Imagery is so rich and varied, and there is so much of it.

One thing, at any rate, we will not do: we will not make a Baedeker catalogue of the most famous beauty-spots. For those who know them, this would be merely boring, while those who do not know them would merely be robbed of the pleasure of discovery.

It will be better to say something, more generally, about Dante's way of using the images, and perhaps to begin, once again, by mentioning some of the things that we shall *not* find in Dante—thus saving ourselves disappointment and preparing our minds to enjoy what is really there to see. A remark made once by Tennyson will do as well as anything else to start from. In a talk he gave to his schoolboy son about Milton, he is reported to have said: "I think that Milton's vague Hell is much more awful than Dante's Hell marked off into divisions." [1] Now Tennyson was a great lover and admirer of the *Comedy*: and although he was at the moment occupied with a eulogy of Milton, he would not have delivered this passing rap at Dante without what seemed to him good and sufficient cause. I know exactly what Tennyson meant: and I think it probable that nearly everybody, coming to Dante after reading the Jacobeans, has a moment or two in which he sympathises with Tennyson. Read the first Book of *Paradise Lost*; read the description of Hell:

> A Dungeon horrible, on all sides round
> As one great Furnace flam'd, yet from those flames
> No light, but rather darkness visible
> Serv'd only to discover sights of woe,

[1] Hallam, Lord Tennyson: *Alfred Lord Tennyson: A Memoir* (MacMillan, 1897): Vol. ii, p. 518.

> Regions of sorrow, doleful shades, where peace
> And rest can never dwell, hope never comes
> That comes to all; but torture without end
> Still urges, and a fiery Deluge, fed
> With ever-burning sulphur unconsum'd . . .

Read of Satan:

> With head uplift above the wave, and Eyes
> That sparkling blaz'd, his other Parts besides
> Prone on the flood, extended long and large
> Lay floating many a rood . . .

Read the great roll-call of the "grand infernal peers", with its thundering invocation of sonorous names, rich in legendary association:

> For never since created man,
> Met such imbodied force, as nam'd with these
> Could merit more than that small infantry
> Warr'd on by Cranes: though all the Giant brood
> Of *Phlegra* with th' Heroic Race were joyn'd
> That fought at *Theb's* and *Ilium*, on each side
> Mixt with auxiliar gods; and what resounds
> In Fable or Romance of *Uther's* son
> Begirt with *British* and *Armoric* Knights:
> And all who since, Baptiz'd or Infidel
> Jousted in *Aspramont* or *Montalban*,
> *Damasco* or *Marocco*, or *Trebisond*,
> Or whom *Biserta* sent from Afric shore
> When *Charlemain* with all his Peerage fell
> By *Fontarabbia*. Thus far these beyond
> Compare of mortal prowess, yet observ'd
> Their dread Commander: he above the rest
> In shape and gesture proudly eminent
> Stood like a Tow'r; his form had not yet lost
> All her original brightness, nor appear'd
> Less than Arch Angel ruind, and th'excess
> Of Glory obscur'd: As when the Sun new ris'n
> Looks through the Horizontal misty Air
> Shorn of his beams, or from behind the Moon
> In dim Eclips disastrous twilight sheds
> On half the Nations, and with fear of change
> Perplexes Monarchs. Dark'n'd so, yet shon
> Above them all th' Arch Angel.

Read in the Second Book the description of the journey through Hell:

> through many a dark and drearie vaile
> They pass'd, and many a Region dolorous,
> O'er many a frozen, many a fierie Alpe,
> Rocks, Caves, Lakes, Fens, Bogs, Dens and shades of death
> A Universe of death, which God by curse
> Created evil, for evil only good,
> Where all life dies, death lives, and nature breeds,
> Perverse, all monstrous, all prodigious things,
> Abominable, inutterable, and worse
> Than Fables yet have feign'd, or fear conceiv'd,
> *Gorgon's* and *Hydra's*, and *Chimera's* dire.

Read this: and read also the description of Death:

> The other shape,
> If shape it might be called that shape had none
> Distinguishable in member, joynt, or limb,
> Or substance might be call'd that shadow seem'd,
> For each seem'd either; black it stood as Night,
> Fierce as ten Furies, terrible as Hell,
> And shook a dreadful Dart; what seemed his head
> The likeness of a Kingly Crown had on.

Then turn to Dante, and you may very well feel as though you had trodden on a step that wasn't there and been let down with a bump. What kind of Hell is this, that people can make maps of—a Hell of four-and-twenty neat concentric circles, all carefully docketed and described with the brisk and remorseless accuracy of a continental guide-book? Look at these gaudy monsters—fine old classical figures absurdly degraded into mediaeval arabesques: these comic demons with fancy names like Graffiacane and Libicocco and Cagnazzo, jabbing at the sinners with pitchforks, saluting their captain by putting their tongues out at him, and marching off to the vulgar and indecorous signal he gives by "making a bugle of his breech". Consider the childish physical crudeness of those torments which Milton leaves so impressively undefined: the wallowings in mud and excrement, the floggings and the boilings and the diseases and the turnings into serpents, limb by limb in laborious detail; the slicings apart and the display of bloody stumps and dangling entrails; the clawings and tearings; Ugolino gnawing the scalp of Ruggieri; Satan champing the head of Judas. And then the giants—not "extended long and large" over "many a rood", but measured as with a yard-tape: "His face seemed to me as long and large as St. Peter's pine at Rome, and his other bones were in proportion, so that from his middle up he showed so much that three Frieslanders could not have reached his hair." (A rough calculation works this out at not more than 40 feet or so.) And Satan? Well— Dante stands in about the same ratio to the giant as the giant to one of Satan's arms (here we do another little sum in the margin): and he has three faces, red, yellow and black, and teeth and talons and six wings, not feathered but batlike: and there is fur all over his body: and our last look at him from the other side of the earth's centre shows him, ludicrously, upside-down—"I only saw his great legs sticking up", says Dante—and then we have a little geography lesson about the Antipodes, and that is that; "we have seen all."

Thinking it over, are we not inclined to say, as many critics have indeed said, that this is mere mediaeval bugaboo and bogey-work? Entertaining, perhaps, if you enjoy that kind of thing, and dull if you don't: but hardly to be taken seriously. Where is the thrill, the exaltation of feeling, the grand gloomy suggestiveness that should accompany the vision of Hell? Where, to put it shortly, is the thing we are accustomed to call "the poetry"? Surely Tennyson is right in saying that "Milton's vague Hell is more awful".

For the moment, let us not dispute this point. Let us instead ask another question—not a "literary" question at all, but one that is quite personal and practical. Instead of asking: "Which of these images is the more awful?" let us simply ask: "Which of them is the more like Hell?" Or—still more personally and practically: "If you were obliged to pass eternity in the one Hell or the other, which would you avoid the more eagerly?"

"A universe of Death", says Milton, "created evil, for evil only good." And so long as he is content only to tell us so, it is so. But when he proceeds to detailed narrative, it turns out that there is much mitigation in Milton's Hell. There are games and jousts and feats of arms: the fiends can dig for metal and build a palace: there is exploration: there is rational debate: there is—yes, strange to say, there is music—

> the harmony
> (What could it less when spirits immortal sing?)
> Suspended Hell, and took with ravishment
> The thronging audience.

Harmony in Hell? What would Dante have said to that? For Dante, who loved music, the chord of harmony could no more sound in Hell than the name of Christ or Mary. From the moment that we step inside the Vestibule, noise—hideous, chaotic and incessant—beats us about the ears almost like a physical blow. Thereafter it varies a little, sinking in Limbo to the despairing sighs of those who live in longing without hope—rising in the ghastly pit of disease to shrieks so piercing that Dante has to stop his ears—muted in Caïna and Antenora to an icy hush, broken only by the chattering teeth of the shades "like storks clattering with their bills"—but it never stops until it is extinguished at last in the deathly silence of Giudecca, where misery can no longer even utter a cry to express itself. The mingled clamour of the Abyss rises out of it like thunder; within, the black wind howls, the tyrants scream in the boiling flood of Phlegethon, the harpies "sit and shriek in the strange trees", through whose torn boughs the imprisoned souls gasp out "lamentations mingled with blood"; the cataract goes thundering over the Great Barrier so loud as to drown speech; hideous sounds go up from the 7th Bolgia—"in a voice not made for human speech"; the tall flames roar;—shouts of defiance and ugly blasphemies, the yells of demons and men quarrelling and cursing, the horn of Nimrod blowing over the grey waste "more terribly than the Oliphant of Roland"—these are the sounds of Hell—not music. There is no music until we stand on the reedy shore of Purgatory in the dawn-light and watch the ship of souls draw near across the shimmering sea and hear the redeemed spirits singing as they come: *In exitu Israel de Aegypto*. From then on, the songs never cease: from cornice after cornice, from heaven above heaven, they mount up—*quale allodetta*—higher and sweeter the farther they go till they reach the throne of God. But in Hell is no song. Neither is there any diversion or any rational occupation; only the meaningless monotony of unending and miserable unrest —a vast series of vain repetitions, "up and down, hither and thither". Interchange? exploration? No: the souls and the devils who torment them are bound and fettered each in their own circle, and all their discourse is quarrelling and hatred. At the bottom is Satan: and certainly nobody could ever accuse Dante of being "of the devil's party without knowing it". All the Satanic façade, all that dark dignity which fascinated Milton in his emotions though he repudiated it with his intellect: which moved Marlowe and deceived Shelley and was exploited with romantic perversity by Byron:—Dante both saw it and saw through it. He saw it in royal Jason, in Farinata, proud and silent, "seeming to hold all Hell in deep despite"; he saw it, proud and voluble, in Capaneus, hurling defiance against the gods; he saw it, savage and degraded, in Vanni Fucci, screaming blasphemies and making the figs in God's face; he saw it, stripped naked, in Satan. The prince of darkness, the "Emperor of the sorrowful realm" is not a gentleman, and very much "less than Archangel ruined"; he stands there, hideous, impotent, obscene, grotesque and miserable—"foul as once he was fair"; his face a preposterous parody of the threefold glory he sought to ape; the six wings of his cherubhood deformed to an animal ugliness:

> and as they flapped and whipped
> Three winds went rushing over the icy flat
>
> And froze up all Cocytus; and he wept
> From his six eyes, and down his triple chin
> Runnels of tears and bloody slaver dripped.[1]

Less "awful", or more awful? We are reminded of the old lady who rebuked someone for saying "What the devil——!" on the ground that "she did not like to hear him speak so flippantly about a sacred personage". Dante does not mean the Devil to become for us a sacred personage, or the object of religious awe. He knew all about that awe, and he knew it to come far too near to veneration. Dante's Hell is indeed a place "created evil, for evil only good". His is not the "poetry of Hell": it is Hell itself. Never for one moment can the imagination be seduced by it; we may shrug it off or laugh it away: but in our worst hours of self-disgust the image of it may obtrude itself with a frightening familiarity; it is too like the barren treadmill of some habitual vice, from which we can no longer extract even the illusion of pleasure, yet from which we neither can nor, in the last resort want to, get free. Young people, perhaps, will not very easily recognise the truth of it; Dante's is an adult Hell, as his Heaven is an adult Heaven: of all the poets who have written about the "Last Things", his mind is perhaps the most mature.

But this is to stray a little from our subject. If I have dwelt so long on Tennyson's passing criticism it is to emphasise the rigid control by which Dante's poetic imagery is subdued to its proper function. It is not there for its own sake, but for the sake of the poem as a whole. It is not that Dante cannot, if he likes, be vague and awful in the Tennysonian or the Miltonic manner. The *Inferno* itself provides one magnificent instance, when Dante and Virgil are waiting on the shores of Styx for the Angel to come down and open the gates of Dis.

[1] *Inf.* xxxiv. 50–54.

E già venia su per le torbid' onde
un fracasso d'un suon pien di spavento
per che tremavano ambedue le sponde———[1]

There is the crash and roar as of a great wind, shaking the banks, and then he comes looming through the mist, with the lost souls fleeing before him like frightened frogs. He comes, not like brightness, but like "glory obscur'd"—not like joy, but like judgment. None of Dante's usual precise measurements here; he might be man-size or thirty feet high. First a sound, then a scattering, then the strong, swift feet, "passing dry-shod over Styx", then a gesture—

His left hand, moving, fanned away the gross
Air from his face, nor elsewise did he seem
At all to find the way laborious———[2]

then the terrible unmoved face; then a voice speaking scorn. As he comes, so he goes: aloof, dignified, and, in Tennyson's sense of the word, awful. But this dignity and this awe are not the attributes of Hell —they are the attributes of Heaven as they appear in the eyes of Hell. And he is only vaguely apprehended; because, though Heaven can know Hell, Hell can never know Heaven.

Dante's imagery, then, is always strictly functional, even when it is at its most pictorial. And pictorial it is. Dante, who was the friend of painters, and who (as we know) sometimes did a little painting himself,[3] had the painter's eye. He had a lightning facility for fixing a scene, a look, a movement, in the fewest possible words, but unforgettably. The pictures from the *Comedy* crowd so upon us that of the mere enumeration of them there would be no end. Dante, startled by the voice suddenly calling to him from the burning tomb and shrinking up against Virgil who rallies him: " 'Come, come, what are you doing?' said he: 'Turn round: that is Farinata—look! he has risen upright and you can see him all from waist to head.' " Chiron the Centaur, using the nock of his arrow to put back his great beard from his mouth before he speaks, and Virgil replying to him, standing "where the two natures join". Virgil's head, we realise, reached about to the Centaur's withers—the horse-part, therefore, was of the percheron type, standing some 16 or 17 hands, and, since Virgil came so

---

[1] Then o'er that dull tide came the crash and roar
    Of an enormous and appalling sound,
    So that the ground shuddered from shore to shore;
                    Inf. ix. 64–66.

[2] *Inf.* ix. 82–84.   [3] *Vita Nuova:* xxxv.

confidingly close, it was presumably friendly, and not disposed to kick. Dante does not say all this—we see it, and see the slant of Virgil's upturned face. Virgil again, sitting with Dante on the steps leading to the Fourth Cornice, discoursing to him about love, and "looking intently into my face to see if I was satisfied"—the whole attitude and expression are there—a grave and tender anxiety, with a kind of meekness, as of great wisdom in the presence of a child. The Ship of Souls seen far across the sea—it is another of Dante's parallel passages, the counterpart of the coming of the Angel over Styx: the heavenly thing seen, this time, by a soul in grace; first the glory about the celestial pilot's head, tiny and glowing red "like Mars setting through a mist": then on either side of it, "a white I knew-not-what": then another whiteness below—the ship is coming up over the horizon: Dante glances away for a moment, and when he looks back it is "bigger and brighter": and still Virgil says no word until it is clear that "those first two whitenesses" are wings: and then: "Quickly, down on your knees, fold your hands—behold the Angel of the Lord."

> And nearer and nearer as he came full sail
> The bird of God shone momently more bright,
> So that mine eyes endured him not, but fell.[1]

The thing is not just described: it is seen. The lovely glimpse of Matelda gathering flowers in the Garden of Paradise, on the brink of that little stream running dark and clear under the swaying trees, and turning, when Dante speaks to her:

> As a dancing lady turns with her toes together,
> Foot by foot set close and close to the ground,
> And scarcely putting the one before the other——[2]

That is pure Botticelli; you may see that dainty liveliness in the feet of the dancing Graces in the *Primavera*. The wonderful, clear, Perugino-like colour which suffuses the first eight cantos of the *Purgatorio*; yet it is nearly all suggested; fewer than a dozen lines in those eight cantos contain any colour adjectives at all, and of these three are accounted for by the picture of the Valley of the Rulers (painted, quite literally, in "paintbox-colours"): two by the description of the dawn in Canto II: and one by that mysteriously magical line with which the story opens after the proem and invocation:

> *Dolce color d'oriental zaffiro.*[3]

---

[1] *Purg.* ii. 37–39.   [2] *Purg.* xxviii. 52–54.
[3] Tender colour of orient sapphire.

Yet the colour is present everywhere, cool and transparent along the reedy shore, shimmering blue-violet across the limitless sea, silvery-green on the dew-soaked grass, pouring in arrowy brightness from the cloudless Northern sky—as unlike the grim iron and granite greys and the smoky reds of Hell as though Dante had ransacked the dictionary for all the chromatic epithets invented since his time. All the strange geometrical pattern of the ten heavens is drawn with a pencil dipped in pure light: and in the Heaven of the Moon there is that lovely harmony of pale colour and reluctant motion whose strange lunar sheen is more moon-like than anything in all literature—except, perhaps, Coleridge's

> The moving moon went up the sky
> And nowhere did abide;
> Softly she was going up
> And a star or two beside.

In the same key, and equally evocative, is Dante's apparition of the spirits in the Moon's sphere:

> *Quali per vetri trasparenti e tersi*
> *O ve per acque nitide e tranquille,*
> *non si profonde che i fondi sien persi,*
>
> *Tornan dei nostri visi le postille*
> *debili sì che perla in bianca fronte*
> *non vien men tosto alle nostre pupille——*[1]

—"as from transparent and polished glass, or from clear quiet waters, not so deep that the bottom is darkened, the outline of our own face looks back to us, so faint that a white pearl on a white forehead comes not more slowly upon our vision——" so they appear, and Dante, taking the substance for a reflection, looks back over his shoulder to see what forms these are, thus glassed in the lucid white moonstuff. And after he has spoken with the shimmering form of Piccarda, she begins to sing, "Ave Maria",

> *e cantando vanio*
> *Come per acqua cupa cosa grava——*[2]

"vanished like a heavy thing sinking through deep water". And at once we are leaning over the side of a ship, tossing some trinket into the sea and watching it sink—so unexpectedly slowly—and glimmering as it sinks.

Over and over again, it is in his similes that Dante displays his

[1] *Para.* iii. 10–15. [2] *Para.* iii. 122–123.

4

astonishing power of catching and fixing a visual impression, fleeting but familiar. Nearly always the simile is drawn from something homely and simple. The exotic and the grandiose are rare—though we must not forget the sudden vision of the Phoenix that breaks in upon the ugly reptilian squalors of the Seventh Bolgia, trailing with it a great waft of oriental perfume:

> Living, nor herb nor grain is food for her—
> Only amomum and dropping incense-gums,
> And her last swathings are of nard and myrrh.[1]

But usually the picture is of something seen every day: and it is this strong, homespun, earthy quality, common to all the circles from Hell to Heaven, that holds the poem firmly to reality and prevents it from ever deviating into a false spirituality.

Under the rain of fire that falls upon the Abominable Sand "as Alpine snowflakes fall in windless weather", the shades peer at Dante and his companion as passers-by eye one another "at dusk, under a new moon", and they squinney with pursed brows "like an old tailor at the needle's eye". In the ghastly pit of Disease, two leprous horrors sit propped against one another "like a couple of pans set to warm at the fireside": they scratch their scabs "just as a scullion's knife will strip a bream or any other fish with great, coarse scales": they work away with such energy that "I never saw currycomb plied so fast by an ostler whose master is waiting, or who has been kept up late and wants to get to bed". Two other wretches lie smoking with fever "like a washed hand on a wintry day": the devils by the river of boiling pitch thrust the souls under with their forks "as cooks make their scullions prod the stew to keep the meat from floating". The thief in the Seventh Bolgia who is turning into a reptile has his face drawn out into a muzzle, and

> inside his head
> He pulled his ears, as a snail pulls her horn.[2]

In the higher spheres of Heaven, the souls have no visible forms; they are living and dancing light. The ruby fire that is the spirit of the great warrior Judas Maccabaeus whirls along the flaming cross of Mars, spinning in ecstasy, "*e letizia era sferza del paleo*—joy was the whip to the top".[3] The soul of our First Father moves within his shrouding brilliance and, says Dante, "sometimes you see an animal covered up in sacking, and you can guess at its form because the cloth moves with its movements—well, that was how it looked". Cutting clean into and

---

[1] *Inf.* xxiv. 109–111.   [2] *Inf.* xxv. 131–132.   [3] *Para.* xviii. 42.

through these immaterial heavens of pure intellectual light comes this concrete, commonplace, almost comic snapshot of something seen in any country town in the world on market-day. Nothing could be more vivid: nothing more characteristically Dantesque. I think, indeed, that this famous simile is a sort of touchstone of criticism. If it troubles you —if you find it, in that context, undignified, incongruous, or in any way offensive, then you may be as learned, earnest, and religious as you like about Dante, but you will never really love him—never learn to roll the sharp, salty tang of him with full delight upon the tongue. But if your heart leaps up when you behold this surprising rainbow in that remote, ethereal sky, then you have a thousand more such enchanting sketches to rejoice in. Here, for instance, is Dante, passing upward from the First to the Second Terrace of Purgatory, and feeling, like Christian in the *Pilgrim's Progress*, that a heavy burden has suddenly been lifted from him, so that he climbs more easily. And Virgil tells him that the going will be easier still when all the seven P's—the signs of the Seven Deadly Sins—marked upon his forehead by the Angel at Purgatory Gate have been erased, like the first.

Then, like a man going along with something on his head which he doesn't know about, till the *cenni*—the signs (pointing and giggling, no doubt)— of the passers-by make him suspicious, and he begins feeling with his fingers for what he can't see, so I passed my outspread hand over my forehead and found that only six of the letters were left.[1]

"Whereat", says Dante, "my Leader smiled." To be sure he did—and so do we, pursued by embarrassing recollections of paper caps playfully assumed and forgotten, honeymoon rice tumbling out of silk toppers, tram-tickets parked in a hat-band and unwittingly worn to a funeral, twigs, straws, or the unwelcome attentions of pigeons—something on one's head which one doesn't know about *until*—— Dear, funny Dante—and at such a solemn moment too!

Or here is another self-portrait—Dante is always catching himself in slightly ridiculous attitudes. He and Virgil have now been joined by Statius, and they are ascending in single file the steep stair from the Sixth to the Seventh Cornice—the two Latin poets in front and Dante at their heels.

> And like a baby stork, that longs to fly
> And flaps its wings, and then, afraid to quit
> The nest, flops down again, just so was I—

---

[1] *Purg.* xii. 127–134.

> On fire to ask, but quenched as soon as lit;
> I got as far as making sounds like one
> About to speak, and then thought better of it.[1]

Is there anybody of so brazen a boldness that he has never caught himself flapping like a little stork—or, as P. G. Wodehouse puts it with another simile from the world of nature, "opening and shutting his mouth in a fishlike manner"?

The *Divine Comedy* is an enchanting picture-book. Riffle the pages where you will, the vivid images leap up and catch the eye—things that Dante has seen, that we have seen and see again with his keen vision. Sometimes they are things which he had seen, and which the civilised world had forgotten, but which we of this war-ridden generation see now with a dreadful recognition of their truth. Here is a grim little sketch from the *Inferno*—the sight, in the Bolgia of Disease, of

> the spirits strewn through the dark valley,
> Heaped here, heaped there, enduring their distress;
>
> This on the back, and that upon the belly
> One of another lay, while some crawled round
> The dismal road all-fours, lethargically.[2]

And here is Sacheverell Sitwell describing, in *Splendours and Miseries*, the aftermath of a modern battle:

> In places the corn has become a sickroom, or the bay of a hospital to which they bring the dying. But there are no screens put round the beds. It is part of the degradation that they lie in heaps as though tipped out of a cart. There is a fatality that forces them to crawl on one another, like puppies in a new-born litter. . . . It is not that they seek company. But theirs is the clumsiness of those who have lost perception through all the faculties being expressed in pain.[3]

Across six centuries, two poets touch hands, looking together upon the same scene. The later of them interprets what he sees: the earlier does not need to interpret; he merely shows. He knew that sight and so did his readers. The one passage did not suggest the other, for Mr. Sitwell assures me that Dante's lines are unfamiliar to him. But the two pictures are one even to the comparison with a hospital— "Valdichiana's spitals".

[1] *Purg.* xxv. 10–15.   [2] *Inf.* xxix. 65–69.
[3] *Splendours and Miseries* (Faber, 1943), p. 121.

Here is another picture—Ugolino nailed up in the Tower of Famine, watching his sons drop dead of hunger.

> Already I
> Was blind; I took to fumbling on them; two
> Long days I groped there, calling on the dead;
> Then famine did what sorrow could not do.[1]

"Already I was blind—*già cieco*"; "with grief", say the nineteenth-century commentators, sitting in their snug libraries after dinner. But we who have seen the pictures of Belsen and Buchenwald know better —we know now, as Dante knew, that starved men lose their eyesight. He knew it, and etched the picture with a pen dipped in gall, and afterwards broke out into his fierce cry for judgement upon the cruel city of Pisa. What words he would have found for the wholesale barbarities of our more enlightened age I cannot imagine; only one thing is certain: that he would not have rendered them tolerable to the reader's sensibility by any poetical verbiage. He is the swiftest of all poets; a single terzain—a single line—a brief word—and the picture flashes by almost before our slow vision has grasped it. Yet in a series of these quick, sure touches of detail he builds up his vast landscapes, as memorable in grand outline as in the "minute particulars".

And whether he is working on the grand scale or on the small scale, his images are not only stereoscopically clear but also extraordinarily consistent; or rather, they are clear *because* they are consistent. No divagation into philosophy, no preoccupation with symbolic values, ever seduces him for the moment into taking his eye off the object. If, by any chance, he has omitted to mention something needful to the story—some theatrical property, as one may say—he does not falsify the picture by suddenly introducing it from nowhere. He makes do with what he has; he will rather risk a slight clumsiness than introduce an inconsistency. When Virgil and Dante are confronted with Cerberus, he remembers that the proper thing to do with Cerberus is to appease him with food—"to give a sop to Cerberus". In the corresponding passage in the *Aeneid*, the Sibyl, who is conducting Aeneas through Hades, has come provided with cakes for the purpose. But, in the earlier part of the poem Dante has said nothing about cakes— either through an oversight, or because the idea of Virgil rising up out of Limbo to meet Dante in the Dark Wood and carrying a picnic-basket full of cakes seemed neither probable nor suitable: or because, in the swift rush of the narrative, there was no place where the mention

[1] *Inf.* xxxiii. 72–75.

of cakes would have come in without awkwardness. So Cerberus is appeased—not with cakes, but with "great handfuls of mire", scooped up by Virgil from the floor of Hell. It is the only thing handy, and it will serve—anything will serve, so long as we do not have to introduce a sudden incongruity into the picture. So too with the much-discussed signal that is flung over the Great Barrier to call up Geryon. Some object is needed—something detachable—something that one of the poets would be carrying or wearing in the ordinary way. Dante's girdle is the very thing. So far so good, if the poet had left it there: but he has thought well to attach a suggestion of symbolic meaning to it. He says that it was a rope-girdle, and that with it he had once hoped to catch the Leopard with the painted skin. Allegorically, this is all very well. A rope-girdle is the emblem of a vow—or at any rate an avowed intention of chastity: the Leopard is a symbolic image of Incontinence; whether or not Dante was ever, as has been suggested, a tertiary of the Order of St. Francis, the signification is clear: some effort at self-control has failed in its effect, and now serves to call up out of the deeps of the soul the image of its own evil perversion—the Fraud and Hypocrisy into which such efforts at repression may degenerate. But from the point of view of the actual *story*, the explanation is hastily and awkwardly contrived. Dante said nothing whatever in the First Canto about trying to *catch* the Leopard—only that it gambolled round him and impeded him, so that he was often forced out of his path. Still, though we are now obliged to add something to our first picture of Dante on the mountain, there is nothing here which definitely contradicts it. Dante had never said he was afraid of the Leopard; he said that he was in a cheerful mood, because of the Spring-time morning, and "had good hopes of the creature with the gay fur—*alla gaietta pella*". We remember that he actually spent the whole day, from dawn to dusk, in his adventures with the Beasts: and he might very well have tried to catch the Leopard, as the best way of bringing it to heel. This is perhaps not very convincing: and I readily agree that the passage about the rope-girdle is not one of Dante's best efforts. But the point I want to make is that although the symbolism has here rather intruded upon the story, Dante has neither introduced into the story anything totally incongruous, nor yet substituted the symbolic for the pictorial image. Let us again compare his method with that of two other masters of allegory.

When Christian and Hopeful are shut up in the dungeon of Giant Despair, we are a little surprised to hear Christian say:

"What a fool am I, thus to lie in a stinking dungeon, when I may as well walk at liberty! I have a key in my bosom called Promise that will, I am persuaded, open any lock in Doubting Castle."

Allegorically, that is admirable: but we feel we should like to know —just to make the literal story complete—where that key came from. Did Christian bring it from his home? or did he get it at the Interpreter's House? Bunyan has not chosen to inform us: and we may think that his reticence was wise and that Dante would have been well advised to be likewise reticent about the girdle. It is a matter of opinion.

Now compare Spenser. Sir Guyon is "faring on his way", accompanied only by his Palmer. Spenser is not very explicit about the "way" itself—whether we are on the high road, or in a wood, or where: but since the following canto mentions that Guyon met a knight, "pricking on the plain", and no change of scene is indicated, we may presume that the landscape is some kind of open country. Here they meet with Furor and the railing Hag his mother, dragging and belabouring the unfortunate squire Phaon. Guyon is told that he cannot conquer Furor till he has first restrained the Hag: he therefore seizes her, throws her down,

> And, catching hold of her ungratious tongue
> Thereon an yron lock did fasten firme and strong.

This is a very different matter from a rope-girdle. Even if it were possible to fasten a person's tongue with an ordinary padlock, we might be somewhat taken aback: but it is not, and so we are forced to imagine a kind of scold's-bridle: and we are entitled to wonder how either Guyon or the Palmer came to have this rather specialised instrument handy. Guyon then goes on to defeat Furor:

> Then him to ground he cast; and rudely hayld,
> And both his hands fast bound behind his backe,
> And both his feet in fetters to an yron racke.

"An iron rack"? Curiouser and curiouser. Spenser proceeds:

> With hundred yron chaines he did him bind,
> And hundred knots that did him sore constrain—

Here imagination boggles. We might pass the knotted rope, but a hundred iron chains are very heavy luggage for a knight-errant and an elderly palmer. Either there was an ironmonger's shop conveniently near (though nothing is said of it) or else we have discovered the original of Lewis Carroll's White Knight:

"I was wondering what the mouse-trap was for," said Alice. "It isn't very likely there would be any mice on the horse's back."

"Not very likely, perhaps," said the Knight; "but, if they do come, I don't choose to have them running all about.

"You see," he went on after a pause, "it's as well to be provided for *everything*. That's the reason the horse has anklets round his feet."

"But what are they for?" Alice asked in a tone of great anxiety.

"To guard against the bites of sharks," the Knight replied. "It's an invention of my own."

It is certainly an invention of Spenser's, and one which shows that he was quite content to sacrifice the probability of the literal story for the convenience of the allegory. The metaphorical controls imposed by temperance on physical and verbal fury have been translated into material locks and chains, and simply superimposed upon the literal story with no attempt at mechanical contrivance. The two levels of interpretation—literal and allegorical—have been fused. I do not know that we need blame Spenser for this. *The Faerie Queene* is a fairy-story, and we need not be over-nice about probability, unless we are very literal-minded people, or lecturers in search of something to carp at. The fact remains that this is not Dante's way of doing things. Even at his clumsiest (and Dante, like other people, has his off-moments) he keeps story and allegory separate, and each complete and consistent in itself. This is one of the reasons why our sense of being personally present with him throughout the whole action of the poem is so curiously strong and convincing.

This brings me to another point which perhaps needs to be emphasised rather specially for the modern reader of the *Comedy*. We are accustomed to poetry in which the language is very highly charged with metaphor, so that the fusion between the symbol and the thing symbolised takes place within the very structure of the image itself. Epithets are transferred from the one to the other; the two significations are not juxtaposed but superimposed—as, for example, in T. S. Eliot's lines:

> There are no eyes here
> In this valley of dying stars
> In this hollow valley
> This *broken jaw of our lost kingdoms* [1]

or in Dylan Thomas's fine poem *After the Funeral*, in which the figure

[1] *The Hollow Men.*

of the simple cottage woman, Ann, is fused with the monumental image which the poet makes of her in his verse:

> Her fist of a face died clenched on a round pain,
> And sculptured Ann is seventy years of stone.

This kind of writing is like the modern kind of music in which each discord is not immediately resolved, as in classical music, but the transition is made directly from discord to discord, taking the resolution for granted. Now, in the *Comedy* we find a few examples of this kind of writing, but they are very few—so few that when they do occur the effect of them is quite startling. Nobody, I imagine, can read the first canto of the *Inferno* without being struck by the fused image "*dove il sol tace*—that place wherein the sun is *mute*": or by its echo in the fifth canto: "*loco d'ogni luce muto*—a place made *dumb* of every glimmer of light", followed immediately by the paradoxical "*che mugghia—bellowing* like the sea in a storm". Again in the *Paradiso*, we have the wonderful compressed image:

> *L'altro ternaro, che così germoglia*
> *in questa primavera sempiterna,*
> *che notturno Ariete non dispoglia,*
>
> *perpetualemente Osanna sverna*
> *con tre melode . . .*[1]

"the second ternary [of angels] which thus buds forth in this eternal Spring which nightly Aries does not despoil, incessantly unwinters Hosanna with three melodies . . ."

Here the angels are first compared to flowers budding in springtime: then, in the same sentence, to the birds which, in the troubadour's phrase, are said to "unwinter themselves" (that is, to put off winter) by breaking into their spring-time songs: finally, and still in the same sentence, the song itself—the "Hosanna"—is made the direct object of the verb. So that, in place of a double simile, we have the impacted metaphor: "They who here bud forth unwinter hosanna."

The rare presence of this kind of writing in the *Comedy* shows that Dante could quite well do it if he chose, but that, on the whole, he did not choose. And that for a good reason. The *Comedy*, as T. S. Eliot has pointed out,[2] is itself one gigantic metaphor, susceptible, as we saw earlier, of a great variety of interpretation. Its content is complex:

---

[1] *Para.* xxviii. 115–119.
[2] T. S. Eliot: *Selected Essays* (Faber, 1932); *Dante*, p. 244.

and it deals, especially in the *Paradiso,* with ideas which are difficult enough, even when straightforwardly stated. If Dante had complicated an already complex theme by highly-complex fused imagery, the effect would have been, from the merely artistic point of view, to irritate and confuse the reader, and to impede the swift pace both of narrative and argument. It would have been, indeed, only a manifestation, at still another level, of the gaily-spotted Leopard of incontinence, tripping and gambolling before the reader's feet and luring him out of the way. Dante's poetic tact was sensitive enough to deter him from all such displays of misplaced brilliance.[1] Or we may go further, and find in this restraint a notable humility.

It has often been remarked that his poetic practice in the *Comedy* directly contradicts everything he had said in the *De Vulgari Eloquentia* about poetic theory. That is quite true: it does. But in those chapters of the *De Eloquentia* which he completed, he was dealing with lyric verse, and in particular with the construction of that highly-elaborated and conventional fixed form, the *canzone.* In lyric verse—brief, intense, and highly-charged with emotion—condensed metaphor and closely-packed imagery is as wholly right as in narrative it is wholly wrong. But there is more to it than that: again and again in his lyrics Dante prides himself openly upon the obscurity of his verse: "Song, I think there will be few to understand thy meaning, so intricate and hard is thy utterance"; "Song . . . deny to all men the sweet fruit for which every one stretches forth his hand . . . but if ever thou find one who loves virtue, reveal thyself to him"; or, condescendingly: "I will express myself in easier sentences, so as to be less hard to understand; for seldom beneath the veil does a dark saying penetrate to the intelligence." But by the time he came to write the great "poem to which Heaven and earth have both set hand", he was older, less arrogant, more eager to be understood by ordinary men and women, and if he is aware that he is being difficult, he apologises for it, excusing himself by reason of the profundity of the theme, the novelty of the task, his own inadequacy, the fact that he is trying to say more than can be put into words, so that in the end he must give up the hopeless attempt "as every artist must when he has reached the end of his tether:

> *come all' ultimo suo ciascuno artista".*

The *canzoni* are indeed difficult: and it is a pity that they have so far received comparatively little critical attention, for though some are

[1] See note at end of this paper.

merely crabbed, others contain imagery of great beauty. In them, unlike the *Comedy*, metaphor is plentiful and simile comparatively rare. Indeed, much that is ostensibly simile is in fact fused metaphor, as in the mysterious and lovely *Tre donne intorno al cor* which fascinates as much as it perplexes:

> *Dolesi l'una con parole molto,*
> *E'n sulla man si posa*
> *Come succisa rosa*
> *Il nudo braccio, di dolor colonna,*
>
> *Sente l' oraggio che cade dal volto.*

"The one makes complaint in many words, and leans upon her hand like a lopped rose: her naked arm, a column of grief, feels the rain-storm which falls from her face." Within the delicately classic outlines of this funerary figure, the images are highly elliptical. She leans upon her hand like a cut rose (in the hand? in a vase?) severed from the branch that nourishes its life: or, perhaps, a broken rose withering upon its stalk. Her arm is a column of grief—the image is that of a mourner weeping at a tomb. Or is it, rather, that we are reminded of that great elegiac outburst in the *Purgatorio*, where Italy is called *di dolore ostello?* This lady also is, as it were, a "house of grief", her arm the column that supports the ruined architrave; here the middle term of the simile has been suppressed, like the resolution of a chord, and we are left with a fused and strongly emotional image. In the *Purgatorio* passage, the image reappears in a simplified and more rhetorical form.

Dante, like nearly all poets, has a way of returning to his favourite images and sources. This same *canzone* also contains the adumbration of that remarkable Virgilian mosaic of protest and consent which we noticed in our last paper, though in this case the Virgilian echo is so faint as to be almost inaudible. Love asks the distracted lady who she and her companions are: "and she, who was so ready with her tears, was kindled to greater grief when she heard him, saying:

> '*or non ti duol degli occhi miei?*'
> *Poi cominciò":—*[1]

Three of the four poems of the *Pietra* group not only contain a whole series of similar images, but are, in fact, variations of the same poem:

[1] "Art thou not sorry for my weeping eyes?"
    Then she began:—
    Canz. Tre donne intorno al cor mi son venute.

while the fourth—the notorious *Aspro parlar*—is so closely connected by its imagery with the *canzone* known as the *Mountain Ode*, that it is difficult to believe that this latter does not really belong also to the Pietra group. The rain and the ice in the *canzone Io son venuto al punto della rota* are as it were the original detailed study from nature which preceded the firm, bold outlines of the pictures in the third and ninth circles of Hell.

But upon the fascinating subject of the sources from which, consciously or unconsciously, Dante drew his imagery, I do not propose to embark. Like all the greatest poets, he took as much from literature as from life. John Livingston Lowes, who devoted an enthralling book of about 600 pages to the literary sources of *The Ancient Mariner* and *Kubla Khan* alone, has observed:

> Well-nigh all the encyclopedic erudition of the Middle Ages was forged and welded, in the white heat of an indomitable will, into the steel-knit structure of *The Divine Comedy*. There are not, in the world, I suppose, more appalling masses of raw fact than would stare us in the face could we once, through some super-subtle chemistry, resolve that superb, organic unity into its primal elements.[1]

It is, at any rate, not a task to be attempted in the last few pages of a short paper. Nor have we the time, even had I the will and skill, to try and extract the content of Dante's unconscious from his prevailing imagery. Indeed, I am not very certain about the reliability of this kind of psychological investigation. I have already issued a caution against too-eagerly hunting the hare of sexuality through the circles of the Three Kingdoms: and after carefully considering Dante's occasional references to mothers, fathers and children, I find myself unable to saddle him with an Oedipus-complex or a mother-fixation. It is true that he lost his father early in life and that his mother married again: that he likes to call Virgil his *dolce padre*, and that he once or twice uses the word "step-mother" with that sinister connotation familiar to us in all folk-tale. It is true also that there were, on his own confession, other ladies in his life besides his wife and Beatrice, and that some of his Odes bear witness to a passionate, and apparently unsuccessful love-affair. But on the whole he seems to me to have been an almost exceptionally normal kind of man, singularly free from any disposition either to idealise or to disparage women as a class or the sexual relation as such.

[1] John Livingston Lowes: *The Road to Xanadu* (Constable, 1930), p. 426.

But, apart from all this, and leaving to others the discovery that Hell is a female symbol because it is hollow, or Mount Purgatory a male symbol because it is a cone, and all that kind of thing which is so easy when you once get the knack of it, we can, of course, discover something about Dante's mind and character from the kind of images he uses. We have already mentioned their concreteness, their conciseness, their earthy vigour, their homely domesticity—natural, perhaps, in a man who for so many years of exile had no home of his own.

There is his passion for light and colour, his love of seas and rivers, his quick eye for the characteristic movement of bird or beast, the readiness with which he seizes on some topical allusion—the fall of rocks at the Slavini di Marco: the institution of a one-way traffic control in Rome—to make his meaning more vividly clear. We may infer from his many images of hunting and hawking that he followed these pursuits: indeed, in Can Grande's household he could hardly have escaped them, and there is a slightly sarcastic sonnet about "the noise of beagles and spurring of horsemen, the starting of hares, and hallooing of people, and fleet hounds slipped from the leash" which gives a very powerful impression of a tumultuous week-end in "huntin', fishin' and shootin'" circles, and makes us wonder what he really, privately, thought of sporting society. He is always accused of being snobbishly aristocratic; and certainly he greatly admired the great Ghibelline nobles with their generosity, their patronage of art, and their magnificent way of life—admired them, perhaps, against his better political judgment. But whenever he writes of humble workingfolk it is with remarkable sympathy: the tired vintager on the hillside, the shepherd whose flocks have run short of fodder, the exhausted peasant-woman, haunted in her dreams by her monotonous task of gleaning. The class he dislikes is that of the pushing and vulgar merchants—the self-made bourgeoisie who were climbing so fast into Florentine society; these he castigates and denounces, but they supply him with no poetic similes—one feels that he has thrown them out of his storehouse of subconscious images. One could speak, also, of the remarkable skill with which he pictures the borderland between sleep and waking: and how the various dreams which he describes in the *Purgatorio*, symbolic though they are, have far more of authentic quality—are much more like real dreams—than the majority of prophetic dreams in mediaeval, or indeed any other literature. Notice, for example, how in the dream about the Siren, it is suggested, though not, of course, explicitly stated, that the voice of Virgil, three times calling to him to wake, both makes and breaks the dream and introduces Virgil himself as a character within the dream.

But although the attempt to reconstruct "the real Dante" from his poem is as tempting as it is perilous, it is well to remember that to read his poem only for what it betrays about himself is to run directly counter to his whole purpose in writing. In so far as his own portrait is necessary to the understanding of the *Comedy*, he has given it in his own words. It is not a flattering likeness: and some people find it repellent, though to me it seems endearing. But the image of Dante, like all the other images, is there for the sake of the poem, and not the poem for the sake of Dante. Long before, when he was quite a young man, writing love-poems about Beatrice, he had suffered a memorable rebuke from a lady, who asked him:

"Pray tell us, wherein lies this beatitude of yours?" And I replied simply: "In those words that praise my lady." And she answered: "If that were true, you would have spoken otherwise; and not in these words which are all about your own feelings." [1]

Whereat, he says, he went away ashamed, and determined thenceforth to write nothing but praise of his lady: to write, that is, about his subject and not about himself. In his lyrics he did not always remain true to this resolution; but in the *Comedy*, he did. The poem is Dante's, and he himself is part of his poem: the images, to quote Mr. Day Lewis once more, "represent what a poet has seen looking outwards at humanity and what he has seen looking into his own heart, focused together to make a whole truth".[2]

(1947)

NOTE

Although the true fused image is rare in the *Comedy*, the running-together of two linked similes by the suppression of the second "like as" sometimes produces what looks like a mixed, but is better called, in H. W. Fowler's phrase, a "fused" metaphor. For example:

> Forth of His hands whose brooding tenderness
> Loves her or ere she comes to be, is brought,
> Laughing and weeping, like a babe that plays,

---

[1] *Vita Nuova*, xviii.   [2] *The Poetic Image:* p. 156.

> The simple infant soul, that, all untaught,
> But moved by a glad Maker, turns with pleasure
> To this or that by which her fancy's caught.
>
> First, she's attracted by some trifling treasure,
> Then runs, beguiled, in hot pursuit to scour,
> Save manage sway her love with the curb's pressure.[1]

"The soul, *like an infant*, turns to what attracts her, and then rushes in pursuit of it [carried away *like a man* on a runaway horse] unless she can curb her love."

On the other hand, the image in the same canto of the "shepherd who chews the cud but does not part the hoof" is probably not a mixed metaphor at all, but a mediaeval grotesque—a "camel in shepherd's clothing"—such as one might see on any carved capital or miserere seat (cf. the famous Fox preaching to the Geese in Beverley Minster).

Occasionally also the trick of synecdoche is exploited to an extent which, even in its own day, must have seemed exaggerated, and to modern taste is ludicrous, as in *Para.* xiii. 37–39, where Adam is designated as, "the breast from which was drawn the rib to form the fair cheek for whose palate the whole world pays".

But in all these passages the intention is clear and the verbal imagery throughout the poem remains on the whole straightforward.

C. Day Lewis (*op. cit.*, p. 54), in the course of an interesting comparison between the "Augustan" and the "Romantic" or "Symbolist" use of images, quotes a "startling and salutary" observation by Louis MacNeice: "Those who practise imagery in the Symbolist manner would do well occasionally to notice *how images are used in ordinary speech*,[2] i.e. to drive home a meaning, to make a point, to *outline* a picture (for an outline is distinct from a suggestion)." Since every poetic revolution advertises and justifies itself as a return to the diction and rhythm of ordinary speech, this may well mean that the next poetic move will be a return from the suggestive to the indicative image, from the unconscious to the conscious, from Symbolism (in the technical sense) to Allegory. If so (and there are already signs that it is so) it will be the "modern" type of imagery that will then appear "artificial", "literary", "frigid", and "conventional". It is always well to be prepared for these things.

---

[1] *Purg.* xvi. 88–93.   [2] Italics mine, D. L. S.

THE MEANING OF HEAVEN AND HELL

IF the reader will take his Bible, either in the Latin Vulgate which Dante knew, or in the English Authorised Version, and turn to the ninth chapter of St. Mark, the 43rd and following verses, he will find this passage:

Jesus said: If thy hand offend thee, cut it off: it is better for thee to enter into life maimed, than having two hands to go into hell, into the fire that never shall be quenched;

Where their worm dieth not, and the fire is not quenched.

And if thy foot offend thee, cut it off: it is better for thee to enter halt into life, than having two feet to be cast into hell, into the fire that never shall be quenched;

Where their worm dieth not, and the fire is not quenched.

And if thine eye offend thee, pluck it out; it is better for thee to enter into the kingdom of God with one eye, than having two eyes to be cast into hell fire;

Where their worm dieth not, and the fire is not quenched.

In some Greek codices and in the English Revised Version, the passage is shortened by the omission of some of the solemn repetitions, but without alteration of the significance.

I have begun with this quotation because there seems to be a kind of conspiracy, especially among middle-aged writers of vaguely liberal tendency, to forget, or to conceal, where the doctrine of Hell comes from. One finds frequent references to "the cruel and abominable *mediaeval* doctrine of hell", or "the childish and grotesque *mediaeval* imagery of physical fire and worms". People who write about Dante are often concerned to sneer at him, or alternatively to pity him, for being compelled by "the crude superstition of his age" to believe in these things under menace of excommunication and torture: or else they eagerly assure us that he was too clever really to have believed in them, and was actually a Gnostic heretic or a nineteenth-century liberal, engaged in debunking the Roman Catholic Church in an elaborate satirical cryptogram.

But the case is quite otherwise; let us face the facts. The doctrine of Hell is not "mediaeval": it is Christ's. It is not a device of "mediaeval priestcraft" for frightening people into giving money to the Church:

44

it is Christ's deliberate judgment on sin. The imagery of the undying worm and the unquenchable fire derives, not from "mediaeval superstition", but originally from the Prophet Isaiah, and it was Christ who emphatically used it. If we are Christians, very well; we dare not *not* take the doctrine of Hell seriously, for we have it from Him whom we acknowledge as God and Truth incarnate. If we say that Christ was a great and good man, and that, ignoring His divine claims, we should yet stick to His teaching—very well; *that* is what Christ taught. It confronts us in the oldest and least "edited" of the Gospels: it is explicit in many of the most familiar parables and implicit in many more: it bulks far larger in the teaching than one realises, until one reads the Evangelists through instead of merely picking out the most comfortable texts: one cannot get rid of it without tearing the New Testament to tatters. We cannot repudiate Hell without altogether repudiating Christ.

And, that being so, it is evident that we cannot reasonably blame Dante, or the Church in his age, or any Christian in any age, for believing with desperate seriousness what Christ so unequivocally said. It is quite fatal to come to the study of the *Divine Comedy* with our minds irrevocably set in a frivolous, or superior, or righteously indignant attitude to the very idea of hell; it will throw all our critical judgment out of focus. If we are ever to make head or tail of the greatest of Christian poems, we must at least be ready to understand what is meant by damnation, and why every believing Christian recognises it as a terrible possibility for and within himself, and why it matters to our comprehension of God and Heaven and Man.

From one point of view it is unfortunate that the *Inferno* is the first of the three books of the *Comedy*. It is right for the story, and it is artistically right; the passage from the Dark Wood of Sin in which we are so catastrophically caught must lead through the knowledge of Hell before it can emerge to ascend the Mount of Purgatory to the knowledge of Beatitude: and to descend from the ecstasy of the *Paradiso* to the squalors of the *Inferno* would be, from an artistic point of view, intolerable. But the order of the books means that the reader—especially the modern reader, with his often very inadequate theology and his inherited tradition of vague and kindly humanism—encounters on the very threshold of his enterprise, this huge block of what, to him, is obsolete, repulsive, irreconcilable with the religion of love, and meaningless. He is therefore apt, in self-defence, to dismiss the whole thing from his serious consideration, and either fall back on

5

enjoying "the poetry" without bothering about the meaning: or, which is far worse, write Dante down as a spiteful politician or a vindictive sadist, and pass on to something else—not, as a rule, to the *Purgatory* and *Paradise*. And that is a pity; because although, experientially, the order Hell, Purgatory, Paradise is correct, yet, intellectually, the understanding of Heaven is the key to the understanding of Hell. As a matter of fact, in Dante's own case, Heaven preceded Hell in his experience also. The *Vita Nuova* is the approach and ante-chamber to the *Divine Comedy*. As a child, and as a young man in love, he had glimpsed the vision of eternity: he had "looked upon the hope of the blessed". Later, he fell away and stumbled into the Dark Wood; the *Comedy* is the story of his return home, and the final vision is infinitely greater than that early, half-comprehended glimpse. But experience differs with different people and different generations. It may even be that for some of the younger people in the Europe of to-day, the theology of Hell will seem more acceptable than the theology of Heaven. We have seen in our time the abyss of wickedness yawn open at our feet: school-children have witnessed things which to our Victorian forbears would have seemed quite unthinkable, though they would scarcely have surprised Dante. However that may be, the *intellectual* understanding of the Three Kingdoms must begin with Heaven: and if I have preluded this paper with a brief consideration of Hell, it is only by way of a promise, or a warning, that I intend to take the question of damnation quite seriously, as Dante takes it and as all Christians must if they take Christ seriously.

What I shall try to set down here, as simply and briefly as may be, is the meaning of Heaven and Hell as Catholic Christians understand it, and I shall try to show how that meaning is displayed in Dante's imagery. The great danger always is that, unless we know the doctrine, we may mistake the imagery for the thing imaged. And here again we shall be greatly hampered if we imagine that educated people in the Middle Ages were childish and credulous. It was an age in which a great many people were illiterate, and when nobody knew as much as the twentieth-century person about the physical sciences. But the culture of a fourteenth-century city like Florence was extremely high, and the things that educated people did know, they knew very well indeed, and theology was one of those things. I have before now tried to explain Dante's conception of Heaven and Hell in simple terms to the kind of modern person who is brought up on smatterings of know-ledge in popular digests, and have been told that "my ideas were very sophisticated". The fourteenth century *does* seem sophisticated to the twentieth when it is talking on its own subject. We have forgotten so much of our theology since Dante's time.

Our explanation must begin with Heaven, because Heaven—or rather God in Heaven—is the only unconditioned reality. All other reality is derived from God, being either immediately created by Him, or engendered or evolved or manufactured by the mediation of His creatures, interacting among themselves. If we ask *why* God created a universe of beings, we have to acknowledge that

> *sì nasconde*
> *lo suo primo perchè, che non gli è guado.*[1]

Nevertheless, knowing by revelation that God is all-goodness and all-love, the Christian may meditate upon the matter: and the best conclusions of Catholic thought have never been more nobly summed up than in the passage in the 29th canto of the *Paradiso*:

> *Non per aver a sè di bene acquisto,*
> *ch' esser non può, ma perchè suo splendore*
> *potesse, risplendendo, dir:* Subsisto,
> *In sua eternità di tempo fuore,*
> *fuor d'ogni altro comprender, come i piacque,*
> *s'aperse in nuovi amor l'eterno amore.*[2]

The reason, Dante says, was *generosity.* God—as Plato had written in the *Timaeus*, which Dante had read—is not jealous; He wanted, and wants, to share His reality. He did not want to gain anything for Himself: that is impossible; for all things come from Him, and He could no more *add* anything to Himself by making a universe than a poet can add anything to *him*self by writing a poem. But He desired that there should be others, derived from Himself but distinguishable from Him, and with a dependent but genuine reality of their own, having each a true selfhood, which should reflect back to Him the joy and beauty and goodness that they received from Him. The image

---

[1]   [His] primal *Why*
Lies so deep hid, no wit can wade so far.
Purg. viii. 69.

[2] Not that He might acquire any gain for Himself, for that cannot be; but in order that His splendour [i.e. the reflection of His glory from His creation] might, shining back to Him, declare "*I am*", therefore in His eternity, beyond all time, beyond all limitation, according to His good pleasure, the Eternal Love unfolded Himself into new loves.

Para. xxix. 13–18.

here, as throughout the *Paradiso*, is the familiar one of light; God is the light: the derived radiance of the creature is the *splendore*, the splendour. The right end of every creature is to shine back to God with that splendour, and to be able to say, thus shining (*risplendendo*); "*I am—subsisto*".

That is a key-passage to Dante's thought, and, indeed, to Catholic thought. Notice how entirely different it is from the Gnostic and Neo-Platonic thought which characterises the great Oriental religions and so often tries to infiltrate into Christianity. For the Gnostic, creation is evil, and the outflowing of the One into the Many is a disaster: the true end of the Many is to lose the derived self and be reabsorbed into the One. But for the Christian, it is not so. The derived self is the glory of the creature and the multiplicity and otherness of the universe is its joy. The true end of the creature is that it should reflect, each in its own way and to its capacity great or small, some tiny facet of the infinite variety comprised within the unity of the One. The Christian Heaven is a populous place. "Behold," says Beatrice.

> *mira*
> *quanto è il convento delle bianche stole!*
> *Vedi nostra città, quanto ella gira!* [1]

The higher the created being is, and the nearer to God, the more utterly it is itself and the more it differs from its fellow-creatures. The lowest and least of created things—the prime matter—is formless and homogeneous: and inorganic matter has very little individuality. Plants have much more; animals are real individuals; and a human being is more than that: he is a person. When we come to the angels, or "intelligences" in Dante's phrase, they are thought of as possessing such super-personalities that the Schoolmen refused to think of them as being merely so many members of a species; they said that every angel was a separate species all to himself. This may seem to us rather a quaint if not absurd way of putting it: but the intention is clear; an angel is so triumphantly and perfectly himself that one of these blessed beings differs from another not as one man from another but as one *class* of terrestrial beings from another. Remembering the four beasts of the Apocalypse, we may even say that they differ as a man from an

---

[1]   admire
How great the company of the robes of white,
Behold our city, how wide it spreads its gyres.
Para. xxx. 128–130.

ox, or an eagle from a lion. However curious this scholastic language may appear, we may at any rate find it a useful corrective to the impression we are apt to carry away from the pictures of many mediaeval and modern artists, which show row upon row of angels, all with the same wings feather for feather, the same white nightgown, the same hair-do, and the same expressionless face. All images are inadequate: but we may use one image to correct the other. An imagery of sameness may properly represent the unity in bliss; another kind of image may as properly present the inexhaustible variety of super-human personality and differentiated power.

With the ultimate destiny of the sub-rational creation, Western thought in the Middle Ages did not much concern itself, neither need we. Dante is clear, however, that the *splendore* shines back from every part of creation, though not equally from all:

> *La gloria di colui che tutto muove*
> *per l'universo penetra, e risplende*
> *in una parte più, e meno altrove.*[1]

The splendour is in some parts less—partly because the "form" stamped on the "matter" is sometimes imperfect, owing to the limitations which attend all finite and created being; partly—and this is the great principle of hierarchy which runs all through mediaeval thought —because, even where all things are made perfect according to their capacity, their capacities differ. This is the conclusion to which Beatrice is leading up through the celebrated passage in *Paradiso* ii about the dark patches in the Moon:

> *Virtù diversa fa diversa lega*
> *col prezioso corpo ch'ell'avviva—*[2]

"diverse power makes diverse alloy with the precious body which it quickens". The *splendore* of, let us say, a beetle is less than that of an angel, even though beetle and angel may each be perfect after its own nature: it is their natures that differ. With this general conclusion we may readily agree; though we may rebel at some of its further consequences. We must bear it in mind, because it is important.

Leaving the lower creation, we come to the destiny of rational beings

---

[1] The glory of Him that moves all things soe'er
   Impenetrates the universe, and bright
   The splendour burns, more here and lesser there.
                              Para. i. 1–3.

[2] *Para.* ii. 139–140.

—that is, of men and angels. The angels are pure intelligences, and Heaven is their native abode. Men are beings of mixed nature, compounded of matter and spirit: Heaven is the abode in which they, too, but at the end of a shorter or longer time-process, will find the home prepared for them, and then at last their true selfhood will be fully realised.

What, then, is "Heaven"? Here, for the moment, let us resolutely dismiss all imagery—even Dante's images of light and music and ecstatic dance: even the rainbow and the wheels and the fire of Ezekiel and the Apocalypse: still more the Rubens-like Miltonic picture of angelic armies and celestial banquets: and most decidedly of all any caricature that may linger in our minds of "sitting on a damp cloud with a halo and harp". Let us dismiss all the geocentric mechanism of revolving spheres and distinct physical heavens—Dante himself will have none of them except by way of analogy. There is, he says emphatically by the mouth of Beatrice, only one true Heaven, and that is the Empyrean:

> *Ivi è perfetta, matura ed intera*
> *ciascuna disianza; in quella sola*
> *è ogni parte là dove sempr'era,*
> *perchè non è in loco e non s'impola—*[1]

"there every desire is perfect, ripe and whole: in that alone is every part there where it always was; for it is not in space and has no poles". It is not limited by time or space, or conditioned by motion or direction (*non s'impola*); in that eternal whole, all parts are present together (notice that multiplicity is again affirmed) and in that eternal instant all times are present together (*è . . . là dove sempr'era*). It is, in the words of Boethius, "the perfect and simultaneous possession of everlasting life". In what, then, does it consist, the everlasting life to possess which is Heaven? In the definition of the Schoolmen: "Heaven is the seeing of God in His essence." That is the Beatific Vision, the true goal of every desire: that is the realisation in which the true self of all spiritual beings is made real: behind all the tumultuous images of poet and musician and painter there lies that little, dry, abstract phrase. The images exist only to bring the significance of that phrase home to us.

I must now try to explain very shortly what the Schoolmen meant by this important phrase, and I will begin by borrowing a definition from P. H. Wicksteed's *From Vita Nuova to Paradiso* [2]—an admirable

---

[1] *Para.* xxii. 64–67.   [2] Manchester University Press, 1922.

little book, of the greatest possible assistance towards getting an intellectual grasp of the *Commedia*. "To know a thing in its essence meant so to understand its inmost being as to see how all its manifestations and effects necessarily flow from it because they are involved in it." Dante elsewhere explains that this is the way in which we understand a logical process, as for example, a series of geometrical propositions, all necessarily flowing out of, because virtually contained in, the fundamental axioms.

Now it is evident that very few things are known to us in this way. Apart from abstractions of the kind just mentioned, most things—the Aristotelians would have said all things—are known to us, not in their essence, but by their effects. Exterior objects make an impression upon our senses, and we deduce knowledge about their properties and behaviour. The minds of other people are made known to us by the actions we see and the words we hear, which we interpret largely by analogy with our own mental processes. There is, of course, the phenomenon called "mind-reading", but it is rare and partial. Of our own minds we have, indeed, direct and intuitive consciousness "from the inside": though even here I think we should have to admit that we do not even know them and their workings as intimately as perhaps we once supposed we did—the psychologists have given us glimpses of unplumbed abysses within ourselves, and we find it hard to tell where our thoughts and emotions come from, or how they interact one with another. When it comes to the mind of some alien species—even of our favourite cat or dog, we have to admit ourselves baffled. We try to interpret their behaviour: we argue about whether they can distinguish colours, and how far they are capable of reasoning: and we very often transfer to them the kind of feelings we have ourselves. But what it really feels like to be a cat: how the world really looks to a dog: and above all, what the values of the animal creation are; these are enigmas, and the more earnestly we gaze into those strange furry faces—so familiar, so uninhibited and open, and yet so curiously secretive, the more we are aware of their remoteness and otherness. Only God, who made all things, knows them and us and all His myriad creatures from the inside—knows them *in their essence* and as they are, and knows how their effects develop out of their essence, with the same intimacy and certainty with which we follow an abstract logical process.

We have imagined trying to enter into the consciousness of a creature more limited than ourselves; let us now imagine it the other way. Let us imagine ourselves able to read the mind of someone much greater than we are—let us say of Dante himself. Instead of wrestling with the text of his poem and trying to work out what it meant, through a mist of our own preconceptions, prejudices, ignorances, and the inevitable misunderstandings which result when two minds of very different temper and capacity are trying to communicate by means of signs and words, we should watch the making of poetry from within, and have immediate insight into the mind itself. We should see the images pouring in through all the gates of sense and memory, linking and weaving and setting to partners in the intricate associative dance and streaming out again, transformed, into the great poetic images: we should know the *Commedia*, that is, in its essence and not merely by its effects. That would not, of course, make us as great as Dante; his would still be the originating mind, and our wonder and admiration could only deepen by seeing it at work. Neither should we be able to understand any more of its working than our own minds were capable of receiving; but what we did understand, we should know directly and intuitively instead of by the indirect process of reasoning upon the data presented to us by the senses. To take a very simple and inadequate analogy. As things are, we stand outside another mind like children looking at the dial of a clock; we see the hands move round and we can tell the time by their movement: but the mechanism is concealed and we can only guess at what makes them move. In the other case, it is as though we saw the clock from within, and directly watched the motion of the pendulum and weights and wheels; but how much we understood of their action would depend on whether we were mechanically-minded children or not.

In Heaven, we see that the knowledge which the blessed souls have of one another is of this intimate, intuitive and essential kind. That is why Dante never needs to formulate a question, for Beatrice and the souls whom he meets in the various spheres enter into his mind and read the question there. Sometimes they wait for him to ask—not because they need to, but for the sheer pleasure of hearing him speak (rather as, in the case I supposed, we should enjoy watching Dante actually make his poem and put it into words). Thus Cacciaguida, filled with delight at seeing the inheritor of his blood, says to Dante;

> *Tu credi che a me tuo pensier mei*
> *da quel ch'è primo, così come raia*
> *dall' un, se si conosce, il cinque e il sei—*[1]

---

[1] *Para.* xv. 55–57.

"Thou thinkest that thy thought makes its way to me from the primal Thought itself, just as, when rightly known, the pentad and hexad are seen to ray forth from the monad" (i.e. as we said before, with the inevitability of a logical geometrical process): *"tu credi il vero".* Nevertheless, he goes on, in order that the sacred love which fills him with longing may be the better fulfilled,

> *la voce tua sicura, balda e lieta*
> *suoni la volontà, suoni il disio,*
> *a che la mia risposta è già decreta.*[1]

The blessed creatures know one another and delight in one another, as they know and delight in Dante and all things:—

As in a fish-pool, still and clear, the fishes draw towards anything that is dropped in from without and seems as though it might be food, so I saw thousand and more splendours draw towards us, and from each was heard: "Lo, one who shall increase our loves—*Ecco chi crescerà li nostri amori*[2]"

All that is within their capacity they know and love perfectly: all that is beyond and above their capacity they know and love to the fulness of their capacity. In his joy at beholding Dante, the splendour that is Folco of Marseilles blazes out "like a fine ruby smitten by the sun"; for light up there is what a smile is here:

> *per letiziar lassù folgor s'acquista,*
> *sì come riso qui—*[3]

and Dante, entering into the spirit of the place, says to him with a mock-reproach that is almost playful:

> *"Dio vede tutto, e tuo veder s'inluia—"*[4]

Why then does thy voice not satisfy my longing? I should not have waited for thee to ask

> *"s'io m' intuassi, come tu t'immii."* [5]

In all these exchanges, the manner in which the spirits see and know is not left doubtful. Their minds behold all things mirrored in the primal Thought: they read by the light which rays out for ever from the

---

[1] "let thy voice, assured and confident and glad, speak forth thy will, speak forth thy desire, to which my answer is decreed already".
Para. xv. 67–69.

[2] *Para.* v. 100–106.
[3] *Para.* ix. 70–71.
[4] *Para.* ix. 73.
[5] *Para.* ix. 81.

eterna fonte, the eternal fountain of light to which, in our last glimpse
of Beatrice, we see her turn her adoring eyes. "If I could in-thee
myself as thou dost in-me thyself," says Dante, courageously coining
new words for the unknown: but he begins by saying: "God sees all
things, and thy sight *in-Hims itself—s'inluia*"—thy seeing sinks into
God—it is "ingodded"; Beatrice uses that very word of the Seraphim
who circle closest to God and know and love Him best: "*dei Seraphin
colui che più s'india*".[1] Is it then possible for the knowledge of a creature
to span the measureless distance between the made and the Maker,
between the finite and the Infinite? Yes—for otherwise that desire and
love for the highest possible good which (as Dante tells us over and
over again) is the main-spring of all human and angelic action, would
remain without fulfilment, and Heaven would not be perfect. How can
this be? I will quote Wicksteed again, because he explains it so well:

> To human or angelic nature it is, in itself, impossible to be or to become
> deiform ["ingodded", in Dante's phrase], but to God all things are possible;
> and by impressing His very self, essentially, upon the created spirit He can
> so transfuse it with the "light of glory" (*lumen gloriae*) that "in that light
> it can see the light". For when assimilated to the essential being of God it
> can, up to the measure of the initial capacity divinely bestowed, see God as
> He sees Himself.[2]

That, we may remember, is what St. Paul says: "Then shall I know,
even as I am known."

Wicksteed adds a reminder:

> "Up to its measure"—For the infinite must remain in infinite excess of
> the finite. But the assimilation within that measure may be perfect and may
> constitute, to that spirit, the absolute fulfilment of its longing for perfect
> vision and for perfect blessedness. . . . [It will be] the direct vision of perfect
> power, wisdom, love; of perfect goodness, truth, beauty; not as abstractions
> or ideals of our minds, but as the very Being of God, who is Being's self.[3]

In other words, what the blissful know is Reality, the ultimate reality
of every good thing that they have imagined, filling them through and
through with itself—and inexhaustible. I suppose that everybody as a
child (as well as some adult people who ought to have put away
childish things) has wondered what one would find to do in an eternity
of bliss. Dante—and it is perhaps his greatest achievement—is able to

---

[1] that one of the Seraphim who is the most in-godded.

Para. iv. 28.

[2] *Op. cit.*, p. 27.   [3] *Ibid.*

convince us that this kind of thinking makes no sense. Eternity is not an unmeaning stretch of endless time: it is all times and all places known perfectly in one deathless and ecstatic present

> *O abbondante graʒia, ond' io presunsi*
> *ficcar lo viso per la luce eterna*
> *tanto che la veduta vi consunsi!*
>
> *Nel suo profondo vidi che s'interna,*
> *legato con amore in un volume,*
> *ciò che per l'universo si squaderna;*
>
> *sustanʒia ed accidenti, e lor costume,*
> *quasi conflati insieme per tal modo*
> *che ciò ch'io dico è un semplice lume.*[1]

"I think I saw it," he says, "the universal form of this complex, because, more largely, even as I say this, I feel that I rejoice." [2] That which for a blinding moment he knew in its essence, he now knows, human-fashion, only in its effects. But he did see that.

From that gaze upon the universe he passes to the Vision of God Himself. This he cannot even attempt to describe, except in that image of the three consubstantial circles or spheres, the rainbow and the fire, and the in-manning of God beheld there as the pledge and means of the ingodding of man. It is the same vision that Ezekiel had, prophetically looking upon Christ before ever Christ was incarnate, seeing the Son of Man exalted between the cherubims:

> Upon the likeness of the throne was the likeness of the appearance of a man . . . and I saw as the colour of amber, as the appearance of fire round about within it . . . and it had brightness round about. As the appearance of the bow that is in the cloud in the day of rain, so was the appearance of the

---

[1] O grace abounding, whereby I presumed
So deep the eternal light to search and sound
That my whole vision was therein consumed!

In that abyss I saw how love held bound
Into one volume all the leaves whose flight
Is scattered through the universe around;

How substance, accident, and mode unite,
Fused so to speak together, in such wise
That this I tell of is one simple light.
Para. xxxiii. 82–90.

[2] *Para.* xxxiii. 91–93.

brightness round about. This was the appearance of the likeness of the glory of the Lord.[1]

But Dante is not yet in Heaven. The power passes. Yet he has looked upon the reality of God, and already, as a wheel is moved equally about its centre, "desire and will are wheeled by love": the love in whose power the Intelligences "by understanding" move the spheres of Heaven, enters into him and makes Him its own. Long ago, in a dream, Love—the Lord of terrible aspect whom he had first encountered in the God-bearing image of Beatrice—had said to him "I am the centre of the circle, to whom all parts of the circle are similarly related: but with thee it is not so." [2] Dante had not then understood this; now he does. Now all parts of his circumference move equally about that central Love of which his first love was the image and the promise. The first love is not denied by the last love; all forms are taken up and integrated into that. So, in the early vision and in the final vision, the image of the circling wheel recurs.

This, then, is Heaven

> *Luce intellettual piena d'amore,*
> *amor di vero ben pien di letizia,*
> *letizia che trascende ogni dolzore.*[3]

The soul, knowing God as He is, knows itself in God as God knows it and as it really is. It knows at last what it was made for, and plunges rapturously into the infinite understanding and love and joy in which every partial end that it had fumblingly proposed to itself—every "loose end", as one might say, of its being—is knit up into the *forma universal di questo nodo.*[4] It was made for this: to mirror the splendour and, shining back, to declare *I am*. Nor, however deeply it in-Gods itself, can it ever come to the end of the knowledge and the love and the joy, for God is infinite and new every day, and His riches unsearchable, and though every created thing brims over with its joy, He still has more.

It is not necessary to go into the details of Dante's Ten Heavens. The important thing is to grasp the central idea of what is *meant* by

---

[1] *Ezek.* i. 26–28.

[2] *Vita Nuova,* xii.

[3] Pure intellectual light filled full with love,
  Love of the true good filled with all delight,
  Transcending-sweet delight, all sweets above.
          Para. xxx. 40–42.

  Para. xxxiii. 91.

the concept of Heaven itself, understood absolutely. There are perhaps two or three points about this concept that we need to emphasise, because they conflict so sharply with our contemporary ideas about what is good and desirable.

First of all, we cannot but be sharply struck by the fact that two of our favourite catch-words have absolutely no meaning in Heaven: there is no *equality* and there is no *progress*. Perhaps I should modify that a little: there is equality in the sense that all the souls alike are as full of bliss as they are capable of being: but between soul and soul there is no formal equality at all. The pint-pot and the quart-pot are *equally full*: but there is no pretence that a pint and a quart are the same thing; neither does the pint-pot ever dream of saying to the quart-pot, "I'm as good as you are"—still less of saying "It isn't fair that you should hold more than I." The old sin of Envy, which unleashed the She-Wolf of Avarice from Hell, is utterly extinguished in Heaven. And there is no progress at all in the sense of "bettering one's self" or "getting even with other people". Dante, in the lowest Heaven, the Heaven of the Moon, specially asks Piccarda about this:

> *Ma dimmi; voi che siete qui felici,*
> *desiderate voi più alto loco,*
> *per più vedere, o per più farvi amici?* [1]

"Do you long to go higher, to gain more knowledge or win for yourselves more love?" She laughs, and all the blessed laugh with her. And she replies in the famous lines:

> *Frate, la nostra volontà quieta*
> *virtu di carità, che far volerne*
> *sol quel ch'avemo, e d'altro non ci asseta.* [2]

"Brother, our desires are stilled by love. We want only what we have. To want more would be discordant with the will of Him who disposes us here, and in these circles there is no room for that, for here our being is in charity and cannot be otherwise (*è necesse*). So that our being thus, from threshold unto threshold, is a joy to all the realm as to the

[1] "But tell me, you who here have your happiness, do you desire a higher place, to see more or to win more love?"

Para. iii. 64–66.

[2] "Brother, our will is stilled by the power of charity, which makes us wish only for that we have, nor do we thirst for anything beyond."

Para. iii. 70–72.

king, who draws our wills to what He wills; *e la sua voluntade è nostra pace*—and His will is our peace."

When he says that, Dante means what he says. Envy and ambition (under the names of equality and progress) are so native to us to-day, that we find this rather difficult to accept. George Santayana, for example, has been betrayed at this point into a most lamentable piece of dishonest criticism. He says:

For Piccarda to say that she accepts the will of God means not that she shares it, but that she submits to it. She would fain go higher, for her moral nature demands it, as Dante—incorrigible Platonist—perfectly perceived; but she dare not mention it, for she knows that God, whose thoughts are not her thoughts, has forbidden it. The inconstant sphere of the moon does not afford her a perfect happiness; but, chastened as she is, she says it brings her happiness enough; all that a broken and a contrite heart has the courage to hope for.[1]

There can seldom have been a more flagrant instance of reading into a poet's lines something that the critic would have said in his place and cannot forgive him for not saying. "Our being thus is a joy to the whole realm—*a tutto il regno piace*". "We love, for love is the necessity of our being."

At this point there is an interesting difference between Dante's conception and that of the Moslem writer Ibn Arabi. It has been argued that Dante's Three Kingdoms owe a good deal of their imagery to Moslem writings about the after-life, which may have reached him either directly, or through the work of the Averroïsts. Ibn Arabi says of Heaven:

Each knows his allotted grade and seeks it as a child seeks its mother's breast, and iron, the lodestone. To occupy or even aspire to a higher grade is impossible. In the grade in which he is placed each sees the realisation of his highest hopes. He loves his own grade passionately and *cannot conceive that a higher could exist. If it were not so, heaven would not be heaven but a mansion of grief and bitter disillusion.* Nevertheless, those in the superior participate in the enjoyment of the lower grades.[2]

In Ibn Arabi's Heaven, envy is excluded, apparently, only by ignorance and lack of imagination. But in Dante's Christian Heaven, it is excluded by love. The lower know that the higher exist, and "it is a joy to the

---

[1] *Three Philosophic Poets.* (Harvard University, 1910), p. 127.
[2] Miguel Asin: *Islam and the Divine Comedy* (John Murray, 1926), p. 159. (Italics mine.)

whole realm": they look up the ranks of the great ones soaring above them, and are filled with rapture and love. They envy them no more than you or I envy Dante or Shakespeare for being great and glorious. Why should they envy, or why should we? We are thrilled with delight to know that beings so noble can exist. One might even say that a principle of equality works here: that the lowest ranks have a special bliss of their own in having so many—so extra many—splendours and joys to look up to.

We may find this very difficult of acceptance: nevertheless we must take it seriously, and bear in mind that for Dante and his contemporaries, this heavenly pattern is also the ideal pattern of earthly order. Nothing in it condones injustice; but justice is not having as much as the next man but having what one deserves. Felicity likewise is not abundance of possessions but perfect congruity with one's function; and that is why Dante is severe upon those who "thrust into the convent him that is born to wear the sword, and make a king of him that should be a councillor"[1]. Had Satan not introduced disorder into the universe, all creation would follow the pattern of the angelic orders, who are "wheeled by love" about that point "on which Heaven and all Nature hangs".

> Cosi veloci seguono i suoi vimi,
>   per simigliarsi al punto quanto ponno,
>   e posson quanto a veder son sublimi . . .

> e del vedere è misura mercede
>   che grazia partorisce e buona voglia,
>   cosi di grado in grado si procede. . . .

> Questi ordini di su tutti rimirano,
>   e di giù vincon sì che verso Dio
>   tutti tirati sono e tutti tirano.[2]

All look upon God in the measure of the knowledge and love which they have by the grace given to them and their own good will; all are

---

[1] *Para.* viii. 145.

[2] Thus swiftly do their withies [i.e. their circling bands] follow one another, that they may assimilate themselves to the point as closely as they can, and they *can* in measure as they are exalted to perceive. . . . And the measure of their perceiving is the merit begotten of grace and good-will, and so from rank to rank it goes proceeding. . . . These orders all direct their gaze upward, and below exert their winning power, in such fashion that all are drawn and all draw up to God.

Para. xxviii. 100–103, 112–114, 127–129.

drawn up with the cords of love by those above them, and themselves draw those below them. The Heavens draw Man; and Man was made "lord of creation" that he might draw up the whole material creation. What Man in his fallen nature cannot do of himself, Christ does in man, until the resurrection of the "holy and glorious flesh" and the "reconciliation of all things" to God in Christ, in a new Heaven and a new earth.

A second point that many people find difficult about Dante's Heaven is that although the blessed remain very closely and intimately concerned with the affairs of earth, and are indeed continually denouncing the sins of mankind, they remain untroubled in their ecstasy. Some critics are disconcerted by this intrusion of earthly matters into the courts of Heaven—Miss Rebecca West complains that the blessed seem to be "worried" all the time by these things; but "worried" is exactly what they are not, and to other critics this in itself is an offence. All Heaven blushes for the sins of him who sits in Peter's seat: yet immediately after, the aether is adorned with the triumph of the ascending flames; upon the great denunciations pronounced in Heaven after Heaven, the song and dance follow swiftly. Not even the knowledge that Hell co-exists with Heaven can make the least wound in the eternal joy of the saints: Beatrice leaves Dante with the prophecy that the divine vengeance will overtake Pope Clement "and thrust him of Alagna down lower", and returns unmoved to her seat amid the petals of the mystic Rose; and we are reminded of that earlier word that she had said to Virgil: "My nature by God's grace is made such that your calamities cannot touch me nor the fire of this burning assail me." [1]

What are we to make of this contradiction, in appearance so harsh, between the anger and the joy, the deep concern and the imperturbable indifference? We must first of all remember the action of the two streams of Lethe and Eunoë, of which all souls drink in the Earthly Paradise on their way to Heaven. Lethe destroys all memory of guilt and shame and sin: Eunoë restores the memory of the sin as a historical *fact*, but the accompanying unhappiness remains forgotten—the sin is remembered only as the glad occasion of God's gracious mercy and forgiveness. As Cunizza explains to Dante, "*lietamente a me medesma indulgo la cagion di mia sorte*" [2]—the blessed "joyously forgive themselves"—a thing, as we all know, extremely difficult in this life, because

[1] *Inf.* ii. 91–93.
[2] "joyously I forgive myself the occasion of my lot".
Para. ix. 34–35.

pride gets in the way. For instance—that dreadfully silly and unkind thing you said to poor Miss Smith when you were quite a child. Even after all these years, it makes you turn hot and writhe on your pillow if you remember it suddenly in the middle of the night; and the fact that Miss Smith was so decent about it makes you feel all the worse. But in Heaven, when you have purged off the sin, you will remember the wretched little episode only as a *fact*: you will be free for ever from the ugly shame that is the protest of your pride against being humiliated in your own eyes; and seeing Miss Smith as God sees her, you will rejoice in her beautiful charity as though it had been something else, and not your unthinking cruelty, that called it forth.

In somewhat the same way, although the unity of Christ's mystical body is such that the blessed dead are deeply concerned with the living, whether to help, pity, pray for them, or to feel indignation at their sins, yet in Heaven the powers of anger and pity are experienced *pure*, and not bound up with a whole complex of confused personal feelings. When God and His Saints are angry, anger does not tear them to pieces, distort their judgment and poison their lives: they pity, but pity does not ravage them with helpless torments and put them at the mercy of the blackmailing egotism which thrives by exploiting and playing upon the feelings of the tender-hearted; in C. S. Lewis's admirable phrase: "The action of pity will live for ever, but the passion of pity will not." [1]

We cannot deal with this subject without touching upon that question of Free-will, which bulks so large in all Dante's thought, as in all discussions upon theology and ethics. Lest we should "find no end, in wandering mazes lost", I propose to skip all the standard arguments about the two freedoms and the validity of choice, and attack the problem from a slightly different angle.

Let us remind ourselves of the lines already quoted about the creation: that God created so that His splendour might, shining back to Him, declare: *I am*. Now, in one sense, all creatures can do this merely by existing: one day telleth another and one night certifieth another. But God has called into existence not only nights and days, and stones and oceans, but also plants and animals, which appear not only to exist but consciously to enjoy existing; and not only these, but

[1] C. S. Lewis: *The Great Divorce* (Geoffrey Bles, 1945), p. 111. (Cf. also *Purg.* xx. 94–96—*la vendetta che, nascosa, fa dolce l'ira tua nel tuo segreto*—
". . . the vengeance which makes sweet
Thy wrath, within the secret of Thy will".)

rational beings—men as we know, angels as we believe—who not only consciously enjoy existing but self-consciously know that they exist and enjoy. Their knowledge and their delight are enriched by their own free assent; they say "I am", and with the whole power of their selves they eagerly mean what they say.

Now the point is this: that this free assent of the creature must be his assent *to reality*. The facts of the situation are that he is a created being; that the end of his existence is to mirror God's glory to the utmost of his capacity; and that he can only enjoy or attain his true selfhood by letting his "desire and will" be wheeled about that centre of reality from which "Heaven and all nature hang". The fall of angels and men is, looked at from one point of view, a refusal of assent to this reality: or what the scientist would call "a lack of humility in the face of the facts". However this may be supposed to have come about, it is fairly obvious that if you make a creature capable of freely assenting, there is always a risk, so to call it—or at any rate a theoretical possibility—that he may refuse to assent, or assent with a bad grace. Assent cannot be forced and free at the same time: it is beyond the power even of omnipotence to produce two incompatible results at once—"the contradiction", as the logical demon very properly said to Guido da Montefeltro, "does not allow it". If we ask why God should have willed to make a free creature, we can only guess that the stature of such a creature is of such nobility, and its ecstatic love and obedience a thing so essentially glorious and so delightful to itself and to its Maker, that God thought it worth the risk to Himself and to the rest of creation. This is to speak in human terms; and we do not, of course, know: though in the Beatific Vision we shall know so far as we are capable of knowing.

But, taking the situation as the theology of creation gives it to us, we see that the mere existence of a "self" that can in a real sense know itself as "other than" God, offers the possibility for the self to imagine itself independent of God, and instead of wheeling its will and desire about Him, to try and find its true end in itself and to revolve about that. This is the fall into illusion, which is Hell. The creature denies, or rebels against, its creaturely status, and at once plunges itself into a situation which is bound to be full of frustration and misery, because it is at variance with the facts.

Scripture does not tell us very much about the fall of Satan and his angels, but the Church has always held that it was due to pride. The good angels, as Dante explains, "were modest to acknowledge themselves derived from that same Goodness which made them swift to so great understanding: wherefore their vision was exalted with grace illuminating and with their merit, so that they have their will full and established".[1] No more than any other creature can an angel be "ingodded" except by an act of divine grace; their "merit" is "to receive the grace by laying the affections open to it". This the rebellious angels would not do: they rejected their derivation, and so fell in the very act of being called into being—"before one could count twenty" as Dante picturesquely puts it.[2] They fell, that is, immediately and for ever; for angels, being pure intelligences and made in the mode of instantaneousness, do not change or develop or progress: they are what they are wholly and immutably, and move, as it were, all of a piece. All that was required of them was to receive their beatitude lovingly, willingly, and realistically, as a free gift of God: but they wanted to be "as God", and so they fell.

The fall of Man, we know a little more about from Scripture. It happens rather differently, because man is not a pure intelligence, but partly material, and it is his nature to develop in time and space and grow gradually into the life of Heaven. Therefore his knowledge cannot be purely intellectual, but has to be gained by experience. He is created good, in a good world; but Satan suggests to him that there is a different way of knowing reality—it can be known not only as good, but also as evil. God, says Satan, knows it both ways; if Adam and Eve eat the forbidden fruit, they also will know like God. Satan, however, carefully omits to point out that God can "know" evil purely as an intellectual possibility, without experiencing it or calling it into existence; but that Man, if he is to know it at all, must know it, as he knows everything else, by experience. Adam and Eve, intoxicated by the idea of being "as gods", disregard all warnings and eat; they have their desire, and know evil.

We need not now examine the Adam-and-Eve myth with the intention of arguing about how far it is pure parable and how far it may represent something that historically happened when a fully self-conscious self first made its appearance on the scene of creation. We may in passing note three things: first, that the fashionable habit of calling the prohibition of the Fruit of Knowledge an "arbitrary taboo" is a quite unjustifiable travesty of the Bible story. There, God is represented as saying to Adam and Eve: "Do not eat: if you do, it will kill you"—and I do not know what else one could reasonably say

---

[1] *Para.* xxix. 58–63.   [2] *Para.* xxix. 49.

to anybody when begging him to refrain from taking strychnine or prussic acid. The second thing is a consideration that naturally would not occur to Dante, with his limited knowledge of the cosmos, but is bound to occur to us; namely, that if there are, in the universe, other rational material beings besides Man, there is no need to suppose that they have fallen into the same error. Thirdly: since Man is, of his nature, a being susceptible of development, it is possible in his case for God (with man's own assent and cooperation) to undo the consequences of the Fall—or rather, not to undo, but to redeem them. This, however, belongs to Atonement Theology, and is not part of our present subject.

What we have now to consider is this: What is the meaning of this illusion of Hell? this knowing of good as evil? It may sound paradoxical; but it is actually something very familiar to us.

If we refuse assent to reality: if we rebel against the nature of things and choose to think that what we at the moment want is the centre of the universe to which everything else ought to accommodate itself, the first effect on us will be that the whole universe will seem to be filled with an implacable and inexplicable hostility. We shall begin to feel that everything has a down on us, and that, being so badly treated, we have a just grievance against things in general. That is the knowledge of good as evil and the fall into illusion. If we cherish and fondle that grievance, and would rather wallow in it and vent our irritation in spite and malice than humbly admit we are in the wrong and try to amend our behaviour so as to get back to reality, that is, while it lasts, the deliberate choice, and a foretaste of the experience, of Hell.

Let us take one or two very simple instances:

When a child falls over a chair, its instant reaction will very likely be to say, "Naughty chair", and belabour it soundly with whatever first comes to hand. That is apt to strike the grown-up Adam, who knows more than the child about the nature of inanimate matter, as funny: but if Adam is sensible he will take the stick away and not encourage the child to expect the material universe to accommodate itself to his wishes.

The grown-up Adam, having laughed at the child, may then go to Piccadilly Tube Station with the intention of taking a train to Stanmore. With his mind fixed on the Test Match or the sins of the Government, he may neglect to consult the indicator which is saying plainly that the train now at the platform is going to Watford, and when, having passed Baker Street in a fond illusion, he looks up at the next station and finds that it is not St. John's Wood, but Marylebone, he will mutter savagely that he has got into "the wrong train". Neither will it for a moment occur to him that what he is saying is as absurd as what the child said. But what is wrong with the train? In the eyes of God and London Passenger Transport, it is a perfectly good train, proceeding on its lawful occasions to the destination appointed for it by a superior power. To be sure, it has got a wrong passenger, who has nobody to blame but himself. But the determination to see the good as evil and the right train as a wrong 'un has entrenched itself in the very core of Adam's language: and it is well for his soul if he confines himself to that merely conventional method of transferring his own errors to the universe, and does not angrily add that "all these damned trains seem to go to Watford".

Let us now take something that cuts deeper. We may perhaps have the misfortune to know a person who is unreasonably jealous. He exacts of his wife, his friends, his animals, an exclusive devotion to himself which only God would be justified in demanding—and indeed his demanding is part of his illusion that he is "as God". As a matter of fact, God is by far the less exacting of the two. God demands of us an entire devotion, but He permits—indeed, He desires—that that devotion should overflow in love upon all our fellow-creatures—*tutti tirati sono, e tutti tirano*.[1] But this is what the jealous man will not have. No expressions of affection can content him, no sacrifice will satisfy him: he wants to possess the object of his jealousy body and soul; and even if he did he would not be content. For he misinterprets everything and is determined to do so, and so sees all good as evil. If his wife likes having other friends and interests, he accuses her of being unfaithful and not finding him enough to satisfy her; if she shuts herself up and waits on him hand and foot, he complains that she is ostentatively making a martyr of herself for the express purpose of putting him in the wrong, and he darkly suspects that she is wishing him dead, so that she can have a good time. If she is cheerful in company, he asks why she keeps all her gaiety for other people; if she is silent, then she is only trying to win sympathy for being so badly treated at home. I need not go on—whether it is husband or wife, parent, or friend, the jealous person makes his own and other people's lives a misery. He will, of course, have moments of remorse, when he says that he is a miserable and accursed wretch and not fit to live, and so forth; but that he is made that way and cannot help it. And it is very usual for

[1] *Para.* xxviii. 129.

people to agree that in fact he *cannot* help it, and that his unfortunate
behaviour is due to his having contracted an inferiority complex in
childhood, through being an only child, or a younger child, or what
not. Very often there is truth in the explanation. But only too often
there is apparent in his very remorse a gloomy self-satisfaction. He is
proud of his unfortunate disposition, which, he feels, confers on him
a kind of distinction. He really thinks that this savage passion of his
is a superior brand of love, which shows him to be much more highly-
strung and sensitive than other people. He is not genuinely sorry;
he only enjoys making a scene. If his remorse were a real conviction
of sin he would go to a psychiatrist—or fall on his knees, which is
cheaper and, as some of us think, more effective—and get himself put
back into touch with reality.

Now, the tendency to this kind of illusion—to the knowing of
good as evil—is what is known as Original Sin: and it is plain enough
that we are in fact all born with it, however we come to be so. (This,
by the way, is what the Church means by being "born in sin"—it does
not mean that sex is sinful or that there is anything wrong in itself
about being born into a material world.) The harbouring of evil
passions and the doing of evil acts as a result of surrendering to this
illusion is Actual Sin: and the effects of sin are very real evils, which
proliferate in a world where all men are sinners and all the victims of
their own and each other's sins. God's way of dealing with sin will
be considered in our paper on the meaning of Purgatory. For the
moment we must confine our attention to Hell.

It is the deliberate choosing to remain in illusion and to see God
and the universe as hostile to one's ego that is of the very essence of
Hell. The dreadful moods when we hug our hatred and misery and are
too proud to let them go are foretastes in time of what Hell eternally is.
So long as we are in time and space, we can still, by God's grace and
our own wills assenting, repent of Hell and come out of it. But if we
carry that determination and that choice through the gates of death
into the state in which there is, literally, no time, what then? Death,
which was the bitter penalty attached to man's knowledge of evil, is
also man's privilege and opportunity. He is not allowed just to slip
away easily, body and soul, into eternity, as the early Fathers imagined
he might have done if he had never lost his innocence. In knowing
evil, Man had to know death as a crisis—the sharp sundering of mortal
and immortal—and in that crisis he sees his choice between reality and
illusion. As it passes out of the flesh the soul sees God and sees its own

sin. This crisis and confrontation are technically known as the Particular Judgment. If, in the very moment of that crisis, the true self is still alive, however feebly: if, deep down beneath all perversities of self-will, the absolute will is still set towards God's reality, and the soul can find it in itself, even at that last moment, to accept judgment—to fling away the whole miserable illusion and throw itself upon truth, then it is safe.[1] It will have to do in Purgatory, with incredible toil and without the assistance of the body, the training which it should have done on earth: but in the end it will get to where it truly wants to be. There is no power in this world or the next that can keep a soul from God if God is what it really desires.

But if, seeing God, the soul rejects Him in hatred and horror, then there is nothing more that God can do for it. God, who has toiled to win it for Himself, and borne for its sake to know death, and suffer the shame of sin, and set His feet in Hell, will nevertheless, if it insists, give it what it desires. The people who think that if God were truly nice and kind He would let us have everything we fancy, are really demanding that He should give us freehold of Hell. And if that is our deliberate and final choice, if with our whole selves we are determined to have nothing but self, He will, in the end, say, "Take it." He cannot, against our own will, force us into Heaven, in the spirit of "I've brought you out to enjoy yourself and you gotter enjoy yourself". Heaven would then be a greater agony than Hell—or rather, Hell *is* Heaven as seen by those who reject it: just as the agonies of the jealous *are* love, seen through the distorting illusion. We might adapt the definition of Boethius and say: "Hell is the perfect and simultaneous possession of one's own will for ever."

"Justice moved my high Creator: Divine Power, Supreme Wisdom, Primal Love made me." That is the inscription over Hell-Gate. Power, Wisdom and Love make Hell by merely existing. The self-centred soul, seeing the eternal Reality, sees it as cruel, meaningless and hateful, because it wills to see it so. We need not really be surprised at this: we are only too well accustomed to these distorted views. When we demand justice, it is always justice on our behalf against other people. Nobody, I imagine, would ever ask for justice to be done *upon* him for every thing he ever did wrong. We do not want justice —we want revenge: and that is why, when justice is done upon us, we cry out that God is vindictive. Neither is it very certain that we

---

[1] *Cf.* in the *Purgatorio* the stories of Manfred (iii. 118–135) and Buonconte (v. 94–108).

shall welcome mercy or charity. La Rochefoucault, in a bitter and memorable maxim, pointed out how hard it is to forgive those whom we have injured. We avoid them, because the very sight of them is an offence to our vanity: and often, the meeker they are, the more savage we feel. The damned cannot bear to stand in the light of God's innocence and "look upon Him whom they pierced". What they want is the old familiar sin. They are like confirmed drunkards; their sin makes them miserable, but they cannot live without it. They press to pass the river,

> *chè la divina giustizia li sprona*
> *sì che la tema si volge in disio*—[1]

"Divine justice so goads them that their fear is changed into desire". God puts nobody in Hell: the damned may wail and weep and curse their parents and the day they were born, blaming everything and everybody but themselves: nevertheless they go, like Judas, "to their own place", because it is the only place where they can bear to be.

Hell, in a manner, is Heaven in reverse; it is Reality seen as evil and seen so far more perfectly than it can ever be in this world. At the bottom of Hell is the Miserific Vision, as the Beatific Vision is at the height of Heaven: and as the Beatific Vision is the knowing of God in His Essence, so Hell is the knowing of Sin in its essence. Dante speaks indifferently of the torments, the pains, the penalties, or the punishments of Hell; and this language often prompts people to suppose that the torments are punishments arbitrarily inflicted, as a man might beat a boy for stealing sweets. But the intimate analogy between the sin and the penalty shows that the suffering of Hell is punishment only in the sense that a stomach-ache, and not a beating, is "punishment" for greed. What has gone is the glamour; gluttony loses its accompaniments of the bright lights and holiday atmosphere, and is known *in its essence* as a cold wallowing in dirt, a helpless prey to ravenous appetites. Covetousness and squandering are no longer dignified by names like "the economy of thrift and the economy of conspicuous waste"—they are known as a meaningless squabble about a huge weight of nonsense; usury and sodomy—however we may like in this world to segregate them in the very different spheres of high finance and high aesthetics— are lumped together on the same scorched earth—sterility left to

[1] *Inf.* iii. 125–126.

scratch in its own dust-bowl. The platform rhetoric, the propaganda, the sloppy romanticism, the endless stream of words, words, words dishonestly used to debase language and extinguish right judgment— it all pours down to the ditch of the Second Bolgia where the flatterers wallow in their own excreted filth. The schism that divides the Body of Christ, the sedition that splits the State, the malice that breaks up homes for the pleasure of making mischief, are experienced in the self: "See how Mahomet is mangled!" The hidden graft which rots community life beneath the surface, only from time to time throwing up a black and oily bubble to burst in a public scandal, still works like a diabolic leaven beneath the "wondrous dark" crust of the boiling pitch; and as the devils thrust the barrator down with their prongs, they cry to him:

> *"Coperto convien che qui balli,*
> *si che, se puoi, nascosamente accaffi!"* [1]

"Behold our City!" says Beatrice, "how wide it spreads its gyres! How great the company of the white robes!" The Città Dolente, too, is a populous place, "co' gravi cittadin, col grande stuolo",[2] but its gyres narrow as they go deeper. Nor, in that great city, is there any citizenship. "We are all citizens of one true city," says Sapìa to Dante on the road up Purgatory: [3] and in Heaven, the blessed, though they may appear to Dante in separate spheres, all have the same home in the Empyrean, where the angels flit between their ranks like bees visiting a bed of flowers. But in Hell, it is each for himself: there is no communication between one circle and another: even the demons are so bound that they may not pass their appointed limits.[4] No soul helps another, or pities another. Occasionally, when sin has been shared, as with the Lustful, or the Avaricious, or (more horribly) with Ugolino and Ruggieri, there is a kind of common grievance against fate. More often, especially in the deeps of Nether Hell, there is only an eagerness to accuse, a snarling vindictiveness of spite. "My beast of a wife is the cause of my torment"; "I wait till Carlin come to make

---

[1] "Go cut thy capers, try down there to do
  Subsurface deals and secret money-grabbing!"
        Inf. xxi. 53–54.
[2] With its sad citizens, its great company
        Inf. viii. 69.
[3] *Purg.* xiii. 94–95.
[4] *Inf.* xxiii. 55–57.

excuse for me"; "Could I but see Guido or Alexander here, I would not miss that sight for all the waters of Branda"; and the spite is extended to Dante too: "That you of all people should see me here!" cries Vanni Fucci, and goes on: "So that you may not enjoy the thought of it I'll tell you something you won't like, and I hope it breaks your heart." [1] Even at his tenderest, Dante deals ruthlessly with this egotism; listen to Francesca: "If the King of the Universe were our friend"—one begins to think it is all God's fault; "Love took hold of us"—well, Love (as Dante had once said) is an abstraction, an accident in a substance; are we to put the blame on an abstraction? "My beautiful body was torn from me, I had no time to repent——" and then, like the lash of a whip, the sudden savage snarl: "Cain's place awaits our murderer!" The soft voice resumes: "You are so kind—I will tell you how it was; we were reading that lovely story —we thought no harm—something came over Paolo and he kissed me—the book was a pander and he that wrote it!" [2] God, Love, Gianciotto, the novelist, were to blame, not we; we were the helpless prey of our own and other people's passions, and now we drift on the black wind.

So piteous are the accents here, and so moving the sheer poetry that it might deceive the very elect. Many, indeed, have been deceived into swallowing Francesca's version of things, hook, line and sinker, and transferring to Dante the resentment they feel on her behalf against God, love, vindictive husbands, "suggestive" literature and all the rest of it. But, as in the case of Piccarda, we must believe that Dante means what he says, when he goes out of his way to write that meaning plain in the very structure of his verse. It is true that he does not comment: he merely shows. But he seldom makes a damned soul sympathetic without slipping in something which would show us—if we were not carried away by our admiration for picturesque sinners— just what it is we are admiring. Jason[3]—"is he not still right royal to behold?" Does he not scorn the whips? A magnificent Byronic figure. Quite so. He is the man who seduced a girl and left her "with child and abandoned". Farinata,[4] holding all hell in contempt—is he not splendid in his dark, unbending pride? There he stands, while old Cavalcanti lifts his head out of the burning tomb to put his pitiful question to Dante and then, thinking his son dead, sinks back into despair added to despair.

[1] *Inf.* xvi. 44–45; xxxii. 68–69; xxiv. 133, 148–151.   [2] *Inf.* v. 91 *sqq.*
[3] *Inf.* xviii. 83 *sqq.*   [4] *Inf.* x. 34 *sqq.*

Ma quell' altro magnanimo . . .
. . . non mutò aspetto,
nè mosse collo, nè piegò sua costa.[1]

That is the "magnanimity" of Hell—to remain totally unmoved by other people's misfortunes. There is no "action of pity" here—only a rigid seclusion in self. . . . What could be more touching than the tale of Pier delle Vigne?[2] Suspected by the Emperor he had served, traduced by evil tongues, he takes his own life. How can God condemn to Hell this poor man distracted by grief? But he himself proclaims that grief had nothing to do with it: it was hurt pride, *disdegnoso gusto*: he would rather be dead than humiliated, and for all eternity he has what he wills. At every turn we find the sinner still hugging the beloved sin and often expatiating upon his punishment with a gloomy relish which is only a continued expression of his egotism. Ciampolo[3] with his trickery and his delighted appreciation of other people's villainy— "Fra Gomita? a sink of corruption!—*barattier fu non picciol ma soprano*";[4] Master Adam of Brescia and Sinon of Troy taunting each other with their crimes and comparing their diseases like a couple of drunks sneering at each other for not being able to carry their drink:[5] Bertrand de Born crying in what sounds like a blasphemous parody: "See if there be any horror like to mine!"[6]—a last hideous twist given to the ambition to be "as God".

It must be remembered about any poet who writes of Satan and Hell that he has a double task to perform: he must show sin as attractive and yet as damned. If sin were not attractive nobody would fall into it; and because pride is its very root, it will always present itself as an act of noble rebellion. It is only too easy, especially in an age when order and hierarchy are perverted or discredited, to persuade one's self that rebellion, *as such*, is magnanimous, that *all* control is tyranny, that the under-dog is in the right *because* he is vanquished, and that evil is to

---

[1] But that great-hearted (*magnanimo*) spirit . . .
. . . his countenance did not move,
Nor bent his neck, nor stirred his side at all.
Inf. x. 73–75.
[2] *Inf.* xiii. 58 *sqq.*
[3] *Inf.* xxii. 44 *sqq.*
[4]   no pretty jobbery
for him—he was a sovereign barrator.
Inf. xxii. 86–87.
[5] *Inf.* xxx. 91 *sqq.*
[6] *Inf.* xxviii. 132.

be pitied the moment it ceases to be successful. But it is not true; "*qui vive la pietà quando è ben morta*".[1] The poet's business is to show both the brilliant façade of sin and the squalor hidden beneath it; his task is to persuade us to accept judgment. Purgation is what happens to the soul which, accepting judgment, moves out of illusion into reality, and this is the subject of the *Purgatorio*.

[1] Here pity, or here piety, must die
 If the other lives:
　　　　Inf. xx. 28–29.

(1948)

THE MEANING OF PURGATORY

WE considered Heaven and Hell together because, although they are more totally opposed to one another than yes and no or black and white, yet they have certain aspects in common, as direct opposites always must have. Both are eternal states—"absolutely elsewhere" as regards our familiar time-space continuum. Both have that finality and absoluteness which our "climate of opinion" finds so uncongenial. Both can be experienced in this life, if at all, only in moods and moments which, while giving as it were a foretaste of the *quality* of beatitude or damnation, are other than, and discontinuous with, the pattern of daily life. Mystics intensely, and many other people less intensely, know these moments of vision which open a window upon a different mode of existence. There are the moments of the going out of the self —such, for instance, as St. Augustine and his mother experienced one evening shortly before her death. They had been talking of the sweetness of eternal life and how it must surpass all other sweetness, and they considered the marvel of God's works, "mounting step by step the ladder of the material order", until they

came to their own minds and passed beyond them into the region of unfailing plenty, where the life itself never comes to be, but is, as it was and shall be evermore, because in it is neither past nor future but present only, for it is eternal, for past and future are not eternal. And as we talked and yearned after it, we touched it for an instant with the whole force of our hearts. And we sighed, and left there impawned the first fruits of the spirit, and heard again the babble of our own tongues, wherein each word has a beginning and an ending.[1]

And there are the moments of the descent into the abyss of the self, such as Gerard Manley Hopkins wrote of in those sonnets which terribly explore the depths:

> O the mind, mind has mountains; cliffs of fall
> Frightful, sheer, no-man-fathomed. Hold them cheap
> May who ne'er hung there.[2]

---

[1] St. Augustine of Hippo: *Confessions*, Bk. ix (Bigg's translation).
[2] Poems of Gerard Manley Hopkins (O.U.P., 2nd ed., 1935), p. 62.

73

and again:

> I am gall, I am heartburn. God's most deep decree
> Bitter would have me taste: my taste was me;
> Bones built in me, flesh filled, blood brimmed the curse.
> Self-yeast of spirit a dull dough sours. I see
> The lost are like this, and their scourge to be
> As I am mine, their sweating selves; but worse.[1]

Such intuitions are not of this world; and however long or short their actual duration, they are in their essence timeless.

But Purgatory is different. Purgatory is not an eternal state but a temporal process, continuous with, and of a quality comparable to, our experience in this world. It should, for that reason, be easier for us to understand and appreciate; yet, oddly enough, of Dante's three *cantiche*, the *Purgatorio* is the least read and (which is by no means always the same thing) the least quoted—although among those who read Dante properly, it is often the most tenderly loved. Various reasons might be suggested for this comparative neglect: the people who like to enjoy the dramatic horrors of the *Inferno*, while at the same time condescending to Dante as a cruel and superstitious mediaeval, are disconcerted by the tender serenity of the *Purgatorio*; finding nothing to be agreeably shocked at, and unwilling to take the subject of salvation seriously, they fall back on saying that the book lacks poetry and variety and is too full of ethical discourses. It is not true that it lacks poetry; it is, to be plain, better written than the *Inferno*—more easily, more competently, and with a more sustained power of poetic narration. But it does not contain so many purple passages which can, at a pinch, be wrenched out of their context and enjoyed as detached "beauties"; neither, on the other hand, can it be so easily pillaged as the *Paradiso* for "jewels five words long" suitable to adorn and illustrate sermons and books of devotion. It might be said briefly that almost everybody has at least heard of Paolo and Francesca, the Last Voyage of Ulysses, and Count Ugolino, as almost everybody has at least seen quoted somewhere *e la sua volontade è nostra pace; vergine madre, figlia di tuo figlio;* and *l'amor che muove il sol e l'altre stelle.*[2] But the *Purgatorio* can only be enjoyed as a whole; and that means the ability to read long stretches of narrative verse and understand what

---

[1] Poems of Gerard Manley Hopkins (O.U.P., 2nd ed., 1935), p. 65.

[2] And His will is our peace (*Para.* iii. 85); Virgin Mother, daughter of thy Son (*Para.* xxxiii. I); the love that moves the sun and the other stars (*Para.* xxxiii. 145).

the poem is about. And unfortunately, the whole doctrine and meaning of Purgatory has become clouded and obscured since Dante's time—and not only in Protestant countries. There it was for a long time discredited and discarded, while in Catholic countries it underwent an alteration of balance, which swung it away from Dante's position; and it is only in comparatively recent years that the balance has been redressed. All this is a pity, not merely because it has impeded proper understanding of the *Purgatorio*, but because the loss of the doctrine has been a great loss in understanding and charity and has tended to destroy our sense of the communion between the blessed dead and ourselves: and for that loss the alteration in balance has been, as I believe, very greatly to blame. Had the doctrine of Purgatory never been presented otherwise than it is in Dante, the Reformed Churches would have found much less reason to repudiate it; it would at any rate have offered far less opportunity for the scandal and abuse of which they complained.

It is true that the doctrine has but slender warrant in Scripture, although we learn that already in St. Paul's time it was a custom among the proselytes of the young Christian churches to be "baptised for the dead"—baptised, that is, as proxies for friends and relatives who, perhaps believing and desiring to embrace Christianity, had died before they could receive the sacrament of purification. St. Paul refers to this,[1] without comment and as a thing established, in the course of an argument about the resurrection: "Otherwise, what would happen about those who were baptised for the dead? If the dead are not raised at all, why are they baptised for them?" Clearly, it was thought that the dead were not in a mere state of suspended animation, but could profit by the prayers and actions of the living. And indeed we find in the Second Book of Maccabees (written about 124 B.C.) that the Jews also, or some of them, had arrived at the same conclusion. We read there how some of the Jews who died in the battle against Gorgias were found to be wearing heathen amulets, and how Judas Maccabaeus took up a silver collection to the sum of 2,000 drachmas, which he "sent unto Jerusalem to offer a sacrifice for sin, doing therein right well and honourably, in that he took thought for a resurrection. For if he were not expecting that they that had fallen would rise again, it were superfluous and idle to pray for the dead".[2] More authentic still, as evidence that the dead are not inert and inactive, is the famous passage in the First Epistle of St. Peter, where he speaks of Christ "being put to death in the flesh

[1] 1 *Cor.* xv. 29.   [2] 2 *Macc.* xii. 43–44.

but quickened by the Spirit, by which also He went and preached unto the spirits in prison, which sometime were disobedient".[1] None of this, of course, points to a doctrine of purgation by suffering, which is what we understand by Purgatory. It is probable that the early Christians, living as they did in expectation of an almost immediate Second Coming, had little occasion to ponder upon the conditions attending the Intermediate State. They believed indeed that, as St. Paul said in the First Epistle to the Corinthians, "the fire should try every man's work", and that "if any man's work shall be burned, he should suffer loss: but he himself should be saved; yet so as by fire".[2] But the words refer, in their context, to the Last Judgment, and this was the trial to which their faith looked forward. Meanwhile, however, they prayed and made sacrifice for the dead. Tertullian, in A.D. 200, speaks of this as an established usage, adding, "if you ask where is the law concerning this custom in Scripture, you cannot read of any such there. Tradition will appear before you as its initiator, custom as its confirmer, and faith as its observer."

As so frequently happens, a practical charity and an intuitive feeling for what was in tune with the Faith preceded the exact formulation of doctrine. But as time went on, the hope of the Second Coming receded: it became evident that Christ had established His Church to do His work in the earth, and not to be immediately snatched up into Heaven. Indeed, He had often said as much; but His disciples had, as so often, misunderstood Him. And as the Church grew, she found herself with many members who were not, in the first ecstatic sense, confessors and martyrs but more like what we should call plain, ordinary Christians. Under these circumstances it was hardly possible that people should not meditate upon the condition of souls who had to wait out the interval between death and the end of the ages, and wonder what was to happen to those who, although baptised and believing, could not exactly be held to deserve the title of saints. It must have become evident that, as a modern writer has put it, "most men when they die are probably too good for Hell, but they are certainly too bad for Heaven".

Von Hügel, whose study of the teaching of St. Catherine of Genoa throws much light on this rather difficult subject, thinks that the doctrine of Purgatory, like much else, came into the Church along the lines of Hellenic thought, and was first clearly formulated by the Alexandrian Fathers. Thus Origen, in the second century, interprets

[1] 1 *Pet.* iii. 18–19; cf. iv. 6.   [2] 1 *Cor.* iii. 13–15.

Our Lord's words about the debtor, "thou shalt by no means come out [of prison] till thou hast paid the uttermost farthing", as a reference to Purgatory, and explains: "These souls receive in the prison, not the retribution of their folly, but a benefaction in the purification from the evils contracted in that folly; a purification effected by the means of salutary troubles." He also takes the passage from St. Paul—"he himself shall be saved, yet so as by fire"—to refer to Purgatory; and he says: "these rivers of fire are declared to be of God, who causes the evil that is mixed up with the whole soul to disappear from out of it." Clement of Alexandria takes much the same line. St. Augustine (354–430), while inclining rather to "the older Christian and Jewish conception of the soul abiding in a state of shrunken joy-and-painless consciousness from the moment of the body's death up to that of the general resurrection and judgment" [1] (i.e. in a kind of Limbo) yet in *The City of God* definitely accepts the idea of Purgatory as an extension and completion of the purifying trials of earth: "As for temporal pain (he says) some endure it here and some hereafter, and some both here and there: yet all is past before the last judgment."

Finally, and omitting for the moment all reference to St. Thomas Aquinas, about whom I shall have to say a good deal in a minute or two, we get the official declarations of the Roman Church: "We are bound, by the Confession of Faith of Michael Palaeologos, 1267 A.D., and by the Decree of the Council of Florence, 1429 A.D., to hold that these Middle souls 'are purged after death by purgatorial or cathartic pains'; and by that of Trent 'that there is a Purgatory' " [2] (i.e. a place of purifying).

I want to be as clear as possible about these early ideas of Purgatory, because there has been a tendency on the part of recent Protestant writers to exaggerate very much the difference between Dante's conception of Purgatory and that which they take to be the official Catholic doctrine. It is quite true that Dante's conception is very unlike, and very far superior to, the crude and melodramatic notions which we find in *popular* literature from the second century onwards; and that it also differs greatly in tone from that later mediaeval teaching which gave rise to the abuses so strongly denounced by the Reformers. But no admiration for Dante's originality and for the loftiness of his mind ought to seduce us into trying to make out that this most Catholic

---

[1] Von Hügel: *The Soul of a Saint*, reprinted in *Readings for Friedrich von Hügel* (Dent, 1928), p. 192.
[2] *Ibid.*

of writers was a kind of anticipatory schismatic or heretic. He was not a "Protestant" in the sense that he desired or contemplated any sort of repudiation either of the authority of the See of Peter or of the traditional doctrine of the Church; he was a Reformer only in the sense that he desired that authority to remain uncontaminated by the temporalities and that doctrine to be maintained in its integrity. The reason why his picture of Purgatory seems to us unlike what we are accustomed to think of as the "official" version, is that a change of emphasis did in fact take place in the teaching, but after his time. The change was, perhaps, already beginning, but it was not as yet marked, although in at least one passage he does take note of it. Dante represents the older tradition. We must not interpret Dante in terms of King Henry VIII, or even of *Piers Plowman*, which was written fifty years after Dante's death. Dante's thought is so mature, and his poetic accomplishment so great, that it is sometimes difficult to remember how early he lived. He was born in the reign of our King Henry III, and died in the reign of Edward II, twenty years before Chaucer saw the light of day.

Thus much having been said by way of warning, we will return to the doctrine of Purgatory: and here I must trouble you with rather a long quotation from St. Thomas Aquinas.

Two things [he says] may be considered in sin: the guilty act and the consequent stain. Now it is evident that in all actual sins, when the act of sin has ceased the guilt remains; for the act of sin makes man deserving of punishment, in so far as he transgresses the order of divine justice, to which he cannot return except he pay some sort of penal compensation which restores him to the equality of justice. Hence, according to the order of divine justice, he who has been too indulgent to his will, by transgressing God's commandment, suffers, either willingly or unwillingly, something contrary to what he would wish. This restoration of the equality of justice by penal compensation is also to be observed in injuries done to one's fellow-men. Consequently, it is evident that when the sinful or injurious act has ceased, there still remains the debt of punishment.

But if we speak of the removal of sin as to the stain, it is evident that the stain of sin cannot be removed from the soul without the soul being united to God, since it was through being separated from Him that it suffered the loss of its splendour, in which the stain consists. . . . Now man is united to God by his will. Therefore the stain of sin cannot be removed from man unless his will accepts the order of divine justice; that is to say, unless either of his own accord he take upon himself the punishment of his past sin, or bear patiently the punishment which God inflicts upon him; and in both ways punishment has the character of satisfaction. Now when punishment is satisfactory, it loses somewhat of the nature of punishment, for the nature of punishment is to be against the will: and although satisfactory punishment, absolutely speaking, is against the will, nevertheless, in this particular case and for this particular purpose, it is voluntary. . . . We must therefore say that, when the stain of sin has been removed, there may remain a debt of punishment, not indeed of punishment absolutely, but of satisfactory punishment.[1]

Now let us see what this means, first of all, in purely human terms, and as simply as possible. We will suppose that in a fit of anger or resentment or merely sheer wicked carelessness you damage something belonging to your friend—we will call it a valuable china teapot. This, of course, gives her in law a claim against you for damages; and if you express no penitence or she is unwilling to forgive you, she can take you into court and make you pay. But in the case we are considering, God is the friend, and He is always ready to forgive: and the sinner is penitent—otherwise he would not be going to Purgatory but to a very different place; so we need not trouble about that aspect of the business. We shall take it that, seeing the fragments of the teapot at your feet, you are overcome with shame and horror at what you have done and want to put matters right so far as possible. Obviously there are two things to be done: the first is to restore the right relationship with your friend which has been broken up by your anger or negligence or whatever the sin was. You go to her at once and confess your sinful feeling and the guilty act to which it led; you say how dreadfully sorry you are, and you beg her to forgive you, and promise that you will try to make it up to her in future. That is, you make an act of penitence: confession, contrition and atonement. She forgives you at once, you kiss and make friends; and that restores the relationship. You are now released at once from the *guilt* of what you did: in technical terms, you have purged the *culpa*. But this does not restore the teapot. In law, she could still, if she chose, take you into court; and although she is perhaps not likely to press her claim, *you* will feel that you ought to do something about it—offer to pay for it, scour the shops to find another teapot like it, or give her something else to make up: otherwise your atonement will not be complete. You will want, that is, to make an act of *compensation*, and the technical term for that is purging the *reatus*. And indeed, if you are *not* anxious to purge the *reatus* one might feel a little dubious about the sincerity of your contrition. But

[1] S.T.I., II^{ae} Q.87, A.7. (English Dominican Translation.)

here it is well to bear in mind that the intention in all this is *to please your friend*. One must not, whether to save one's face, or in order to wallow in the sensation of doing something spectacular, insist on making one's amends in embarrassing, unwelcome, or inappropriate ways. You may remember Léon Bloy, called upon to endure a miserable and degrading poverty. "I asked God", he wrote, "to let me suffer for my friends and for Him both in body and soul. But I had envisaged noble and pure suffering, which, as I now see, would only have been another form of joy. I had never dreamed of this infernal suffering which He has sent me." This illuminates what St. Thomas says about the sinner; "the stain cannot be removed unless *either* of his own accord [the sinner] take upon himself the punishment, *or* bear patiently the punishment which God inflicts upon him." Since God is the injured party, it lies with Him to say in what way the *reatus* is to be purged: and if the sinner is truly penitent, he will be eager to purge it in any way God may appoint, so that the stain may be removed and the relationship fully restored *on both sides*. For one must never forget that there are two parties to any act of forgiveness. However ready the injured party may be to forgive, the forgiveness cannot be effective—that is, the right relationship cannot be restored—unless the offender is prepared to accept forgiveness. It is quite true that God's forgiveness is immediate and unbounded but it is frivolous and foolish to imagine Him as saying casually: "Oh, that's all right—don't mention it", every time we commit murder. When we sin, we alienate ourselves from God; and if we are ever to be happy in His presence again, it is something in *us* that has to be altered—not anything in Him.

Now it seems to me quite clear from what St. Thomas says that he looks upon the purging of the *reatus* as being, first, last, and all the time for the sinner's own benefit, as a means to purifying away the stain and so making fully effective the purging of the *culpa*. In *this* life, of course, purging the *reatus* involves making atonement to man as well as to God; we must compensate the person we have injured as fully as we are able, and we must also set ourselves right with the Church, whom we have offended in his person; that is the reason—or at any rate the original and best reason—why penitent sinners bestow alms, or give statues and ornaments to churches and monasteries, or build chapels or what-not, as a way of showing their contrition. But the soul in Purgatory cannot in that sense "compensate" God. He has not injured God in the sense of having damaged Him or taken anything from Him: nor can he benefit God by giving Him anything, since all he has is God's already, and God wants for nothing. The only way in which the soul can injure or 'grieve" God is by injuring itself; and the only thing it can restore to God is itself. It can only restore itself and purge the stain, which is the separation from God, by accepting judgment and gladly submitting to have the stain scoured off it by any means however painful: and this "cleansing of the filth" as Dante calls it *is* itself the making of the satisfaction. In that moment of illumination which is given to it at death, the soul says, as it were: "Lord, I see You and I see myself; I am dirty and disgusting; even though in Your infinite goodness You were ready to receive me as I am, I should not be fit to stand in Your presence and my eyes could not bear to look at You. Please clean me—I don't mind what You do to me—I'll go through fire and water, anything, to be more like what You want me to be." We may remember the opening of Donne's great sonnet:

> Batter my heart, Three-personed God, for You
> As yet but knock, breathe, shine and seek to mend;
> That I may rise and stand, o'erthrow me, and bend
> Your force, to break, blow, burn and make me new.

That is the passion and poetry of St. Thomas's precise and scholastic definition. Dante's elect spirits utter it with less vehemence and more security, freed as they are from temptation and the world's stress: "Now go; I would not have thee stay longer, for thy tarrying disturbs my weeping, whereby I ripen that without which one cannot turn to God"; "thus soon have I been led to drink the sweet wormwood of the torments"; "we are so filled with desire to speed that stay we cannot"; "then certain of them came towards me as far as they could, but ever on their guard not to issue out of the fire"; "divine justice sets their desire toward the torment, as once toward the sin".[1]

"Divine justice", it is the counterpart of that other and more terrible phrase: "Divine justice so goads them that their fear is changed into desire." In the case of the damned also the desire is set toward the torment as once toward the sin; but differently. In Heaven, Hell, or Purgatory, we have what we choose, in the way in which we choose to have it. That is God's justice; and there is nothing arbitrary about it.

It is true that, in strict justice, the whole *reatus* of man's guilt can never be purged by Adam's seed, either here or hereafter. When one looks at the complicated network of wickedness and misery in which

---

[1] *Purg.* xix. 139–141; xxiii. 85–86; xviii. 115–116; xxvi. 13–15; xxi. 64–66.

men have contrived to entangle themselves, it is clear that no individual purgations, however eagerly and humbly undertaken, can ever really "make it up" either to God or to mankind as a whole. For one thing, the offering can never be wholly disinterested; it is, after all, one's self that is cleansed, and most of us will have enough to do to bring *that* about. Few are such saints as to have anything left over to offer up in satisfaction for others, or for mankind as a whole. But that part of it has been seen to. The *culpa* and the *reatus* for mankind were purged once for all in this world by the one Man who, being Himself perfectly sinless, could make satisfaction with all that He had and was, receiving into Himself the total evil and returning the total good. This, says Dante, in that seventh canto of *Paradiso* which is one of the noblest statements of Atonement doctrine ever uttered, this was God's generosity, that He did not simply remit the debt, but by becoming Man, gave man the means to satisfy justice:

> *La pena dunque che la croce porse,*
> *s'alla natura sunta si misura,*
> *nulla giammai si giustamente morse—*[1]

That which suffered on the cross was all mankind; in St. Paul's strange and memorable phrase: "He was made sin for us"; He accepted the *culpa* and purged the *reatus*. It was justice, because He was Man.

> *e così nulla fu di tanta ingiuria*
> *guardando alla persona che sofferse,*
> *in che era contratta tal natura.*[2]

It was injustice, because He was God; but because of that, He alone was able to do, as Man, what man can never do—make a free gift to God of a greatness commensurate with the crime committed. That gift, having been made in man's nature and on his behalf, is man's for the asking. Each penitent soul, offering itself to God, can come with that gift in his hand, and so offer the full satisfaction which, of himself, he cannot by any means make.

That is Dante's famous doctrine of the just vengeance—"*la giusta*

---

[1] If, therefore, the penalty inflicted by the cross be measured by the [human] nature which was assumed [by Christ], then never did any bite so justly.
                                                                    Para. vii. 40–42.

[2] And, in like manner, never was any so undeserved if we look to the Person of the sufferer into whom this nature was taken up.
                                                                    Para. vii. 43–45.

vendetta". It does not properly belong to our subject: but I have mentioned it because it is frequently misunderstood—chiefly because we have got hold of a distorted idea about arbitrary "punishments" (in the legal sense) for sin, and have lost hold of the teaching of St. Thomas about what the purging of the *reatus* really means.

This brings us to that shift of emphasis—that alteration in the balance —of the doctrine of which I spoke earlier. Here I think it will be best simply to quote what von Hügel says about it:

> It is interesting to note how—largely under the influence of the forensic temper and growth of the Canonical Penitential system, and of its successive relaxations in the form of substituted lighter good works—Indulgences,— the Latin half of Christendom, ever more social and immediately practical than the Greek portion, came, in general, more and more to dwell upon two ideas suggested to their minds by those two, Gospel and Pauline, passages. [That is, the "paying the uttermost farthing", and the "being saved so as by fire".] The one idea was that souls which, whilst fundamentally well-disposed, are not fit for Heaven at the body's death, can receive instant purification by the momentary fire of the Particular Judgment; and the other held that, thus already entirely purified and interiorly fit for Heaven, they are but detained (in what we ought, properly, to term a *Satisfactorium*), to suffer the now completely non-ameliorative, simply vindictive, infliction of punishment,—a punishment still, in strict justice, due to them for past sins, of which the guilt and the deteriorating effects upon their own souls have been fully remitted and cured. . . .
>
> This form of the doctrine was found greatly to favour the multiplication among the people of prayers, masses, and good works for the dead; since the *modus operandi* of such acts seemed thus to become entirely clear, simple, immediate, and, as it were, measurable and mechanical. For these souls in their *Satisfactorium*, being, from its very beginning, already completely purged and fit for Heaven, God is, as it were, free to relax at any instant, in favour of sufficiently fervent or numerous intercessions, the exigencies of His entirely extrinsic justice.[1]

The writer goes on to say that one may find what he calls this "highly artificial, inorganic view" emphasised "with even unusual vehemence" in certain sixteenth- and seventeenth-century writings, and also among certain more modern theologians. He adds that, while the penitential system of the Latin Church and the doctrine and practice of Indulgences "stand for certain important truths liable to being insufficiently emphasised by the Greek teachings concerning an intrinsically ameliorative *Purgatorium*", yet "as between the primarily forensic and

[1] *op. cit.*, p. 222.

governmental, and the directly ethical and spiritual, it will be the former that will have to be conceived and practised as, somehow, an expression and amplification of, and a practical corrective and means to, the latter".[1] And further on he says: "It is very certain that the marked and widespread movement of return to belief in a Middle State is distinctly towards a truly purgative Purgatory, although few of these sincere seekers are aware ... that they are groping after a doctrine all but quite explained away by a large body of late Scholastic and Neo-Scholastic theologians."[2]

It should by now, I think, be pretty clear that those writers are mistaken who, thinking to do Dante honour, claim for him an "originality" amounting to a breach with received Catholic doctrine, in that he lays so strong an emphasis upon the ameliorative aspect of Purgatory. He is simply laying the emphasis where the older, Greek tradition laid it; and we must remember that in Dante's time that Greek tradition was still very much alive in Italy. Old Rome and New Rome had not been so long or so deeply severed as to blot out all memory of Constantine and Justinian; the twin streams of Neo-Platonic Christian mysticism and of Greek Patristic theology poured through St. Augustine and the pseudo-Dionysius to water the garden of the Franciscans and Victorines. Moreover, as we have seen, that emphasis is to be found in St. Thomas Aquinas himself. The two elements in all just punishment—the purgation of *culpa* and *reatus*, amelioration and satisfaction, ethical and legal, internal amendment and external amends—are both there; but in Dante as in the passage we read from St. Thomas they are fused and blended together, with the *emphasis* lying always on the purification of the heart and the eager consent of the will. You pay the price—but you pay it because you want to, and because that is your only means of expressing your love and sorrow: and in paying you grow clean and fit to receive the forgiveness freely offered and to return to that right relationship which nothing but your own folly ever disturbed.

I think that the perpetual arguments about penal systems and methods of dealing with crime would be greatly illuminated if it could be clearly grasped that the important thing in every case is to induce the criminal to *accept judgment*. If that point can be gained, then the whole distinction between ameliorative and retributive punishment tends to disappear; for the culprit then understands that the penalty is the opportunity offered to him to purge the *reatus* and by so doing

[1] *op. cit.*, p. 223.   [2] *op. cit.*, p. 226.

to put himself back into right relations with society. But society, on the other hand, must be willing to take him back.

Now that we have understood the meaning and value of purgatorial pains, it is easier to see just how Dante works out his theme. The difference, and the balance, between purgation and satisfaction is perhaps most clearly marked at that point where Dante really is most original—namely, in his invention of Ante-Purgatory, and the contrast between the sinners without and within the gate kept by the Angel with the Keys. Outside the gate are the souls who, though saved by accepting judgment in the moment of death, are for one reason or another not yet allowed to begin their purgation. Some died excommunicate; others were cut off in their sins and had only time to turn their wills to God *in articulo mortis*; and others delayed "doing anything about religion" until the imminent approach of death frightened them into action, and so on. An elementary sense of justice suggests that these people should not be put on the same footing as those who all their lives have struggled to do their best and make their repentance for sin, and bring themselves as near as they can to a fitness for God's presence. Accordingly, they are punished for their negligence—and this is, in fact, the only punishment in Dante's Purgatory that is purely retributive. And in what does it consist? Well, like everybody else in the Three Kingdoms, these souls have what they chose. They chose delay and they have it. They are punished by being held back from the "cleansing pains" which they so earnestly desire, and for various terms corresponding to their own delays they are obliged to wander idly about the green slopes and flowery valleys of the sun-and-wind-swept hillside.

In these dwellers in Ante-Purgatory, Dante, with delicate touches, shows how, though sin and the temptation to sin are past, the stain of the sin remains. He deals most tenderly perhaps with the Excommunicate, who refused obedience, and now wander like shepherdless sheep, startled at every strange sight and not knowing what they are doing or why, for their leaders are as ignorant as themselves. We do not of course know what sins they may have to purge when they are admitted by the Angel; Manfred admits that his sins were horrible (as indeed they were); and he still shows perhaps some pride of ancestry, some resentment against the Bishop of Cosenza; we may guess that he will spend some time on the cornices of the Proud and of the Wrathful. Lazy Belacqua is Lazy Belacqua still, nor has he lost his indolent cynicism and his touch of malice. Those heedless warriors who fell in battle, unprepared and unhouselled, are impetuous still and still egotistical, sweeping down on Dante like a charge of cavalry and clamouring for his attention; only poor little Pia, whose husband murdered her at Maremma, says modestly: "When you have rested from your hard journey, remember me." (One wonders why so sweet a soul did not die at peace with God; perhaps she was too unhappy and so gave way to despair—if so, the Cornice of the Slothful will correct her too-great passivity.) The rulers and men of affairs who pushed God into the background while they worried and fussed about their importance and their position in life and the enormous busyness of public office, sit there carefully retaining rank and privilege and still, as it were, talking business and fretting about politics and the sins of "the pest of France". It is to them that we see the serpent come nightly; whether it goes to other parts of the island we are not told—but to them at any rate it comes, as though sin, thrust out for ever from the will and the waking mind, might yet (but for the guardian angels) slip into their subconsciousness and trouble their dreams. The stain of sin rests on them all—yet not so as to shake their hope and confidence or alter their blessed courtesy and good-will.

All these spirits ask eagerly for the prayers of the living, that their term of exile may be shortened.

"It is useless for me to go up," says Belacqua, "the bird of God who sits at the gate would not admit me to the torments. I must stay here for as many years as I lived on earth, unless prayer aids me from a heart in grace." And Manfred: "The excommunicate must stay outside for thirty times the period of their presumption, if holy prayers—*buon preghi*—shorten not the time. Go, thou, tell my kind Constance, explain about the ban laid on us—*chè qui per quei di là molto s'avanza* —you people there can help us here so much." "Ask them to pray for me in Fano," says Jacopo del Cassero, "*per ch'io possa purgar le gravi offese.*" [1] And Buonconte: "Pity me, help me; no one loves me, I have no one to pray for me, *per ch'io vo tra costor con bassa fronte.*" [2, 3]

Since *this* part of the punishment is purely retributive, God is, in von Hügel's phrase, "free" to remit some portion of it "of His sole courtesy", accepting the love and prayer of living souls in grace as a full satisfaction for what the sinner omitted in this life. And we find indeed that this charitable exchange is permitted and welcomed. "In

[1] that I may purge away my heavy offences.
[2] therefore I walk among these [spirits] with downcast brow.
[3] *Purg.* iv. 127–135; iii. 136–145; v. 70–73; v. 85–90.

my last hours I repented," says Sapìa, "but I should not be where I am now" (i.e. already within the gate and on the Cornice of the Envious) "but that Pier Pettinagno was sorry for me and remembered me in his holy prayers." There is one other possibility: a heroic act of charity and conquest of the besetting sin may graciously be accepted to make up for many years of negligence; thus Provenzan Salvani, though he put off repentance to his last hour, is admitted quickly to the Cornice of the Proud because of the one great act of humility which he performed out of pure love for his friend. But, generally speaking, the souls in Ante-Purgatory must wait patiently upon the love and prayers of the living. Charity is the rule: the charity of others, one's own charity towards others—this breaks the ban and privileges the soul to enter upon its suffering.

But once we are past the gate, there is a subtle difference. Prayers are indeed asked for, and their effect will, in fact, be the shortening of the period of purgation. But there is no more question of asking that God may remit the suffering—only that the souls may perform their penance better. "So may grace quickly cleanse away the scum of your conscience" is Dante's greeting; and the spirits, eagerly embracing their pains, say only, "Go thy way now: I would rather weep than talk. Pray for me." And again: "I pray thee pray for me when thou hast reached the summit"—And: "If thou art so largely privileged as to enter the cloister whose Abbot is Christ, say a Paternoster for me so far as is needful to us who can be tempted no longer." [1] And Forese, on the Sixth Cornice, says: "Not once only as we circle this road, is our pain renewed: I say pain, but I ought to say comfort, for our pangs of hunger lead us to the tree of Christ's cross. My wife by her prayers drew me forth from the place of waiting and liberated me from the other circles." [2] Notice the distinction: from the Ante-Purgatory he is simply removed—*tratto fuore*; from the lower cornices he is set free —*liberato*. The force of the distinction is seen when we look back to the all-important passage in which Statius explains how a soul is "set free" from purgation, so that the whole mountain quakes and a shout of joy goes up from top to bottom:

> *Tremaci quando alcuna anima monda*
> *sentesi, sì che surga o che si mova*
> *per salir su, e tal grido seconda.*

---

[1] *Purg.* xiii. 88–89; xix. 139–141; xxvi. 145–147; xxvi. 127–132.
[2] *Purg.* xxiii. 70–75; 87–90.

Della mondizia sol voler fa prova,
che, tutta libera a mutar convento,
l'alma sorprende, e di voler le giova.

Prima vuol ben; ma non lascia il talento
che divina giustizia contra voglia,
come fu al peccar, pone al tormento.[1]

There is no point, you see, at which God says: "Your term's up", or "all things considered I think that will do now", or, "I have received a great many prayers and offerings on your behalf, so I'll let you off the rest". Nobody comes to release the soul; it is its own judge, and when it *feels* that it is clean—*sentesi monda*—it simply gets up and goes. It knows itself clean because it is free to follow its will. Did it not always will to go upward? Yes; the absolute will—that which wills the final end—was always set towards the ascent. But it was tied and bound by the conditioned will—*il talento*—that part of the will which wills the means to the end—and *that* was "turned to the torment as once to the sin". When you as a child were invited to a delightful party your will was simply to go there; but your parents said: "Not so fast; you can't go like that, in shorts and sweater and looking like nothing on earth. You must have a bath and change and submit to having your hair done, and then you can go." That is rather like the ordinary idea of after-life punishment: an exterior power forcibly imposes conditions. But Dante's idea corresponds to the working of the adult mind. When you are grown-up, though your *voler* is still simply to go, your own *talento* imposes the salutary restrictions, demanding perhaps the tedium of a permanent wave or the discipline of a boiled shirt. You may, as Statius and St. Thomas both point out, dislike these things in themselves, but you choose *contra voglia*, to do them as the means to the end. Your own judgment tells you when you are really ready—the last curl in place, the finger-nails properly attended to, the white

---

[1] But when some spirit, feeling purged and sound,
Leaps up or moves to seek a loftier station,
The whole mount quakes and the great shouts resound.

The will itself attests its own purgation;
Amazed, the soul that's free to change its inn
Finds its mere will suffice for liberation;

True, it wills always, but can nothing win
So long as heavenly justice keeps desire
Set toward the pain as once 'twas toward the sin.
Purg. xxi. 58–66.

tie sitting correctly; then your *talento* takes the fetters off your *voler*, and you are *liberati*—free to call a taxi and go. So Statius explains: "I who have lain under this torment five hundred years and more only just now felt my will free—*sentii libera voluntà*—to seek a better threshold." [1]

In all this, Dante is still following St. Thomas; and in making the soul's own sense of freedom the signal of release from the torment, he is, I think, rather working the doctrine of penitence out to its natural conclusion than initiating an original conception of his own. But in him the effect is startlingly original; partly because we are accustomed to the later shift of emphasis towards the "forensic and external" concept of satisfaction, and partly because we are apt to think in terms of the "popular theology" expressed in writings like *St. Patrick's Purgatory* and in the illuminations to mediaeval Books of Hours. In those popular conceptions, Purgatory is usually a dark and smoky place, like Hell, populated by demons with toasting-forks; indeed, very often Hell and Purgatory are the same place, the only distinction being that the saved souls are let out at the end of their sentence, whereas the lost remain there for ever. The open-air imagery of Dante's great Mountain, with the sea bathing its reedy shores, and the wide sky where the Sun's chariot drives by day, and the seven blessed stars wheel by night till the moon comes up "like a burnished mazer"—this is what takes us so far from anything we are accustomed to connect with mediaeval visionary literature. This—and not only this; but also the enchanting good manners of all the inhabitants of the place, their delight in praising one another and their charming candour when they have occasion to speak about themselves. For Dante, the circles of Purgatory are not suburbs of Hell, but milestones on the road to Heaven. Here, indeed, he may be said to have departed from St. Thomas, who suggests, rather dubiously, that Purgatory is probably situated in the neighbourhood of Hell. But then St. Thomas was writing plain prose, and was not claiming to be a specialist in poetic imagery. In this respect Dante is nearer to the Moslem tradition, by which he may or may not have been directly influenced. One Moslem book does indeed situate Purgatory upon a mountain in an island—though no further off than Taprobane (that is, Ceylon). Nobody, I believe, has succeeded in discovering what prompted Dante to transfer the venue to the Antipodes.

The geographical imagery is, however, less germane to our purpose

[1] *Purg.* xxi. 67–69.

than the symbolic figures of the sinners themselves. They are not yet heavenly, but they are the width of the world away from Vanni Fucci and Adam of Brescia and Filippo Argenti. In Hell, Dante's appearance arouses surprise and antagonism; in Heaven it is "here is one who shall increase our loves"; in Purgatory there are marvel and praise at the wonderful grace that shines upon him and eager wishes for his good speed. In Hell, each soul ignores its neighbours, or bites them, or hastens to accuse them; in Purgatory, each praises his neighbour and is frank about his own sins. Touches of Dante's delicate humour are not wanting: listen to Umberto on the Cornice of the Proud:

> *Io fui Latino, e nato d'un gran Tosco:*
> *Guglielmo Aldobrandesco fu mio padre:*
> *non so se il nome suo giammai fu vosco—*[1]

"I was son to a great Tuscan—Gwillim Aldobrandeschi was my father"—he pulls himself up and adds, modestly, "I don't know if you ever heard of him. I am here to make satisfaction for my insolent pride of race."

And Oderisi, "honour of Agobbio and the illuminator's art": "Brother, Franco Bolognese is a better painter than I; he gets all the honour now—though I still get a little. Fame is a breath of wind." [2] And he goes on to tell of Provenzan Salvani's great act of humility. Sapìa, on the Cornice of the Envious, gently rebukes Dante for asking "whether anybody there is Italian":

> *O frate mio, ciascuna è cittadina*
> *d'una vera città; ma tu vuoi dire,*
> *che vivesse in Italia peregrina.*[3]

One hears the echo of the *De Monarchia*: "the human race is most likened to God where it is most one",[4] and the outcry against the troubles caused by princes contending for supremacy. Sapìa herself took only too fierce a part in these envious contendings, and envied the prosperity of her own countrymen, so that when Provenzan Salvani defeated them at Colle she "lifted up her impudent face, shrilling to

[1] *Purg.* xi. 58–60.
[2] *Purg.* xi. 82–84, 158 *sqq.*
[3] "O brother mine, citizens all are we
    Of one true city; any, thou wouldst say,
    Who lived a pilgrim once in Italy".
                            Purg. xiii. 94–96.
[4] *De Mon.* I. viii.

God: 'I have nothing to fear from Thee now', as the blackbird does for a few days of fine weather".[1] Wasn't she absurd? she says—one would hardly believe anybody could be so demented. But there! her kinsfolk are a foolish set of people. She is sweet and serious—yet, if her eyes were not stitched like a wild hawk's, one would almost expect to see a twinkle in them: in Heaven she will, no doubt, be very ready to forgive herself and "laugh at her own error". The two spirits with her are distressed by the degradation of the quarrelsome towns in the valley of the Arno—dogs and wolves and swine all of them, perpetually snarling and fighting among themselves. Perhaps the tone of these remarks is a little acrimonious for souls on the way to Heaven—but then one remembers that they have not yet purged the sin of Wrath.

I would not like to affirm that, at every step up the Mountain, Dante has laboriously considered which faults should be shown to have been already purged and which still remain. But certainly, as the way ascends, the temper of freedom and purity and joy pours itself into the verse, until, at the last encounter on the Cornice of Fire where the lovers purge their passion, there is only that lyric greeting which, in its courtesy, sadness, sweetness and jubilation sums up the whole quality of Purgatory:

> *Tan m'abelis vostre cortes deman*
> *qu'ieu no'm puesc, ni'm vueil a vos cobrire*—[2]

it is almost the accent of Francesca, the woman who couldn't say No —but in the tone of it there is an enormous difference. Listen to it for a moment. Here is Francesca:

> *O animal grazioso e benigno*
> *che visitando vai per l'aer perso*
> *noi che tignemmo il mondo di sanguigno,*

> *Se fosse amico il re dell'universo,*
> *moi pregheremmo lui la tua pace,*
> *poi che hai pietà del nostro mal perverso.*

> *Di quel che udire e che parlar ti piace,*
> *noi udiremo a parleremo a voi . . .*

> *. . . Nessun maggior dolore*
> *che ricordarsi del tempo felice*
> *nella miseria; e ciò sa il tuo dottore,*

---

[1] *Purg.* xiii. 121–123 *sqq.*   [2] *Purg.* xxvi. 140 *sqq.*

> *Ma se a conoscer la prima radice*
> *del nostro amor tu hai cotanto affetto,*
> *farò come colui che piange e dice.*[1]

"It is kind of you to ask: I am willing to answer"—the same words in the Infernal and the Purgatorial circles of the Lustful: the one in the plangent, long-drawn-out, wailing Italian periods; the other in the quick, dancing, gay Provençal.

Ieu sui Arnaut, que plor e vau cantan—"I am Arnaut, who weep and go singing"—that is the whole climate and atmosphere of the mountain-top.

> *consiros vei la passada folor,*
> *e vei jausen lo jorn qu'esper denan*—

jausen—jauchzend: there is no English word which quite conveys the sense of the Provençal or the German; it is "the shout of them that triumph, the song of them that feast" in two clamant syllables. "Exulting" is perhaps the nearest equivalent.

> *Ara vos prec, per aquella valor*
> *que vos guida al som de l'escalina,*
> *sovegna vos a tem da ma dolor* [2]

---

[1] "O living creature, gracious and so kind,
    Coming through this black air to visit us,
    Us, who in death the globe incarnadined,

Were the world's King our friend and might we thus
    Entreat, we would entreat Him for thy peace,
    That pitiest so our pangs dispiteous!

Hear all thou wilt, and speak as thou shalt please,
    And we will gladly speak with thee and hear . . ."

Then she to me: "The bitterest woe of woes
    Is to remember in our wretchedness
    Old happy times; and this thy Doctor knows;

Yet, if so dear desire thy heart possess
    To know the root of love which caused our fall,
    I'll be as those who weep and who confess."
                Inf. v. 88–95; 121–126.

[2] So well your courteous request pleases me that I neither can nor will conceal myself from you. I am Arnaut, who go weeping and singing. Regretfully I look upon my past, exulting I look forward in hope towards the day to come. Pray you now, by that Power that shall guide you to the summit of the stair, be mindful in good time of my sufferings.   *Purg.* xxvi. 140–147.

"I pray you by——"—it is a title for God: goodness, virtue, power—all three together, and with them the notion of worth, value, preciousness, and a kind of gaiety in the word too—"I pray you by Him who, being all this, leads you to the top step of the stair, when the time comes, be mindful of my griefs."

Poi s'ascose nel foco che gli affina.[1]

What Dante comes to "at the top step of the stair" is the Earthly Paradise. And this brings us to the question: When all the penitence and all the purgation are done, in this world and the next, where exactly does mankind find itself? The answer—a disappointing one perhaps for those who make a fetish of progress—is that it finds itself exactly where it originally set out from. Like Chesterton's traveller who went all round the world to discover England, man has journeyed through the troubles of Earth and the vision of Hell and the steep ascents of Purgatory simply to come home. His relationship with God is restored, he has recovered the primal innocence, he stands where the First Adam stood; Paradise is regained. Not quite as it would have been if Adam had never wished to know good and evil, for with God nothing is ever lost or wasted. The innocence is now enriched by all the bitter experience; the evil is not simply blotted out, it is redeemed. But the will, which throughout its temporal probation has been thwarted and hampered and terrified and tyrannised over by the disorderly lusts to which it enslaved itself, and which has had in consequence to be put in subjection to the Law, is now free. It can go to its own true place as swiftly and certainly as the stone falls downward or the fire mounts upward. It no longer needs the sober wisdom of Virgil to guide and instruct it, for it cannot go wrong; its every motion is directed to God without effort; therefore it needs no rule but itself to guide it—neither human law nor ecclesiastical discipline.[2] It can do what it likes, for it cannot but like what it ought.

"Thus far," says Virgil, "have I brought thee by discernment and skill—*con ingegno e con arte*—now take thine own pleasure for guide.

---

[1] Then he hid himself in the fire that refines them.
Purg. xxvi. 148.

[2] Or perhaps, more exactly, it finds in obedience to these disciplines simply the full expression of its own will. See paper on *The Fourfold Interpretation of the Comedy*, p. 115 *sqq.*

8

"Non aspettar mio dir più, ne mio cenno.
Libero, dritto e sano è tuo arbitrio,
e fallo fora non fare a suo senno:

per ch'io te sopra te corono e mitrio." [1]

So far, then, so good. But at this point Dante springs rather a surprise on us. He enters the lovely wood; as his earthly pilgrimage began in the Dark Wood, so it ends in this one, where the trees whisper all day with the wind of the turning spheres and make a harmony with the bird's song, and where the little stream runs rippling under cool shade, and Matelda plucks the red and yellow flowers, singing the psalm *Delectasti*, and turning, when Dante greets her,

come si volge, con le piante strette
a terra ed intra se, donna che balli,
e piede innanzi piede a pena mette—[2]

Something like this we might perhaps have expected. And there, shining through the trees comes the pageant of Revelation, the unfolding from beginning to end of God's purpose—and this, maybe, is the way in which Man should have come to know that purpose, had he not chosen to experience it after another and more bitter manner. And here at last there comes to Dante the unforgettable, unforgotten first Image of Love, the God-bearing Image in which he had first seen the light of the true Reality. She is the same—how could he fail to recognise her, even under the veil? Yet not the same; for he sees now, what he once divined by love, the body of glory in which God had always seen her. This, too, we had expected—what else had he come all this way to see? He turns to Virgil—but Virgil is gone, and "not all that our First Mother lost" can stay his tears. And then the voice that had once saluted him in the streets of Florence speaks to him again, and speaks swords:

"Dante, perchè Virgilio ne se vada
non piange anco, non pianger ancora
chè pianger ti convien per altra spada. . . .

---

[1] "No word from me, no further sign expect;
　Free, upright, whole, thy will itself lays down
　Guidance that it were error to neglect,

Whence o'er thyself I mitre thee and crown".
                    Purg. xxvii. 139–142.

[2] As a dancing lady turns with her toes together,
　Foot by foot set close, and close to the ground,
　And scarcely putting the one before the other—
                    Purg. xxviii. 52–54.

> *Guardaci ben: ben sem, ben sem Beatrice.*
> *Come degnasti d'accedere al monte,*
> *non sapei tu che qui è l'uom felice?"* ¹

That, I think, we had not expected.

> Dante, weep not for Virgil's going—keep
> As yet from weeping; weep not yet, for soon
> Another sword shall give thee cause to weep. . . .
>
> Look on us well; we are indeed, we are
> Beatrice. How didst thou deign to climb the hill?
> Didst thou not know that men are happy here?

And he looks at himself mirrored in the clear water, and draws back from the sight—*tanta vergogna mi gravò la fronte.*² He had seen himself not so long ago, mirrored "just as he was" in the first polished step that leads up to Purgatory Gate; but that time he was not so overcome. Now Beatrice reproaches him, accuses him, strips him so naked that the Virtues and Graces at her side are filled with pity, spares him nothing, wrings confession out of him: "Is it not true? What do you think yourself? Answer me; for the memory of wretchedness has not yet been taken from you by this water." He breaks down:

> *Confusion e paura insieme miste*
> *mi pinsero un tal "si" fuor della bocca,*
> *al quale intender fur mestier le viste.*³

She has not finished with him yet. "Why, why, why did you do it? What snares were in your way? What charm or what profit was there to be had from those other things that you needs must go wandering after them?" He can only falter back his answer:

> "Things transitory with their false delight,"
> Weeping I said, "enticed my steps aside,
> Soon as your face was hidden from my sight." ⁴

She is a little mollified: "You have confessed—it would have been just the same if you had kept silence or denied it—we know all about you

---

¹ *Purg.* xxx. 55–57, 73–75.
² such shame weighed down my forehead
    Purg. xxx. 78.
³ Terror and shame inextricably knit
    Forced from my miserable lips a "Yes"
    Such that the sight must needs interpret it.
        Purg. xxi. 13–15.
⁴ *Ibid.* 34–36.

here; but in this court confession blunts the edge of the axe. Stop crying and listen. Once, in me, you saw and loved your true good. The image of it was taken from you when I died—but you had seen. Was there any mortal thing that should have drawn you to lust after it, once you had seen *that*? Are you a grown man that you behave like a child? Lift up your beard and look at me." He looks, and he cannot bear it, and falls unconscious.

This, I think, one would not have expected. Theologically, it seems as though Dante had transferred the crisis and confrontation of the Particular Judgment from the moment of death to the moment when purgation is already complete.

One ought not, perhaps, at this point to hold Dante too rigidly to the official theology of the After-Life. That, after all, is not what he is describing in his own case. Dante the Pilgrim is not, in fact, dead, except in a symbol: he is only having a vision of these things. We could only know what Dante the Poet thought happened to the *literally* dead if he had told us here what happened to Statius. But this he has not done. We conclude that Statius, like Virgil, saw the Pageant of Revelation approaching; but after the arrival of Beatrice, Statius fades out of the picture. Presumably he too drank of Lethe, for we know that all souls must do so; and later on, after the second Pageant of Church and Empire has been shown, we find Statius with Dante on the other side of the stream and invited by Beatrice to come and drink also of Eunoë. That is all. One must not read into people's poems what they do not choose to put there. I have a private theory that the Image of Beatrice, as Beatrice, is for Dante alone; and that what Statius saw was not she, but a personal vision of that Image, whatever it was, that had been for him the God-bearer. It is, of course, fused into Beatrice at the end, since we see everything through Dante's eyes, and he could not see it otherwise. All this is mere speculation—a meditation on the text, and not exegesis. It is with Dante that we are concerned; and for him neither death nor judgment nor purgation has as yet taken place in fact. Consequently, we need not be surprised if, in his vision, there is not an exact correspondence at every point with "the real thing".

Still, when all this is said, there may still be a profound symbolism in that sudden terrible humiliation when he sees himself glassed in the clear water *after* the regaining of Paradise and the reversal of the Fall. It would mean that for the first time it was possible for him to see sin in its full horror, as it is seen by one who is wholly innocent, in whom there remains not one thought, not one little motion of the will which gives the smallest consent to sin; as Christ saw it when He endured to bear the guilt of it and felt the desolation of it drop down between His Manhood and His Godhead, so that He cried *Eloi, eloi, lama sabacthani*; as God sees it always. That is a thing of which no living human being can ever have the experience; for in the greatest saint there is always some taint of Original Sin, some remnant of the false self that is on the Devil's side and gives treacherous assent to evil. But the nearer one is to innocence, the more hideous does sin appear: that is why great saints so often seem to us to have an exaggerated and even morbid idea of their own sinfulness. If one can imagine a person with the innocence of a very young child, combined with the understanding of a grown man; a person totally stripped of all the cynicism, callousness, indifference, wilful incredulity, love of sensation and sneaking sympathy with destructiveness which the habit of seeing ugly things folds round us like a defensive armour; if we can imagine such a person confronted with the naked fact of something like Belsen or Hiroshima—then we may get some faint idea of what sin would look like to a spirit made totally clean.

It would, of course, be wholly unbearable. No finite creature could endure it. Dante faints away: "What became of me then she knows who was the cause of it." [1] And immediately he is plunged into Lethe, and that final, unmitigated knowledge of evil in its essence is taken from him, to be restored by Eunoë as Adam's original knowledge of all things as good. "In Heaven," said the Lady Julian of Norwich, "the token of sin is turned to worship. . . . For right as to every sin is answering a pain by truth, right so for every sin, to the same soul is given a bliss by love." [2] And, in considering the *Paradiso*, we saw that it was so.

Dante, when he made the unclouded vision of sin the first effects of the return to innocence, may have meant that this experience must necessarily befall any spirit that is fully purged. If he did, there is, so far as I can see, nothing in this idea that is inconsistent with the Catholic faith, though I do not know that it is anywhere explicitly made part of the doctrine of Purgatory. Or he may have meant it to be looked upon only as a result of his whole vision upon himself. If so, it does not, strictly speaking, belong to the literal, but rather to the allegorical meaning of the poem.

[1] *Purg.* xxxi. 89–90.
[2] Julian of Norwich: *Revelations of Divine Love* (ed. Warrack, Methuen, 1940), *Thirteenth Revelation* (ch. xxxviii).

In these two papers I have dealt only with the *literal* meaning, which is, as Dante said in the *Epistle to Can Grande*, "the state of souls after death". The *allegorical*—that is, the real meaning of the poem—is the experience of the soul in *this* world: or rather, the universal experience of the soul in its relation to God's Reality—the universal pattern of which the life after death is at once an instance and a symbol.

It is in this life, and not only in the next, that we can, by glimpses, have experience of Hell and Heaven, and that it is our business, by confession, contrition, and satisfaction, to purge the *culpa* and *reatus* of sin, and give that willing assent to God's grace which restores the primal relationship and brings the life of man back to something approaching its lost innocence. In reading Dante, this precedence of the allegorical over the literal must never be lost to sight. It explains, for example, two points which may at first perplex us when reading the *Purgatorio*. One is that Dante seems to take it for granted that Purgatory is an experience through which *all* souls have to pass on their way to Heaven: whereas theologians for the most part hold that a holy soul, dying in grace, may have completed its purgation in this world and be admitted immediately to the Beatific Vision. In the literal sense, Dante might well allow this: but for the allegorical meaning, the ascent of the Mountain is clearly necessary for all, since the Earthly Paradise is—theoretically at any rate—the goal at which the penitent in *this* world has to aim. The second point is the rather surprising intrusion into the Earthly Paradise of the symbolical Pageant of Church and Empire which is shown to Dante under the Tree of Knowledge. The allegory applies, not only to the individual soul of each man, but also to Man-in-Society; and Church and Empire (according to Dante) are the two institutions, of equally divine appointment, by which Society ought to be so guided as to enable man to attain the fruition of earthly blessedness, and the establishment in this world of a true Kingdom of God. The failure of these institutions is, therefore, highly relevant to the allegorical significance of the Earthly Paradise, and that is why Dante put the pageant where it is.

There is also, of course, the "anagogical" or mystical interpretation of the *Divine Comedy*, for which every stage in Dante's journey corresponds to a stage on the Illuminative Way. But this belongs to the field of Mystical Theology, and would have to be dealt with separately.

If I have restricted myself on this occasion to expounding, as best I can, the literal meaning of the poem, it is because I have found that misunderstanding about it so often proves a barrier between Dante and his readers. If we allow our minds to be influenced by crude and distorted notions of what the Church really *means* by Hell and Heaven and Purgatory, we shall find the literal story always getting in our way. When we see the word "punishment" we shall automatically think of savage reprisals; when we see the word "prayer" we shall think of somebody trying to bribe or wheedle God into letting people off part of a whipping; when we see the word "dance" or "hymn", we shall think of Heaven as a kind of glorified Three Choirs Festival. And these irritating fancies will continually fret us, and make us waste our time carping at the imagery instead of coping with the allegory.

I ought perhaps to say one word about the question which still sometimes bothers people, namely whether the Church officially teaches that the pains of Hell and the joys of Heaven are physical or "only" spiritual. On this side of the Resurrection, the souls have no bodies: [1] consequently the question has no meaning—or at most resolves itself into the rather academical one, discussed with some ingenuity by St. Augustine, whether and how a spiritual being can suffer pain from a physical fire. After the Resurrection, there will be a body; but it will be, as St. Paul says, "a spiritual body", and since we do not know at all what it will be like, we cannot tell how it may be able to suffer or rejoice. The danger of saying explicitly, as some theologians have always said, that the pains and joys of spirits are wholly spiritual is that the sort of person who reads *The Freethinker* is then moved to say: "Oh, merely figurative"—as though nothing were really real except the pleasure of sun-bathing and the pains of toothache. What is meant by the stress sometimes laid upon the physical aspect of both pain and joy is that it is *real*, and that it involves the whole personality.

Thus far, then, to quote Virgil again, I have brought you, with what *ingegno ed arte* I can command. You have "seen the temporal fire and the eternal",[2] and the *"luce intellettual piena d'amore"* [3] which is the one Reality of which those fires are the perverted experience—the experience of the good known in its opposite aspect of evil. To appreciate Dante it is not, of course, necessary to believe what he believed, but it is, I think, necessary to *understand* what he believed, and to realise that it is a belief which a mature mind can take

---

[1] For the mediaeval doctrine of the "aery body" ordained to the spirit for the express purpose of enduring the purgatorial pains, see *Purg.* iii. 31–33, xxv. 20 *sqq.* This doctrine is, of course, not *de fide.*

[2] *Purg.* xxvii. 127.   [3] *Para.* xxx. 40.

seriously. The widespread disinclination to-day to take Hell and Heaven seriously results, very largely, from a refusal to take *this* world seriously. If we are materialists, we look upon man's life as an event so trifling compared to the cosmic process that our acts and decisions have no importance beyond the little space-time frame in which we find ourselves. If we take what is often vaguely called "a more spiritual attitude to life", we find that we are postulating some large and lazy cosmic benevolence which ensures that, no matter how we behave, it will all somehow or other come out right in the long run. But Christianity says, "No. What you do and what you are matters, and matters intensely. It matters now and it matters eternally; it matters to you, and it matters so much to God that it was for Him literally a matter of life and death."

Here, to end up with, are three quotations from the Lady Julian:

To me was shewed no harder hell than sin.

In every soul that shall be saved is a godly will that never assented to sin, nor ever shall. . . . Though the soul be healed, his wounds are seen before God,—not as wounds but as worships.

As verily as God is our Father, so verily God is our Mother; and that sheweth He in all, and especially in these sweet words where He saith: "I it am." That is to say, "I it am, the might and the goodness of the Fatherhood; I it am, the wisdom of the Motherhood; I it am, the light and the grace that is all blessed love; I it am, the Trinity, I it am, the Unity; I am the sovereign goodness in all manner of things. I am that maketh thee to love; I am that maketh thee to long; I it am, the endless fulfilling of all true desires."

THE FOURFOLD
INTERPRETATION OF THE *COMEDY*

IN the summer of 1950 the Columbia University Press enlivened us by announcing the names of the Ten Most Boring Classics, chosen (according to newspaper reports) by "hundreds of editors, writers, booksellers, librarians, literary critics and ordinary readers". Top marks for dullness were allotted to the greatest allegory in English prose—*The Pilgrim's Progress*. This was followed, in order of demerit, by *Moby Dick*, which (if not explicitly allegorical in form) has certainly a *significacio* beyond its literal meaning; and by *Paradise Lost*, the greatest religious poem in English verse. Thence, by way of Boswell's *Johnson*, *Pamela*, *Silas Marner*, and *Ivanhoe*, we come to *Don Quixote*, the greatest novel of Spain, whose signification also is not entirely on the surface: and *Faust*, the greatest poem in the German language, and certainly allegorical, especially in its second part. One may perhaps tentatively conclude that religious allegory is not the most popular branch of literature in the United States—or at any rate among such of their citizens as enjoy filling in questionnaires. *The Divine Comedy* was not included in the "Lower Ten"; but this may have been merely because none of the hundreds of voters had ever tried to read it.

Having myself a peculiar fondness for allegory, I can only hope that if a similar enquiry were put out in this country, it might produce less mortifying results. I admit, however, that I am not very sanguine about editors, booksellers, librarians and literary critics. Some writers would, I know, be on my side; but I should pin my faith to the common reader. All the same, I am very much aware, and have indeed frequently said, that in our present day the art of reading, as of writing, allegory has been to a very great extent lost. The ordinary reader, unaccustomed to this kind of picture-writing, is not always quite sure what the picture represents, or what he is supposed to look for. And the commentators are not always as helpful as they might be, because, lost in a maze of controversial detail, they often forget to make clear the broad outlines of the scheme of interpretation. Perhaps they feel that these are too obvious to need pointing out; but it is always curiously easy to overlook the obvious. The present paper is concerned with what I conceive to be the most prolific source of confusion where the *Commedia* is concerned; and, after what I have said, I hope I may be forgiven if I am sometimes very obvious indeed.

An allegory, as we all know at any rate in theory, is a story (whether veracious or fictitious) whose literal meaning is a symbol to convey the greater signification for whose sake the story exists. That is the first and most obvious thing to bear in mind; and the prime source of error and misunderstanding in reading allegory is to confuse the literal with the allegorical meaning—the sign with the thing signified. And the second, though less obvious, is like unto it. In most great and richly significant allegory, the literal story may find its allegorical interpretation at more levels than one; and error and misunderstanding result when the levels are confused. In a well-constructed allegory (and the *Commedia* is supremely well constructed), story and significance are lines which run parallel, never fusing or crossing one another; and the pattern is one of such universal truth that the signification remains valid and consistent at all levels of interpretation.

Now, Dante himself, in the *Epistle to Can Grande*, has told us that his poem has a literal meaning which is to be interpreted at three levels—the allegorical, the moral and the anagogical. This division is not a personal whimsy of his own invention. It was the recognised method of interpreting Biblical narrative, particularly the narrative of the Old Testament, and goes back to the early Christian Fathers. Dante's three levels are identical with those enumerated and explained by St. Thomas Aquinas (S.T.I., Q.I., A.10), who says: "That first signification *whereby words signify things* belongs to the first sense, the historical or literal. That signification *whereby things signified by words have themselves also a signification* is called the spiritual sense, which is based on the literal and presupposes it. Now this spiritual sense has a threefold division. . . . So far as the things of the Old Law signify the things of the New Law, there is the allegorical sense; so far as the things done in Christ, or so far as the things which signify Christ, are signs of what we ought to do, there is the moral sense. But so far as they signify what relates to eternal glory, there is the anagogical sense." If you will compare this extract from the *Summa* with the passage in the *Epistle* which sets out the four meanings of the text "In exitu Israel",[1] you will see how closely Dante is following St. Thomas, and how he works the principle out in practice.

Now, it is certainly arguable that the original authors of the Old Testament did not in the least expect or intend their books to be

---

[1] See *Dante's Imagery (Symbolic)*, p. 10.

interpreted in this complicated way. But there can be no argument about what Dante intended to be done with *his* book. He wrote it with that fourfold system of interpretation consciously and deliberately in view, and he said so in the plainest possible manner.

Let us, then, look a little more closely at what St. Thomas has to say. First, as to the *literal or historical* meaning. He uses the word "historical", and Dante follows him in this. I rather wish he had not, because by doing so he has deprived me of an adjective which would have come in more usefully in another place. However, there is the word, and it may be taken in either of two senses. It may mean, in the modern sense, "matter of history", something which really happened; or it may mean, in the wider sense of the Latin word *historia*, something which is narrated—a *story*, whether fact, myth, or fiction. For St. Thomas, either sense would do equally well; Dante, I think, probably intends it in the wider sense, seeing that, although in the *Epistle* he gives an instance from actual history (the return of Israel from Egypt), in a parallel passage from the *Convivio* he says that the literal story may be a poetical figment, a *bella menzogna*. In any case, in their literal meaning, whereby they "signify *things*", the words *tell a story*. There will be episodes, in which characters speak and act in character, and their words and actions make up the story.

Now we come to the "spiritual sense", "whereby the *things signified* by words have themselves a signification". The "things signified" are, as we have just seen, the *story*. It is most important to remember this. If we want to know what the spiritual sense of the whole work is, we must look, first, foremost and all the time, at the movement of the story as a whole—not, primarily, to *obiter dicta* thrown out by the characters, who may be speaking *in* character. If we do this, we shall be saved from much misunderstanding. We shall not, for example, imagine, like Professor Whitfield in his book *Dante and Virgil*,[1] that Dante started off by accepting Virgil, who represents Humanism at its best, as a sufficient guide in himself to the perfection of the active life on earth, and that he then, discovering half-way through that this conclusion would be unorthodox and that earthly perfection was unattainable, jettisoned Virgil for Beatrice, Humanism for Grace, and the Active Life for the Contemplative. Whatever praises Dante the pilgrim, speaking in character, may address to Virgil, Dante the poet knew and intended from the beginning that Virgil and his Humanism were inadequate to salvation. The action of the story tells us so. From

[1] J. H. Whitfield: *Dante and Virgil* (Blackwell, 1949).

the very beginning, Humanism is presented to us as damned. In its own strength, it can never rise higher than Limbo; in its own wisdom it can only show us Hell. Grace sends it on its errand of salvation; even as far as Purgatory it can come only in company with a soul in grace, and there it does not of itself know the way and is subject to the authority of all the Ministers of Grace. The spiritual signification resides in the action and development of the story as a whole; and it follows from this that no interpretation of any detached passage can possibly be valid if it conflicts with the general tenor of the story.

Having got this point clear, we can proceed to examine the three levels of interpretation. The first, both Aquinas and Dante call "allegorical"; though Dante goes on to add that all three senses "may in general be called allegorical, since they differ from the literal and historical". It is a little tiresome of Dante to have given two meanings for the same word—especially as the second, more general, meaning is the one in which we to-day always use the term "allegorical". In the rest of this paper I shall use "allegorical" always in its general meaning, and we will find something else to specify the first level of interpretation. For St. Thomas, we are at this level when we see an event in the Old Testament symbolising an event in the New. But we cannot, obviously, apply this test as it stands to the *Divine Comedy*, for the plain reason that it *is* the *Divine Comedy* and not the Old Testament. But when we look at the Old Testament in the light of Christian Revelation, what we see is a series of events, which symbolise or foreshadow another series of events actually taking place in world-history: namely, the story of God's Incarnation. If, then, the literal story of the *Comedy* is taken to be a parallel to the Old Testament, what signification are we to find for it which will be a suitable parallel to the signification which the Old Testament finds in the New? Presumably it will be a parallel in world-history. At this level, the story of Dante's fictitious pilgrimage signifies something actually happening, or that ought to happen, in the real history of mankind. For this reason, I should like to call this first level of interpretation the "historical" level. Unhappily, that word has been used by Aquinas and Dante as a synonym for the literal meaning. I find myself, therefore, obliged to call it the "political" level—understanding the word in its widest sense, as applying to the whole life of man in all its social relationships and historical development. At the first level, the *Comedy*, being interpreted, shows us the way of the *polis*: we may call it "the Way of the City", or perhaps "of the Empire".[1]

The second level—the moral sense—involves no difficulties of nomenclature and needs little explanation. It is the meaning which we most naturally attach to religious allegory—the experience of the "common Christian" in his passage from a state of sin to a state of grace. We may call it quite simply, "the Way of the Soul".

The third level—the anagogical or mystical—is one well-known to all students of religious experience, though it does not lie within the compass of every soul. It concerns that immediate apprehension of the divine which is enjoyed by those who have the gift, and it is known as the Way of Contemplation. Although, as we shall see, Dante's map of this way differs in at least one essential feature from the map made familiar to us in the writings of the later mystics such as St. Theresa of Avila and St. John of the Cross, the Way itself is one which almost every developed religion recognises; and although the souls who follow it are, comparatively speaking, few, the mystical gift is not so rare and remote from daily life as is usually supposed. It is, for example, probably a good deal less rare than the gift of genius.

It is at these three levels, then—the Way of the City, the Way of the Soul, and the Way of Contemplation—that the literal story of the *Commedia* is to be interpreted throughout the poem. I want to emphasise that: *throughout the poem*. These three different levels are not stages on the same way; they run parallel at every point from starting-place to goal. One can, so to say, cross this Atlantic at three levels—by submarine, by steamer, or by aeroplane, and all three routes go the whole way: one does not need to transfer, part-way across, from one conveyance to the other. In theory, I suppose, every Dantist would admit this; but there is, in practice, a quite marked tendency for comment to slip, instinctively and unconsciously, from one level to another. It would hardly be too much to say that there is a constant temptation to interpret the *Inferno* at the political level, the greater part of the *Purgatorio* at the moral level, and the *Paradiso* at the mystical level. This is not always by any means explicitly avowed. But we do find writers concentrating on the *Inferno* as a picture, or a satire upon, this world, with special attention to quattrocento politics. We do find comment on the *Purgatorio* centring about the three steps at Peter's gate, and the moral aspects of self-examination, contrition

---

[1] For Dante's preoccupation with the themes of "City" and "Empire", see A. P. d'Entrèves: *Dante as a Political Thinker* (Clarendon Press, 1952).

and satisfaction—until we arrive at the Earthly Paradise, where the political aspect again becomes dominant. We do find a kind of silent assumption that the *Paradiso* has chiefly to do with what is called the· "more spiritual side" of religion—an assumption coupled with astonishment that Dante should have thought fit to intrude into the heavenly regions denunciations of sin and outbursts of political spleen which are (it is felt) out of place in this rarefied celestial atmosphere.

English people are, perhaps, peculiarly liable to fall into this error of confusing the three levels with one another, and even with the literal meaning—and that for a very simple and natural reason. Our conception of religious allegory is unconsciously dominated by the powerful influence of Bunyan, whose theme, clearly announced upon his title-page, is "The Pilgrim's Progress *from this World to that which is to Come*". All our childhood and school-day memories lead us to expect that in any allegory the pilgrim soul will begin in this world, and pass through death to finish up in the next. But Dante's theme, in spite of the superficial likeness introduced by its involving a journey, is quite different. He says: "The subject of the *whole work* (*totius operis*) taken in the literal sense only is 'the state of souls after death', without qualification (*simpliciter sumptus*). Whereas if the work be taken allegorically the subject is 'man, as by good or ill deserts, in the exercise of the freedom of his judgment, he becomes liable to rewarding or punishing justice'." There is nothing here about passing from one world to the other. The *whole work*, in its literal acceptation, is about "the state of souls after death"; the *whole work*, taken allegorically, is about man's rendering himself liable to the awards of justice by the exercise of his free will—its exercise, that is to say, in *this* world: for in the next world one no longer "renders one's self liable" to anything. In the moment of death the will's choice is fixed, and as the tree falls, there it must lie. And it will not do to say that Dante began with this idea and ended up with another: for the words I have quoted were written as an introduction to the *Paradiso*—at a time when he knew very well what the theme of his book had turned out to be.

Dante's visionary journey, then, unlike that of Bunyan's Christian, is, in the literal story, a journey in the *other* world from beginning to end; in the allegorical significance, it is a journey in *this* world from beginning to end, at whichever level we like to consider it. And since, in the words of St. Thomas, the spiritual sense "is based on and presupposes" the literal, let us begin by considering the literal story.

The story of the journey is prefaced by an introductory passage describing Dante's adventures in the Dark Wood. This is the only part of the narrative which is placed in this world at all four levels. From a merely formal point of view, and for numerical symmetry, this introduction is usually regarded as comprising the first canto only of the *Inferno*; but from our point of view it actually covers the first two cantos and the beginning of the third. Our first contact with the verities behind the veil is made, of course, at the meeting with Virgil; but it is not until Virgil "with a joyous countenance" lays his hand on Dante's and leads him in "among the hidden things", that we cross the boundary between this life and that other.

The literal story is conceived as a blend of truth and fiction. The threefold "state of souls after death"—damnation, purgation, beatification—is a reality, as Africa is a reality. The details of Dante's journey are fiction—as Alan Quatermain's adventures in quest of King Solomon's Mines are fiction. In both cases there are convincing geographical and other details, worked out with a great air of scientific solemnity, which blur the frontiers between fact and fiction and help us to the desirable "suspension of disbelief". Whatever we, personally, may think about the state of souls after death, we must, in reading the poem, accept Dante's belief in Hell, Purgatory and Heaven as post-mortal states; we need not believe, nor need we suppose him to believe, that Hell is physically situated at the centre of the earth, Purgatory on an island in the Southern Hemisphere, or Heaven above the fixed stars. On several occasions, Dante warns us against attributing to him any such naif conceptions. The journey, as such, is a *bella menzogna*: it is just a story.

In the story, we pass through the Gate of Hell on the evening of Good Friday, and descend through the twenty-four circles of the Pit of Hell. Leaving behind us in the Vestibule the Souls who refused to make any definite choice between good and evil, we cross Acheron and come to Limbo, the dwelling of those who, by human and rational standards, lived innocently, and even nobly, but who never knew the great supra-rational Christian graces of faith, hope and *caritas*. With many adventures by the way, all of which have their own exciting place in the fictional narrative, as well as their allegorical signification, we proceed, first through the circles of the incontinent—those who never pulled themselves together to make an effective stand against sin—and next, through the circles of sin deliberately willed and chosen: heresy, violence, fraud simple and fraud complicated by treachery. At the centre of the earth we are brought face to face with

Satan himself. Climbing along his body, and passing upwards through a long subterranean shaft, we emerge at the Antipodes, on the morning of Easter Day. We are now on the island from which arises the great mountain of Purgatory.

We are still in the post-mortal world, but we have passed out from an eternal state to a temporal process. In Hell—although for the sake of the poetical picture, we are obliged to exhibit it in terms of endless duration—neither time nor process has any real meaning. There is only the static monotony of the soul's fixed choice of its own darling sin. No soul ever proceeds from one circle of deepening evil to another; only Dante, the living man who still has time at his disposal, can journey through them and survey them all.

But in Purgatory, time and process are all-important. The souls are hastening to complete their purgation, and their cry is always, "Lose no time! Pray that my time be shortened! Hinder me not!"—so eager are they to speed their progress from circle to circle up the height. Into this realm, Virgil could not go without Dante; he is still his companion but no longer in the strict sense his guide. Yet Dante needs him, since in the story, Virgil is his "contact" in the spirit-world, and lends him eyes to see those "secret things" which are hidden from mortal view. For although both Hell and Purgatory are places with a terrestrial geography, they cannot be apprehended as spiritual places except by those who have gained the entrée. They are places where two planes of existence meet. We shall grasp this better if we think of the fairy rings of folk-lore: in the ordinary way, just places—green marks in a common field; but go there on a particular night of moonlight, speak the ritual words, make the ritual gesture, step into the ring, touch the hand held out to you—*make contact*, and you are transported at once into the Absolute Elsewhere: into a world which occupies the same space as the visible world without displacing or penetrating it at any point.

The journey takes us up the Mountain, past the souls of the excommunicate and the late-repentant who are anxiously waiting to begin their purification, up the three steps through St. Peter's Gate, up by the seven cornices where the stain of the seven Capital Sins is cleansed away, till we come to the bird-haunted forest at the summit. And here Dante meets Beatrice.

Up to this point, the journey has, in general outline, been very like those imaginary surveys of the Other World which were so popular in Christian and Gnostic literature from the second century onwards. But into this basic story, Dante has skilfully woven the threads of another kind of other-world journey—well known to folk-lore—the one in which the wife or mistress is carried away by enchantment, and the lover has to seek her through the under-world and the realms of faerie. The story is common to every folk-literature, and lies, more or less disguised, at the base of all those tales of Arthurian and chivalric adventure which Dante knew so well, and which we speak of as "the matter of Brittany". Beatrice, the real girl whom Dante loved and lost in Florence, is here the Lady; the enchanter is Death; the journey is through Death's kingdom. As in many of the tales, it is the Lady who from afar guides her lover to her; Virgil is the messenger despatched by Beatrice to bring him to her in that other kingdom, and having fulfilled his mission, he vanishes. The Lady upbraids her lover for his lack of faith and his contributory negligence (this, too, is often a feature of the folk-tales); he confesses his fault; and they are reconciled and reunited under the trees of the enchanted wood.

But what is the enchanted wood? Here we must take pains to be exact; for it is here that many interpreters have gone astray, wandering from one level to the other, confounding the literal with the allegorical, and losing themselves in a labyrinth of conjecture. Literally, the Wood is the Earthly Paradise—the Garden of Innocence from which Adam and Eve were driven, through their own fault, at the Fall. It is the original starting-point of mankind. That is the crux of the matter; it is a *starting-point*. It is the point from which Man ought to have started his journey to God—from which every individual man would start now, but for the legacy of original sin, which has exiled him and obliges him to start as best he can from the wilderness, and sometimes from the Dark Wood which is sin's deadly substitute for that other. It is also the point to which every man must return, in order to make his fresh start. It is reached by way of the Mountain of Ascent. Some —those who have kept in the right way—are able to take "the short way up the Hill—*del bel monte il corto andar*"; others who, like Dante, have gone so far out of the way that they cannot pass the Beasts, can only come to it by the long way that leads through Hell and up the Purgatorial path on the other side of the world, which is also the road taken by the blessed Dead. They come to the Earthly Paradise, but they do not stay there. Once there, once purged and restored to the lost innocence of their original nature, they start again, where Adam started, on the road that Adam should have taken. All the journey, all

9

the toil, all the passing through the little and the greater death, is done that man may come back to his true beginning, to the original starting-place from which he may "leap to the stars".

From the Earthly Paradise, under the guidance now of Beatrice, Dante makes that leap, and passes through the seven planetary spheres. Here the spirits of the Blessed are displayed to him. The first three spheres lie within the cone of earth's shadow. In that of the Moon, he sees those who, although their wills were truly vowed to Heaven, yet broke the letter of their vows. In that of Mercury he sees those whose work for God was a little tainted by earthly ambition; yet they "maintained the state of the world" [1] and gave it laws to live by. In that of Venus, he sees the lovers and poets; in them, too, though their love has been purged of self, the love of the creature was a little for its own sake and not wholly for the love of God; and though they have their bliss, their souls' stature remains slightly diminished on that account. Next, in the sphere of the Sun, he sees those whose work lay in the realm of the intellect—the great theological and secular doctors, and the pattern of kinghood. The fifth sphere, Mars, is that of the patriots—the soldiers and the householders, who served God and man in the works of war and peace; the sixth, Jupiter, is the abode of those who supremely loved justice—the builders of true Empire, who whenever they say "I" think "We". Then comes a change. We pass to the sphere of Saturn, from which Jacob's golden ladder reaches up into the ultimate heavens, with "the angels of God ascending and descending on it". In this, the seventh and last of the planetary spheres, dwell the souls of the contemplatives, whose prayer is their whole life. Let us make a special note of that—we shall see why in a moment:—the Contemplatives do not appear until the *seventh and last* of the planetary spheres. Above that, the sphere of the Fixed Stars is inhabited by the great saints—the Apostles who knew Christ in the flesh—and Adam who walked and talked face to face with God in the Garden. Beyond this again is the Primum Mobile, where Dante sees, circling in their ninefold hierarchy, the Angels who live from everlasting to everlasting in the unveiled presence of God. Yet, as Beatrice explains the appearances in the nine physical heavens are only a symbolic presentation to help Dante's understanding. All these blessed beings, from the least and lowest in the sphere of the Moon to the most in-Godded of the Seraphim, to the greatest of the Saints, to Mary herself, inhabit one and the same Heaven, the Empyrean of God, that is neither in time nor

[1] *Eccles.* xxxviii. 34.

in space nor turns on poles,[1] and "has no *where* but in the mind of God".[2] Dante is shown Time, flowing like a river of light; and when his eyes have drunk of it he sees it as a circle, the Rose of Eternity—for Eternity is the mode of Heaven, as it was of Hell. Here he sees all times and all places present at once in the state in which all desire is perfectly fulfilled; and here he is privileged to gaze for an eternal moment upon the Beatific Vision and the unveiled mystery of the Incarnate Godhead. He has reached journey's end.

This is the literal story of the *Commedia*—the story of the journey through the realms of the dead. I have, of course, reduced it to the bare bones. I have left out all the adventures and nearly all the characters, and I have also left out all the descriptions, discourses and conversations. What we are interested in at the moment is the general movement of the action and the fact that this journey is a tour of the *world after death*. I should like to make this further point: that all the characters, considered *as* characters, together with the conversations and the various political, moral and scientific discourses in which they from time to time indulge, belong primarily to the literal story. They are, that is, characters in a dramatic action; and what they say is said in character, and need not be taken to represent the final conclusions of the poet, except in so far as it agrees with the general tone and development of the action itself. Thus, in *Inf.* xxiii, Virgil speaks of "reputation" (*fama*) as that without which man's life is "but as foam in water or straws upon the wind"; but in *Purg.* xi, Oderisi speaks of it as being itself but "a breath of wind, which comes and goes, and as it changes quarter changes name". This implies no contradiction in Dante's own mind: Virgil is made to speak as a pagan humanist; Oderisi as a penitent Christian. Oderisi is the Christian judgment upon those humanist values, which, as we have seen, are from the very start of the poem proclaimed to be inadequate. So too, in *Purg.* xv the vision of the dying St. Stephen praying for his murderers opens up the all-embracing largeness of Christian charity beyond the noble yet limited scope of Virgil's discourse on reciprocal love. Just as Dante is about to say "thou dost satisfy me—*tu m'appaghe*", the vision comes. No writer could more clearly express his judgment in the very structure of his poem.

It is now time to look at the three levels of allegorical interpretation.

[1] *Para.* xxii. 67.
[2] *Para.* xii. 30. This is said, actually, of the Primum Mobile, but applies, of course, equally to the Empyrean beyond it.

The first that Dante mentions is what I have called the political sense or the Way of the City. This is the sense that has aroused the greatest interest in recent years; it is also, as I think, the one into which the worst confusion has been introduced. It is therefore a difficult one to begin with; on the other hand, if we succeed in making it clear to ourselves we shall have little or no trouble in working out the others.

Now, if we hold fast to the principle that, just as the *literal* meaning of the *Commedia* deals exclusively with the life of man after death, so the *allegorical* meanings deal exclusively with the life of man in *this* world, we shall be led at once to a very simple conclusion. We shall conclude that, where the political meaning is concerned, the *Inferno* will show us the picture of a corrupt society—*Città Dolente*, the City of Destruction; the *Purgatorio* will show society engaged in purging off that corruption and returning to the ideal constitution which was God's intention for it when He created man as a "social animal"; the *Paradiso* will show the ideal constitution in working order—the *Civitas Dei*. And that, I believe, is precisely what they do show us. It really is just as simple as that. But I am aware that in saying this I am setting up my opinion against that of many modern scholars who are far more learned and authoritative and better equipped than I am. These other writers all show a strong disinclination to carry the perfected social life on into the *Paradiso*. They are inclined to take it as far as the Earthly Paradise and abandon it there; and some of them suggest that Dante, despairing of, or changing his mind about the feasibility of, a perfected social life on earth, ended by preaching that man should withdraw from the world and find perfection either in a purely contemplative religious life, or only in Heaven after death. (The former of these alternatives involves a confusion of the political and moral levels; the second involves a still more drastic confusion of the literal with the allegorical sense.)

Now I believe that a number of long-standing and almost con-secrated errors have combined to produce this unhappy confusion. The first is an error of critical method—a determination to bring the political theory of the *Commedia* at all costs into line with that of the *Convivio* and the *De Monarchia*.[1] I agree that it is sound to "interpret

---

[1] The operative passage is *De Mon.* III. xvi. "Providence, then, has set two ends before man . . . viz: the blessedness of this life, which consists in the exercise of his proper power and is figured by the terrestrial paradise, and the blessedness of eternal life, which consists in the fruition of the divine aspect, to which his proper power may not ascend without the help of the divine light. And this

Dante by Dante"; but between the earlier works and the later there is, if not contradiction, at least a considerable development of thought. It is not fair to a man to interpret his mature work by his less mature; where the two agree, one may use them for mutual elucidation: where they disagree, one must take the mature work as definitive. Another error is one at which I have already hinted—that of looking on the Earthly Paradise as a point of arrival rather than a point of new departure. There are also some very curious errors of fact, which I confess I find it hard to understand—one being the statement, frequently repeated by people who should know better, that Dante thinks Virgil a sufficient guide in himself to bring men to the perfection of the Active Life. Even if we suppose the Earthly Paradise to represent the perfection of the Active Life (which I am sure it does not) it is abundantly clear from the literal story that Virgil is *not* of himself sufficient to bring his pupil here.

It is also an error of fact to suggest that in the *Convivio* and the *De Monarchia* the perfection of the Active Life is considered as a thing wholly distinct from and equal to, the Contemplative Life. On the contrary, even in the *Convivio*, the Active Life is held to exist to a certain measure for the sake of the Contemplative and to be inferior to it.[1] By the date of the *De Monarchia*, Dante's conception of the Contemplative Life has acquired a definitely more religious content; accordingly, although the authority of the Emperor derives directly from God, he is said to be in so far subordinate to the Pope, "as mortal felicity is in a certain sense ordained with reference to immortal felicity".[2] Bound up with all this, there is a fundamental error about the Church's attitude to the Active Life—a persistent assumption that Catholic Christianity, like any Oriental gnosticism, despises the flesh and enjoins a complete detachment from all secular activities. Such a view is altogether heretical. No religion that centres about a Divine Incarnation can take up such an attitude as that. What the Church enjoins is quite different: namely, that all the good things of this world are to be loved because God loves them, as God loves them, for the love of God, and for no other reason. That is the right ordering of love, about which so much is said in the *Purgatorio*. A full Active Life,

---

blessedness is given to be understood by the celestial paradise." On the development of Dante's thought in this connection, see D'Entrèves, *op. cit.* But the distinction made here is not between the Active and the Contemplative Life, but between the Natural and the Spiritual Life, which is quite a different matter.

[1] *Convivio.* ii. 5; iv. 17.   [2] *De Mon.* III. xvi.

rightly ordered, is therefore in no way incompatible with holiness or even with a rich Contemplative Life. Indeed, many of the greatest Contemplatives have been masterly men and women of business—one need only instance St. Augustine of Hippo, St. Theresa of Avila, or St. Gregory the Great.

But all these errors I have mentioned, acting upon one another and proliferating misunderstandings, have produced such a tissue of confusion that I shall do better to leave them, and to say briefly how I understand the allegory of the City. You will then be able to judge whether my interpretation makes sense or not.

That the *Inferno* is a picture of human society in a state of sin and corruption, everybody will readily agree. And since we are to-day fairly well convinced that society is in a bad way and not necessarily evolving in the direction of perfectibility, we find it easy enough to recognise the various stages by which the deep of corruption is reached. Futility; lack of a living faith; the drift into loose morality, greedy consumption, financial irresponsibility, and uncontrolled bad temper; a self-opinionated and obstinate individualism; violence, sterility, and lack of reverence for life and property including one's own; the exploitation of sex, the debasing of language by advertisement and propaganda, the commercialising of religion, the pandering to superstition and the conditioning of people's minds by mass-hysteria and "spell-binding" of all kinds, venality and string-pulling in public affairs, hypocrisy, dishonesty in material things, intellectual dishonesty, the fomenting of discord (class against class, nation against nation) for what one can get out of it, the falsification and destruction of all the means of communication; the exploitation of the lowest and stupidest mass-emotions; treachery even to the fundamentals of kinship, country, the chosen friend, and the sworn allegiance: these are the all-too-recognisable stages that lead to the cold death of society and the extinguishing of all civilised relations.

Nor need we spend much time over the process of redintegration which, for society as well as for man, means a recognition of error, repentance, and the purging off of evil states of mind. We might note just two points. First, that for Dante the restoration of society must come from within and not from without: the change of heart must precede the establishment of right institutions. Secondly, Virgil's account of the capital sins is worth some consideration. The evil loves that have to be purged are (*a*) the pride that seeks domination and cannot bear to see any other person, class, or nation enjoying equal or superior privileges; (*b*) the envy that is terrified of any sort of competition, lest another's gain should be one's own loss; (*c*) the anger that exacts vindictive reparations and cannot forgive past injuries. Then there is sloth, which may take the forms either of indifference, delay, or despair. Then come the disordered loves for things right in themselves but wrong when they are made an end in themselves: (*a*) avarice, which is the love of money, whether in the sense of grudging thrift or conspicuous waste, and the lust for that power which money gives; (*b*) the greed of a high standard of living; and (*c*) the *lussuria* which is the exaltation of emotional and personal relationships above all other loyalties, human or divine.

Now, it is only when society has discovered its right aim, pressed towards it at all costs, and extinguished these evil or disordered passions, that its will is made right and free, and it can be "crowned and mitred over itself". This famous passage is usually explained by saying that when the will is made free, the need of external rule disappears: "government will wither away" in a correctly Marxian manner.[1] But if Dante means this, at the political level, what becomes of all his insistence upon the God-appointed Emperor and the universal Imperium? The answer often given is that by this time Dante had despaired of the establishment of a perfect government in this world, and was preaching a retreat from the world and postponing the universal Empire to the Last Judgment. This, however, involves a total confusion of all levels of interpretation, and makes one wonder why, right to the end of the poem, he should go on denouncing wicked popes and neglectful emperors, and worrying about a problem of whose solution he has already despaired. But one could take the passage in another way, and say: It is only when society has learned to will its true end that the joint rule of Church and Empire can be established. And since it is true that a visible Church and a secular Empire are in one aspect human institutions, although of divine (in Dante's view equally divine) origin, it is fitting that the visible symbol of crown and mitre should be bestowed by the hand of Virgil. I will add that I think it very likely that Dante had by now come to the conclusion that a special intervention, human or divine, would be needed to bring about the regeneration of society. The Veltro and the DXV may symbolise either a human saviour, or an outpouring of the Holy Ghost and the coming of

---

[1] This interpretation, again, is founded upon the passage in the *De Monarchia*, about the two regimens (of Church and State) of which man would have had no need "if he had remained in the State of innocence" (*De Mon.* III. iv).

the Joachimite Third Kingdom; but the event, whatever it is, must be an event within the time-scheme: the Millenium, if you like, but not the Second Coming at the end of time.

It is well to remember here the current contemporary ideas about the "goal of history". Mediaeval thinkers believed themselves to be living in the "Sixth Age" of humanity, in which, under a great champion of the Faith, the great work of consolidating Christendom should be accomplished and society indissolubly incorporated with the Church. Nobody could foretell its duration; but everybody knew that after it would come the "great tribulations" and the reign of Anti-christ. These, however, should be but the prelude to the opening of the Seventh Age, the Sabbath of Creation. "Then", says St. Bonaventure, "shall descend from Heaven this city—not yet the city that shall be on high, but the city here below—the militant city as conformable to the triumphant city as may be in this life. It will be reconstructed and restored as it was in the beginning, and then also shall reign peace. How long that peace will endure is known to God."

If the crowning and mitring refer to the establishment of the perfect Church and Empire, then the relevance of the pageant of Church and Empire in the Earthly Paradise becomes very much clearer.

In the Earthly Paradise, then, always supposing that human society can contrive to reach that point, the return is made to the constitution ordained for it from the beginning. The agony of rage and frustration that throbs through the *Commedia* always makes itself felt most poign-antly at the politico-social level—and for a very good reason. At this very moment, as at all moments in the world's history, it is more than possible—it is probable and even certain—that there are many indi-vidual men and women who by the moral and the mystical ways are working out their redemption and entering into beatitude. But a perfect *society* has never been seen on earth. Faint approximations, in the fabulous Age of Gold, and in the small circles of the early Christian community or the primitive Franciscan order, are all the examples to which Dante can point, in a society which, so far as he can see, shows no symptoms whatever of repentance or amendment. Nor, perhaps, can we, scanning the headlines in to-day's news, find the signs of the times very encouraging to hopes of religious concord and political peace and order. The vision of the high triumph passes, and Beatrice is left desolate and lamenting beneath the Tree of Knowledge.

But say that the new starting-point is actually reached, the social sins repented and the common will made free, the memory of the unhappy past washed away in Lethe and restored in Eunoë only as factual history, a record full of quiet interest and occasions of thanksgiving: what would the regenerate world be like? The plan of it is in the *Paradiso*. Never yet known on earth, its eternal type is in Heaven:

> *mira*
> *quanto è il convento delle bianche stole!*
> *Vedi nostra città, quanto ella gira!* [1]

The gyres of the City revolve about God. The Angels move them as they move the spheres, each order drawn by love to those above, and drawing those below. In this ordered and happy society there is hierarchy, but no envy. There is only perfect fulfilment of the function for which each soul was made. Some men are greater than others, but the happiness of all is equally great, since for each it is perfect and complete; and this equality in difference is "the joy of the whole realm". And although in every sphere there is seen a different kind of activity, yet in their eternal aspect all these activities are one; for all are worship and delight.

The first six heavens are devoted to the Active Life. It is surely a mistake to look for the perfection of the Active Life in the Earthly Paradise. That, as we have said, is a starting-point not a staying-point. Those who have supposed it to represent the Active Life are, naturally enough, surprised to find that it has in it only one "permanent resident", and that her only occupation is that of picking flowers. From this, they have proceeded to various strange conclusions. But I am convinced that this is all a mistake. Matelda very likely does represent the Active Life, as in Dante's dream of Leah and Rachel; but there is no need to suppose that she, or anybody else, is a permanent resident in the Earthly Paradise. She is the friend and handmaid of Beatrice, whose office it is to bring souls to her greater sister. So Jacob had to wed Leah before he could wed Rachel; so the Active Life exists in a manner for the sake of the Contemplative. But although the Contemplative life is the better part, the Active, too, is blessed. It is also, in a sense, more necessary; for Martha can live without Mary, but Mary must be nourished by Martha. So it is in the life of the City, as it is in the life of the individual soul. Therefore, in the perfected City, there are more

---

[1]   admire
How great the company of the robes of white,
Behold our city, how wide it spreads its gyres.
Para. xxx. 128–130.

circles of the Active Life than of the Contemplative, and they live by exchange of honour and charity.

It is particularly interesting that the first heavenly sphere should be allotted to those who, though called to the Contemplative Life, have failed to achieve it, and have had to be content to fulfil themselves in the Active. I must confess that until I had entertained the idea of this distribution of the heavens between the two lives, I had never grasped why Dante should have given so much space and attention to monks and nuns who had broken their vows. But from my present point of view it appears to me perfectly reasonable. These souls do not quite attain the stature they might have attained; yet they live holily after another mode. It is only required of them that, having failed of the greater service, they should devote themselves with extra energy to the humbler service—they must give, says Beatrice, one-and-a-half times as much. One may well be reminded here of the passage in *The Cocktail Party* in which Mr. T. S. Eliot contrasts the way of the great saint with that of the ordinary man or woman. The second way has not the supreme pains nor the supreme ecstasies of the other, yet:

> It is a good life. Though you will not know how good
> Till you come to the end. But you will want nothing else,
> And the other life will be only like a book
> You have read once, and lost. In a world of lunacy,
> Violence, stupidity, greed . . . it is a good life.[1]

That is the life of the souls in the Moon, who glimpsed the greater life but could not stay the course. What they have is enough for them; it suffices for bliss, and they are blessed.

That the dwellers in Mercury, Venus and Mars all take part in the active life of the City scarcely needs demonstration. A word may be needed about the Sun, which displays the City's intellectual activities. It is often called the "Heaven of the Doctors"—but it contains not only theologians and members of the great teaching orders but also historians, grammarians, logicians and other persons celebrated for secular learning, as well as Solomon, whose wisdom was all in the practical art of kingship. This choice of names, odd if theology or piety sets the standard, is understandable enough if we grant that the sphere of the Sun is intended to give us a representative view of the active intellect in operation. A minor passing perplexity may be caused

---

[1] T. S. Eliot: *The Cocktail Party* (Faber, 1950): Act II (p. 124).

by the translators' habit of rendering the line about Richard of St. Victor as "who was in *contemplation* more than man". But Dante does not say *contemplar* but *considerar*; the word *contemplare* does not occur in this specialised sense anywhere in the *Paradiso* below the sphere of Saturn.[1] Richard of St. Victor never claimed the mystical gift for himself; and I think he takes his place in the circle of St. Thomas for his active work as a writer on mystical theology.[2]

In the sphere of Jupiter, the whole hierarchy of the Active Life is included under the Eagle, the sign of the perfect Empire. Where those who say "I" mean "We", *there* is Justice, *there*, here and now, is the Empire, whether or not the universal monarchy is visibly established. But if and when it is established, the mark of it will be Justice,[3] and its justice will be of that kind. And there, in the very eye of the Eagle, Trajan, the great heathen Emperor, who in loving Justice loved the Christ whom he did not know, sits waiting for the great Christian Emperor who shall bring Justice and Peace to the world we live in.

So that, if anyone asks, "Where, in the *Commedia*, has Dante found room for that perfection of the Active Life, and the Perfect Universal State of which his earlier writings are so full?" the answer is: Here; not in the Earthly Paradise, but in the Heavenly, where all perfection is. Here, with its law-makers and lovers and poets, its scholars and warriors; here, with its civic decencies and family affections; here, with its order and empire and justice. This is the picture of this world as it might be; as, if the Kingdom come, please God it will be; as, in so far as

---

[1] Dom Cuthbert Butler writes in *Western Mysticism*, p. 148 (2nd ed., Constable, 1927): "In one place St. Bernard gives a definition of contemplation in general, as contrasted with consideration or meditation: 'Contemplation is concerned with the certainty of things, consideration with their investigation. Accordingly contemplation may be defined as the soul's true and certain intuition of a thing, or as the unhesitating apprehension of truth. Consideration is thought earnestly directed to investigation, or the application of the mind searching for the truth' [the modern 'meditation'] (*de Consid.* ii. 5, trans. G. Lewis)." Dante was of course acquainted with the writings of St. Bernard.

[2] Edmund G. Gardner in *Dante's Ten Heavens*, p. 110 (2nd ed., Constable, 1904), writes: "It has been said that Richard's mystical writings are a scientific attempt to systematise the facts of the contemplative life"; and in *Dante and the Mystics*, p. 164 (Dent, 1913), refers to Richard's "repeated declaration that he knows nothing, by personal experience, of the ecstatic devotion that he sets forth".

[3] The Latin *justitia* and the Italian *giustizia* have a wider connotation than "justice" has in modern English usage, and might equally well be translated "righteousness".

the Kingdom is already here and at work, it already is. Here, not here-after; though it shall be hereafter; and in the Heaven which knows neither before nor after, here it eternally exists.

Beyond the Active Life, beyond Eagle and Empire, in the seventh and last of the planetary spheres, we come at length to the Contem-platives whose life, here and now, is lived on the borders of two worlds. That life is, in a sense, beyond Empire, for it has that in itself which needs neither law nor government; yet it is bound in love to the active life of the Empire, which is under its feet and sustains it. Beyond the Contemplatives again are those great Saints who, even in this life, are at every moment consciously in the presence of God. And all these manifold lives are brooded over and visited by the Angels; and all of them, each after its own manner, treads out the joyous measure of its perfection and enjoys the vision of God.

That is the Way of the City. The second Way is the Way of the Soul. It is the way of the City, lived by the individual as well as it can be lived in a world where the City is divided and Church and Empire impotent or at odds. Nobody knew better than Dante the difficulties which the corruption of the City puts in the way of the good life, and the bitterness of his anguish comes ringing down to us through six centuries of strife and greed. Nevertheless, in the ultimate resort, the Way and the choice are in the human heart. Heaven and Hell are not without, but within.

We must not, for instance, think of taking the *Inferno* at the political level and the *Purgatorio* at the moral level, in one and the same inter-pretation. At the moral level, the vision of Hell is the deep of corruption which each of us, from time to time, may glimpse as a horrifying possibility inside himself. Such moments of self-knowledge have the quality of eternity. It is not everyone who experiences them acutely; but such knowledge is an invariable part of the experience known as "conversion", and it is because of this that we find the greatest saints accusing themselves—with what seems to us like exaggeration—of being the chief of sinners. The story of the *Commedia* is the story of a conversion, and the stages of the process are those which the accounts of many such experiences in real life have made familiar to us. Peculiar, perhaps, to Dante, is the part played by Virgil. The sinner, who has fallen so far that he can no longer hear the call of religion, is reached, through the grace of God, at the rational level. He realises, one may say, that he is on the point of betraying even the ordinary human decencies; and that salutary shock opens his eyes to his condition and

starts him on the road to repentance. This recognition of the co-opera-
tion of Nature with Grace is characteristically Catholic. Protestant
theology, which postulates the total depravity of human nature, can
find no room for it; and that is why *The Pilgrim's Progress*, for
instance, which is a Protestant allegory, has no figure in it which
corresponds to Virgil.

We need not follow in detail all the steps of the soul's journey.
Heaven, like Hell, is within it—it has to choose which possibility it
will embrace, and, having chosen Heaven, it must die to sin with
Christ and make free its will so that it may become one with the will
of Christ within it. This done, it can be crowned and mitred over
itself—not necessarily in the sense that it can dispense in this world
with Church and State, but in the sense that it can freely accept the
demands which Church and State rightfully make upon it. "Love",
said Christ, "is the fulfilling of the Law"—and He added that no jot or
tittle of the Law should pass away. "Love", said Augustine, "and do as
you like." If love is rightly ordered, that is, it will keep the Law
because it wants to keep it, and find its freedom in that service. Thus
there is—or should be—no opposition between the Crown and Mitre
within and the Crown and Mitre visibly exalted without: that is why
the corruption of visible Church and political State puts such stumbling-
blocks in the way of the soul.

The blessed life is lived in this world in its appropriate sphere of
the Active or Contemplative Life. As the City in its division includes
all types of sin, so the City in its unity includes all types of the good
life; but the individual soul finds its own place, whether secluded in its
own egotism or exchanging blessedness in community. Either way, it
experiences God after its own manner—whether as wrath and judgment or as mercy and joy—since, as St. Catherine of Genoa says, the
fire of Hell is simply the light of God as it is experienced by those who
reject it.

Of the Way of Contemplation, as shown in the *Commedia*, there is
so much to say that a book would be needed to do it justice. Briefly,
there are two mystical ways known to those who practise the presence
of God. The one, which we associate with the majority of great
mystics, is known as the Negative Way, or the Way of the Rejection
of Images, and it has been very fully mapped out by such writers as
St. Theresa of Avila, St. John of the Cross, the author of *The Cloud
of Unknowing*, and others whose names are familiar. The characteristic
of that Way is that it proceeds through a great darkness and solitude

of the spirit, and uses a form of contemplation in which every image of the Divine is rejected.

Dante's Way is different: it is the Affirmative Way, in which all the images are accepted as valid, in so far, that is, as any finite image of the infinite can be valid. This Way, though it is perhaps more typically Western and might appear to be more typically Catholic and Incarnational than the other, has, I believe, never been fully mapped by any mystical theologian—unless we count Dante. Dom Cuthbert Butler, in his book *Western Mysticism*, says that "the Eastern tradition in contemplative life, contemplation, mysticism, has differed from the old authentic Western tradition, and has during these past few centuries obscured it, even in the West".[1] And he distinguishes the Western from the Eastern tradition by the fact that it does not, as the Eastern tradition sometimes tends to do, segregate the mystical element in religion from the other three: the institutional and sacramental; the intellectual and dogmatic; and the active service of others. It lays, that is, more emphasis upon the Active Life as a necessary basis for and factor in the Contemplative. This in itself would account for the attention given to the Active Life in the *Paradiso*, and the insistence throughout the *Purgatorio* on the need for "good works" as well as "good prayers".

But I fancy that there is another direction in which we may need to look for the map of the Way of Affirmation of Images. It is essentially the way of the artist and the poet—of all those to whom the rejection of images would be the rejection of their very means to intellectual and emotional experience; and it would seem to follow from this that the great Masters of the Affirmative Way will tend to be secular, and that they will be more concerned to record their experience than to analyse it in the manner of the regular theologian. It seems possible, indeed, that Dante is so far the only real Doctor of the Affirmative Way; though others have mapped the Way in places. I can think of four English names: Thomas Traherne the Anglican priest, who is particularly interesting because he comes in some respects curiously close to Dante, without showing any signs of having read him, and is therefore an independent witness; Charles Williams, an Anglican layman, who was consciously Dante's disciple and interpreter; William Wordsworth, also an Anglican layman, who would seem to have started by Dante's Way, but never quite to have arrived by it; William

[1] *op. cit.*, p. 324.

Blake, an unorthodox and perhaps heretical Christian, but after his manner also a follower of the Way.

Here, then, is a very short outline of the Affirmative Way as we find it in these five poets. It begins by an experience (usually in childhood) in which the Divine Glory is perceived and apprehended as immanent in some created person or thing: that, to use Williams's vocabulary, is the First Image. The creature is beheld, *sub specie aeternitatis*, bathed in and suffused with the light of its true and eternal nature—it is seen as God sees it. Dante sees Beatrice, and it is as though all Heaven were walking down the street; Traherne sees the corn as "orient and immortal wheat" and men and women as "immortal cherubims"; Wordsworth sees "meadows, grove, and stream . . . apparelled in celestial light"; Blake cries out " 'What!' it will be questioned, 'when the Sun rises, do you not see a round disk of fire somewhat like a guinea?' O no, no, I see an Innumerable company of the Heavenly host crying 'Holy, Holy, Holy, is the Lord God Almighty'."

Then comes the period which Traherne calls his "apostacy", and of which Blake sang in his *Songs of Experience*. The first Image is lost; Beatrice dies and Dante is ensnared by the "things of this life with their false pleasure", and finds himself in the Dark Wood and on the brink of Hell; for Wordsworth the glory "fades into the light of common day".

This is followed by the appearance of the Second Image. A kind of faith is recovered, but slowly, by means of the intellect, and at a lower level. This Second Image is symbolised for Dante in the *Vita Nuova* by the "Donna Gentile", in the *Convivio* by the "Lady Philosophy", but in the *Commedia* by Virgil. For Traherne too, the recovery comes by means of the reading of philosophy at the University. Wordsworth seems to have found it in Anglican orthodoxy;[1] I do not know whether there is anything to correspond with it in Blake. Charles Williams, in *The Figure of Beatrice*, has dealt very suggestively with the phenomenon of the Second Image, though without autobiographical reference.

The third stage on the Way is the triumphant return of the First Image, but at a much higher and more universal level than before. The glory which was once known only in the beloved creature is

---

[1] Or possibly, in the optimistic Theism of his middle period; his final acceptance of a fully incarnational-redemptive Christianity representing a recovery, though imperfect, of the First Image. See John Jones: *The Egotistical Sublime* (Blackwell, 1954), chapter 4, *The Baptised Imagination*.

diffused upon all creation, and taken up into its Eternal Source. This is the reunion, after the toilsome climb up the Mountain, with a Beatrice who is more than herself; and the ascent by her means to the Vision in which all the shining Images are seen "transhumanised" and summed up in the final Image—the Image of the Incarnate Christ in the very centre of the Unimaginable Godhead.

From the first step to the last of this Way the Images remain with us: there is nothing to correspond with the "naughting" of images characteristic of the Negative Way, unless it is the temporary blinding of Dante's eyes in the Eighth Heaven, which by some writers is held rather to correspond to the "Dark Night of the Soul", of which St. John of the Cross speaks. Nearer to that "naughting" is perhaps the moment in the Primum Mobile when "the triumph which ever plays about the point which overcame me, little by little extinguished itself from my sight, seeming embraced by that which it embraces".[1] Yet, in that moment when all other images are withdrawn, the First Image remains to nourish and support the soul, "wherefore", as Dante ingenuously observes, "the fact that there was nothing to see—and love—constrained me to turn myself and my eyes to Beatrice".[2] Neither is there in the *Comedy* anything that corresponds to the "flight of the alone to the Alone", nor any of these private intimacies between God and the soul which occur so frequently in other mystical writings: at every stage of Dante's journey the whole City and Church are with him. And in the last ecstasy, when the Beatific Vision is accorded to him, his longing is winged by Our Lady, through the intercession of St. Bernard and all Paradise: "See, Beatrice, and how many Saints with her, lay palm to palm to aid my prayer." [3] The Way of Affirmation has nothing esoteric about it; it is not a secret path—it might almost be called a public thoroughfare. And the final Vision is not the Abyss of the Divine Darkness, but the Express Image of the Glory.

There are, of course, certain general affinities between the Negative and the Affirmative Ways, and it is possible to recognise in the *Commedia* certain of the stages by which all souls who have the mystical gift accomplish their journey. We may say, for example, that in the *Purgatorio* the Mountain corresponds to the Purgative Way, and that in the *Paradiso* the Heavens of the Active Life correspond to the Illuminative and those of the Contemplative Life to the Unitive Way. And nearly all mystics appear to have experienced at some time the

[1] *Para.* xxx. 10–12.   [2] *Para.* xxx. 14–15.   [3] *Para.* xxxiii. 38–39.

Vision of Hell. But I believe it would be unwise to try and fit the anagogical interpretation of the *Commedia* too exactly into the frame of the Mystical Way of the Negative tradition. The difference made by the approach through the Image is too important to be ignored.

One point, however, I ought to make, to avoid misunderstanding. The contemplation of and by means of the "Image" as it is understood by Dante, is not the same thing as that contemplation of and by images which occurs at the outset of the Contemplative Way in all mystical practice, forming its earliest and simplest exercise, and is afterwards exchanged for the higher form of contemplation without images. Let me put the difference in the crudest and simplest way. In the ordinary method of meditation on, let us say, the kingship of God, we might form in our *imagination* a picture of God seated on a throne like a king; and we might think about the attributes of kingship, such as power and authority and splendour and so forth; and we might perhaps further meditate how all earthly kingship is derived from God. But if we were following in Dante's steps, we should do almost the direct opposite. We should look, perhaps in imagination, or more likely with our bodily eyes, upon an actual king—it might be our own late King George VI—in some ordinary, perhaps trivial situation, at a football match or a garden-party; and we should suddenly see, burning and shining through the mortal body and the modern clothing and all the solemn absurdities of Court ceremonial, the glory and authority of all kings, and of the King of Kings, made known in His fleshly Image, focused in that point and diffused upon the whole City. The scriptural type of the former kind of image is the Vision of Isaiah: "I saw the Lord sitting upon a throne, high and lifted up, and His train filled the temple." But the scriptural type of the second kind is Our Lord's Transfiguration: "He was transfigured before them: and His face did shine as the sun, and His raiment was white as the light." The bodily presence is not withdrawn—it remains planted where it was in earthly time and space; but it is known for an instant as it is known in Heaven, in its awful and immortal dignity.[1]

But the full implications of Dante's Way of Contemplation, and his affinities with other mystics who have gone by the same Way have yet to be worked out.[2]

---

[1] Charles Williams: *He Came Down from Heaven* (Heinemann, 1938), p. 108.

[2] "[Mysticism] has been identified also with a certain outlook on the world—a seeing God in nature, and recognising that the material creation in various ways symbolizes spiritual realities: a beautiful and true conception, and one that

10

We have now covered the same ground four times; and all four ways are, of course, in the end one Way, and the same soul may go to God by two or three or all of them at once. But in interpreting the poem, we shall do better not to swap horses in crossing the stream, or we may find ourselves carried out of the road altogether, and lost in an ocean of conflicting theory.

was dear to St. Francis of Assisi, but which is not mysticism according to its historical meaning"; Dom Cuthbert Butler: *op. cit.*, p. 2. This intellectual appreciation of natural symbolism, whereby *invisibilia Dei per ea quae facta sunt, intellecta conspiciuntur* (*Rom.* i. 20), and which forms the basis of Dante's allegorical method (see *Dante's Imagery: Symbolic*, p. 8 *sqq.*), must be carefully distinguished from the actual *mystical experience*, to which it is related rather as consideration is to contemplation.

THE CITY OF DIS

I SHALL never cease to be grateful that my first introduction to Dante came through the late Charles Williams, himself, like Dante, a poet, and, like Dante, a lay theologian of a very original and creative turn of mind. There are many ways of approach to the *Divine Comedy*: the scholarly, the dogmatic, the historical, the linguistic are all good of their kind, and anybody who intends to make a serious study of the poem must explore each of them in turn if he is to become familiar with the terrain. But one's *first* approach to any place has a unique quality; nothing that happens afterwards will ever quite efface that primal impression stamped upon the blank metal of the mind. If that impression has been significant and right, one may thereafter wander along any by-ways one likes, without fear of stumbling into the dark forest of irrelevance where "the right road is lost".

In the first paragraph of his book, *The Figure of Beatrice*, Charles Williams notes: "Dante is one of those poets who begin their work with what is declared to be an intense personal experience." In the last paragraph he says, in speaking of Dante's affirmation of the womanhood of Beatrice: "This is what Dante insisted on, and . . . we ought perhaps to take Dante's poetry as relevant to our own affairs. . . . If we ought, then the whole of his work is the image of a Way not confined to poets." In those two sentences we have, I think, a guide to the first principles of all literary criticism. Our main business is to ask ourselves: "What did this poem mean in the experience of the poet? And what does it mean in our own experience?" So long as we keep these two questions clearly before us, we can ask any subsidiary questions we like, and it will all be to our profit. But unless we ask those, and can answer them satisfactorily, the poem, as a poem, will be dust and ashes to us, however many little jackdaw pickings we manage to extract from the dump.

I do not mean, of course, that such pickings are useless. The historian's pickings are useful to history; the grammarian's pickings to philology; the theologian's to theology; and the scholar's to scholarship. But they are not useful to poetry unless we have first seen the poem in its native poetical significance. When we have, then we can use all these other things as aids to a fuller understanding; when we have not, then they serve only to bury understanding beneath the dust-heaps of antiquarian learning.

During the last few years, I have been engaged in widening and deepening my acquaintance with the *Divine Comedy*, including, of course, the *Inferno*. I have by now read the *Inferno* innumerable times; I have toiled to translate it into English (and there is no better way of finding out whether one understands a thing or not than translating it); and I have gone through it again in order to compile the necessary minimum of explanatory notes. In the course of these labours I have had, naturally, to read a great many of the critical works which, in my first flush of enthusiasm for Dante I, almost deliberately, ignored—because I did not want to read them until I had made something out of the poem for myself. It was, I remember, while trying to write a helpful note upon the Giants who stand round the Well which forms the division between Malebolge and the frozen Lake of Cocytus at the bottom of the Pit, that I found myself asking the question: "Why in the world did Dante put the Giants just here?" And while looking for the answer, I quite suddenly saw a vision of the whole depth of the Abyss—perhaps as Dante saw it, but quite certainly as we can see it here and now: a single logical, coherent, and inevitable progress of corruption. When I had once seen it so, innumerable small conundrums—*più di mille*,[1] as Dante would say—seemed promptly to solve themselves, the answers clicking quietly into place as they occasionally do in a cross-word when, after long puzzling, one has hit upon some central fifteen-letter word which crosses and clues them all. I do not, of course, mean that I discovered a code or a cipher—that kind of thing belongs to detective fiction, not to poetry. I mean only that I saw the whole lay-out of Hell as something actual and contemporary; something that one can see by looking into one's self, or into the pages of to-morrow's newspaper. I saw it, that is, as a judgment of fact, un-affected by its period, unaffected by its literary or dogmatic origins; and I recognised at the same moment that the judgment was true.

I cannot say I was surprised; because, as I have explained, I was so brought into Dante's presence that I expected his poem to be a judg-ment of fact. What does surprise me, now that I have read more books about Dante, is to find that this expectation is so rare. I have been looking for a critic who should examine the arrangement of the *Inferno*, in detail, with a view to determining whether it is, or is not, justified as a judgment of fact; and I am still looking. What writers usually

[1] over a thousand.

discuss is, however interesting, something quite different. Witte, for instance, was apparently the first to inquire why the arrangement of Hell was not simply that of Purgatory in reverse. There is, of course, one very obvious answer: namely that, from the purely narrative point of view, no poet, not even Dante with his passion for symmetry, could easily face the task of going through *exactly* the same list of sins twice over with no variation except that between upside-down and right side up. Ignoring this artistic consideration, with its corollary that, since Virgil is the guide through the *Inferno*, a classical arrangement is clearly more appropriate in the context than a Christian one, de Witte and Wicksteed point out very rightly the dogmatic reason for the difference: namely, that whereas in Hell evil *deeds* are *punished*, in Purgatory evil *tendencies* are *corrected*; and that these two things are by no means the same thing. Furthermore, there is a fascinating argument about how much of the arrangement is based upon Aristotle and how much upon Cicero, and whether, in conflating two separate classifications, Dante was not led, by an unfortunate mistranslation in the mediaeval Latin version of the *Ethics*, to use the word *malizia* ambiguously in two slightly different senses (a position learnedly combated at very great length by W. H. V. Reade).[1] All this is great fun, and sheds a lot of light on Dante's method of work; I would not be without it for the world. But it sheds no light at all upon the gradation of sins within the three main divisions of Incontinence, Violence, and Fraud (Simple and Complex)—a gradation for which, in default of other evidence, we must presume Dante responsible. And it does seem to me curious that, having traced the disposition back to its classical origins, and decided whether it could be reconciled with scholastic doctrine, it should so seldom occur to anybody to ask: "However Dante arrived at this infernal arrangement, is it sound? is it relevant? does it correspond to anything at all within the living experience of you and me *now*? of the soul and state of Man at all times?" Because, if it does not, our enjoyment of Dante may be aesthetic or historical or political or antiquarian, or anything at all except poetically complete; and whatever the *Comedy* does to us, it will assuredly not fulfil the purpose for which Dante says he wrote it: "To remove those living in this life from the state of misery and lead them to the state of felicity".[2]

The book, after all, is an allegory. It is certainly literature; but—by its author, at any rate—it is no more "intended to be read as literature"

[1] Reade: *Moral System of Dante's Inferno:* Clarendon Press, 1909.
[2] *Epistle to Can Grande.*

than the Bible is so intended—if by "literature" we mean something as irrelevant to belief and conduct as "Three Little Kittens they lost their Mittens". And, being an allegory, it is not primarily "about" the condition of souls after death; that, as Dante points out, is only the literal meaning, and the least important. Considered as a story, the literal meaning is full of entertainment: it is interesting to know what Dante thought of Boniface VIII, to account for his rather surprising choice of Cato as the guardian of Mount Purgatory, to wonder who the blazes Matelda is, and to work out the complicated geography of that "whole quadrant of the first climate" through which Dante found himself "rolling with the eternal Twins".[1] That geography, like his astronomy, was no doubt defective by twentieth-century standards, his embryology would not pass muster among modern medical students, he appears to have got muddled about the dates of Hugh Capet, and to have mistaken the character of Thaïs in a play by Terence for the historical lady of the same name and profession; moreover, he was very likely wrong about the post-mortem destination of most of the people he wrote about, and so, very likely, are his critics. But nothing of all this *really* matters. To the topography and the administration of Hell many sources contribute: Homer and Virgil, the Bible, the apocryphal Scriptures, Ovid, St. Patrick's Purgatory, the matter of Brittany—to separate all these elements out, and see how they are marshalled by a master-hand is to receive a liberal education in the art of narrative construction; but the validity of the *Inferno* does not depend on these things. If a concept is false it will remain false, from whatever authority it can be shown to be borrowed; if it is true, then it will carry the same conviction, whether based on tradition or invented from top to bottom. The truth of the *Inferno* is to be sought in the allegory and not in the literal story. The map of Hell is the map of the black heart; if we want to verify it, we cannot do so from books. At most, we may profit by the title of a little household handbook very popular in my childhood, which professed to instruct one in everything, from the care of babies to "How to Make a Will": it was called *Enquire Within*. The Kingdom of Hell, like the Kingdom of Heaven, is within you. The road from the Vestibule to the Centre lies open to anybody to take.

"It is of course true", says Charles Williams, "that no single soul commits all these sins, nor does Dante say so. But there is a sense in which his single soul, following Virgil, creates for us an opposite vision of a single shade, without Virgil, clambering, stupidly, obstinately,

[1] *Para.* xxvii. 79–81; xxii. 152.

and painfully, from ridge to ridge of deepening evil. The progress of that perversion is seen in many incidents, but it is true essentially of each; there is no place yet where the weary spirit can stop. The earlier plagues still torment it and drive it on to more."[1]

"No single soul commits all these sins"; true. But the interpretation of the allegory need not be confined to the level of the individual soul. It can be made also at the level of society, and Dante himself would be the first to approve our making it so. The City of Dis remains always the image of the City—of the Empire, of community, of man-in-society—the perverted image of that heavenly Rome which spreads its gyres so wide in the Empyrean. "Behold our city," says Beatrice of that, "how great is the company of the white robes"; and Virgil says of this: "Behold . . . the City that is named of Dis, with its sad citizens, its great company." This is the Città Dolente: as the Mystic Rose spreads upward and outward in a timeless eternity, so this narrows inward and down in a "bad infinity" of endless time. It is the image of things to come: but it is also the image of things present. Let us walk about the infernal city and tell the towers thereof; it may be that we shall recognise her public monuments, that as we pass through a street we shall say suddenly, "I have been here before"; that we shall turn a corner and come unexpectedly upon our own house.

The City of Dis is extended in time and in space. She is all simultaneously present at every moment of time, from her respectable suburbs (never more respected than to-day) inward to that withdrawn and secluded centre where

> in that black spot,
> Core of the universe and seat of Dis,
> The traitors lie, and their worm dieth not.[2]

But we may see her otherwise: as a progression in time from suburbs to citadel—a corroding and inevitable process of destruction. Whichever way we look at it, it is all one. Hell is a funnel, continually sucking and drawing all heaviness downwards and inwards towards that centre "upon which all weights downweigh".[3] That which to-day is in the suburbs will be within the walls to-morrow. Everything shifts and slides with the steady centripetal pull towards the bottomless gulf "where there is no more downward";[4] at the end of the descent is the "great Worm" which devours and is never satisfied.

---

[1] *The Figure of Beatrice*, p. 133.
[3] *Inf.* xi. 64–66.
[2] *Inf.* xxxiv. 111.
[4] *Inf.* xiv. 118.

Let us, then, begin the journey—the journey of self-knowledge into the possibilities of depravity. We may find the gate anywhere in the Dark Forest, and there are no bolts upon it. It is, says Dante, "the wide-open door", "the gate whose threshold is denied to none".[1] We enter; we are in the Vestibule. This is not yet Hell, though it is the way to Hell. It is the outer fringe of the suburbs; it is almost, we might say, the junction from which we may take the train for Hell. It is populated by those whom both Heaven and Hell reject: those who were "neither for God nor for His enemies". Virgil speaks contemptuously of "this dreary huddle" whose "blind life trails on so low and crass" that it would welcome everlasting death.

> "No reputation in the world it has,
>   Mercy and doom hold it alike in scorn:
>   Let us not speak of these, but look and pass." [1]

Dante looks, and recognises. We too may recognise—perhaps with some astonishment. The Vestibule is very crowded—more so, indeed, than in Dante's day, and the numbers surprised *him*. Here are the people who never come to any decision. Do we despise them? or do we admire their wide-minded tolerance and their freedom from bigotry and dogmatism? They discuss everything, but come to no conclusion. They will commit themselves to no opinion, since there is so much to be said on the other side. Like the Duke in Chesterton's play, *Magic*, they never give a subscription to one party without giving one to the opposite party as well. They never abandon themselves wholeheartedly to any pursuit lest they should be missing something: neither to God, lest they should lose the world, nor to the world, because there might, after all, be "something in" religion. They shrink from responsibility, lest it should bind them; they condemn nothing, for fear of being thought narrow. They chose indecision, and here in Hell they have it; they run for ever after a perpetually-shifting banner; the worry and fret that torments them as of old stings them like a swarm of hornets. They sweat blood and tears, but in no purposeful martyrdom: the painful drops fall to the ground and are licked up by worms. Let us not speak of them—let us at any rate not commend their wavering minds and their twittering little indecisive books. "But surely," they cry, "*all* experience is valuable! All good and evil are relative! All religions are the same in essentials! One mustn't draw hard-and-fast distinctions! One must be free to try *everything*!" Look, and pass.

[1] *Inf.* v. 20; xiv. 86–87.   [2] *Inf.* iii. 49–51.

We pass. We come to Acheron. Acheron is the passage into Hell itself—it is the act of the will consenting to evil. The dead souls long to pass it, for beyond it lies the place of their choice. They hate what they chose, yet because they chose it they cling to it, as the drunkard clings to drink or the lecher to lechery; as the tired millionaire can get no kick except out of making yet more money that he cannot enjoy; as the tyrant glutted with blood can only stimulate his jaded senses by inventing more complicated forms of torture. "All their fear is changed into desire" because, although their choice has become their punishment, it is yet the only tolerable existence for them; because, though all the savour of the sin is gone, they cannot live without it. Their will consents to judgment, and Charon ferries them over the river. But Dante, the living man, swoons; and when he wakes he is at the other side. Critical ingenuity has exhausted itself in discussing how he got there. But the whole point is that he does not know. How often does a man know the precise moment when his will consented to sin? By what obscure interior resolution did the thought, "I wish my brother were dead" give place to the settled intention: "I mean to murder him"? or the speculative premeditation of murder become a foregone conclusion, crystallising into an act? There is a point at which the dark desire, struggling out of the depths of the subconscious, passes the warder who, in Dante's phrase, "guards the threshold of assent".[1] As a rule, the assent to evil is not recognised until after it has been ratified by the conscious mind.

Acheron passed, we enter the First Circle. It is a place, not of pain, but of grief—a sighing for eternal loss. Here is the Limbo of the unbaptised and the great pagans—people, we may think, who had no opportunity to choose. Yet they are placed on the far bank of the River of Assent. Why? Because, Virgil explains, "they had not faith". Literally, because they lacked faith in Christ; but allegorically because they lacked faith in a more absolute manner. Some of the noblest minds are in that Limbo. They cannot trust the universe; they are strangers to ecstasy. Whether, like Thomas Hardy, they accept this world, or whether, like A. E. Housman, they shrink from it, they are alike in the rejection of eternal joy. In the *Paradiso*, Dante worked out to its conclusion the great Catholic affirmation that those who passionately aspire by faith to beatitude are baptised into Christ by desire: Trajan and Rhipeus are exalted into the Heaven of the just.

[1] *Purg.* xviii. 63.

> They died, not pagans, as thou deemest it,
> But faithful Christians, clinging, he and he,
> To the passion-pierced, to the yet-to-be-passible feet.[1]

But with the great pagans of Limbo it is not so. They show in their mien "neither joy nor sorrow"—they would not let themselves go. Because they dared not abandon themselves to faith they chose not to have hope; therefore they have their choice: "without hope they live in desire". They have honour in Hell, for they gave great gifts to men. Yet they belong to the City of Sorrow, and Satan can use them for his work of corrupting society; for by precept and example they can make men afraid of hope.

In the Limbo of the Pagans there is light—the cold and clear light of a dutiful though unecstatic morality. But now we pass into darkness. In the Circle of the Lustful there is no light at all—only the black air and the howling whirlwind. Upon that wind and exposed to its buffetings the lovers drift for ever. This is appropriate; for all these circles that we are now passing through are the circles of drift. We are not yet within the walls of Dis which ring the inner city with the iron ramparts of an obdurate and malignant will. We are still in the suburbs, among the sins (as Dante will presently explain) of Incontinence, where a defective will, too inert to march in pursuit of the good, trails helplessly after the appetite.

In this Second Circle, the image is sexual; it is the obvious and convenient image for what it figures, but we need not confine it to the sins of sex. The circle of the Lovers is the circle of *shared* sin. It still preserves mutuality: the love that was exchanged does not leave Paolo and Francesca—they chose to be together, and so they are. That is the mercy in their punishment, but it is also part of the punishment, for they now know to what pass each has brought the other, and their mutuality has become their reproach. The sin is mutual indulgence—the self-indulgence of indulging other people. One gives way—partly, no doubt, for one's own pleasure, but partly because it would hurt the other person to say "No". Francesca cannot say "No" to anybody. Because Dante speaks kindly to her, she will do anything for him: "Hear all thou wilt, and speak as thou shalt please, And we will gladly speak with thee and hear."

> "The bitterest woe of woes
> Is to remember in our wretchedness
> Old happy days, as well thy Doctor knows;

---

[1] *Para.* xx. 103–105.

> Yet, if so dear desire thy heart possess
> To know the root of love which wrought our fall,
> I'll be as those who weep and who confess." [1]

The sin, you see, looks convincingly like self-sacrifice. One gives way to one's lover out of pity, and damns him with the kindest intentions. One indulges one's children to their hurt because one cannot bear to give them a moment's unhappiness. One writes and speaks no matter what foolishness, because one's public turns up an eager face and must not be disappointed—"Hear all thou wilt . . . and we will gladly speak". We listen to the claims of humanity, and wallow in the yielding of ourselves to their lusts, lusting ourselves for their grateful appreciation. We love them, we say, and like to see them happy. We devote ourselves . . . It is a sweet and swooning agony of pity and self-pity; and Dante swoons in sympathy.

When he wakes, the mutuality of indulgence has mysteriously vanished. The indulgence has become a solitary indulgence of appetite. He is in the Circle of the Gluttons. The appetite, once offered and shared, has now become appetite pure and simple, indulged for its own sake. Like all the sinners we have so far met, the Gluttons are people of whom our present civilisation is inclined to think highly. They have an engaging egotism; they demand so amiably and seem to get so much out of life that we feel they have hit on the right attitude to the world of things. They have, in fact, a high standard of living—and that, we agree, is the thing to aim at. If we are ever inclined to envy or resent them, it is not really because their standards are wrong, but because our own standard of living is too low. It is true that something in the nature of things seems reluctant to concede these standards. If Dante had seen a civilisation that understood beatitude only in terms of cinemas and silk stockings and electric cookers and radiators and cars and cocktails, would it have surprised him to find it all of a sudden waking to the realisation that, having pursued these ideals with all its might, it was inexplicably left cold, hungry, bored, resentful and savage? Probably not, for he described Gluttony so. For Dante, the punishment of sin is the sin itself; the Gluttons lie prostrate under an eternal drench of rain and sleet and snow, and Cerberus, the embodied appetite which ruled them, rules them still, yelping and tearing them.

In this cold and sensual wallowing, there is no mutuality. Each shade

[1] *Inf.* v. 121–126.

suffers his greed, as he enjoyed it, by himself and blind (it is Dante's word) to his fellows. But appetite cannot so indulge itself without encountering the thrust and pressure of other, conflicting, greeds. So in the next circle the Greed of Hoarding and the Greed of Squandering are chosen as the types of those opposing greeds. Here a perverted spirit of community reappears: it is a community of opposition. The greeds of either sort combine in gangs; they roll great stones against the other party:

> They bump together, and where they bump, wheel right
> Round, and return, trundling their loads again,
> Shouting: "Why chuck away? Why grab so tight?" [1]

They are united in nothing but hatred, and their combination is to no purpose; for

> . . . round the dismal ring they pant and strain
> On both sides back to the point where they began,
> Still as they go bawling their rude refrain;
>
> And when they meet there, back again, every man,
> Through his half-circle to joust in the other list . . . [2]

It is sheer futility. Dante says that their faces are unrecognisable; and indeed they have nothing distinctive about them, except what they derive from a gang and a party-slogan. Even as gangs they are barely distinguishable—the economy of accumulated thrift and the economy of conspicuous waste are counterparts of one another and issue in the same economic deadlock. And indeed, among nations, combines, parties and gangs of all descriptions we may find the same spurious alliances against the common enemy, and the same ominous family resemblance.

Spurious alliances do not hold together; community of opposition is no lasting bond. The clash of greeds dissolves and disintegrates into an anarchy of hatred, all against all. Beneath the Circle of the Hoarders and Spendthrifts is the Marsh of Styx, where the Wrathful are plunged in a muddy slough. On the surface, the souls, "naked, with looks of savage discontent", [3] rend and snarl at one another: this kind of wrath is active and ferocious; it vents itself in sheer lust for inflicting pain and destruction—on others if it can; on itself, if it can find no better object.

---

[1] *Inf.* vii. 28–31.   [2] *Inf.* vii. 31–36.
[3] *Inf.* vii. 111.

The other kind is passive and sullen; it lies at the bottom of the marsh, gurgling its inarticulate hymn of hate:

> ". . . Sullen were we; we took
>   No joy of the pleasant air, no joy of the good
>   Sun; our hearts smouldered with a sulky smoke;
>
> Sullen we lie here now in the black mud." [1]

This is the last of the Circles of Incontinence; this savage and impotent frustration is the end of the indulgence that began so tenderly with the mutual yielding of Paolo and Francesca—which can be traced back even further, to a morality without joy, or, beyond that, to a mere habit of tolerance and indecision. The beginning of it all seemed to promise well enough—by what inexorable steps did society reach this point? Dante, when he was wandering in the Dark Wood, met with three beasts: the first of them was a gaily spotted Leopard, which gambolled about him so prettily that he had, he says, "good hopes of the animal with the dappled hide",[2] and scarcely noticed that it was tripping him up and turning him out of the way. The Sins of Incontinence are the sins of the Leopard, and we are rather apt to take a hopeful view of them. Tolerance and open-mindedness are surely rather desirable than otherwise; there is much to be said for good Paganism; love makes the world go round, and as for a high standard of living, is not that the very charter of the City of the New Jerusalem? Thrift and generosity—and, of course, all those other pairs of incompatible opposites—call them the Hegelian dialectic of thesis and antithesis, and it is clear that out of a concentrated effort to push each to its logical conclusion there will come—well, a clash, certainly, but equally certainly a reconciling synthesis. Wrath and hatred——?

It is noticeable that in the passage from mutual antagonism to wrath, the path which Dante follows is, for the first time, described in detail. The first stages of the descent into Avernus are almost imperceptible —we pass oblivious, or swooning; we dream our way into damnation. But with the drop into wrath and war we begin to be aware that something is seriously wrong with society; we begin to see just where it is we are going.

> So to the farther edge we crossed the rink,
>   Hard by a bubbling spring which, rising there,
>   Cuts its own cleft and pours on down the brink.

---

[1] *Inf.* vii. 121–124.   [2] *Inf.* xvi. 107–108.

> Darker than any perse its waters were,
> And keeping company with the ripples dim
> We made our way down by that eerie stair.
>
> A marsh there is called Styx, which the sad stream
> Forms when it finds the end of its descent
> Under the grey, malignant rock-foot grim . . .[1]

The way is plain, and from now on we can deceive ourselves no longer. But in Hell, once we have given ourselves over to the will to destruction, there is no way back. We must go on. Now, however, evil has become conscious of itself. There is a change. We have, in fact, passed through the suburbs of Upper Hell and reached the moat of the City itself. We come to a watch-tower, from which our approach is signalled to the garrison of Dis. A boat is sent to fetch us. We step in. This time there is no doubt about how we make the crossing; the will is awake and the consent deliberate.

And here, in the poem, comes an episode which all the critics have conspired to misunderstand. As the boat is ferried across Styx, a hideous shape rises from the mud and confronts Dante,

> Crying: "Who art thou that com'st before thy time?"
>
> "Tho' I come," said I, "I stay not; thou who art made
> So rank and beastly, who art thou?" "Go to;
> Thou seest that I am one who weep," he said.
>
> And I: "Amid the weeping and the woe,
> Accursed spirit, do thou remain and rot!
> I know thee, filthy as thou art, I know."
>
> Then he stretched out both hands to clutch the boat,
> But the Master was on his guard, and thrust him back,
> Crying: "Hence to the other dogs! Trouble him not!"
>
> And after, laid his arms about my neck
> And kissed my face and said: "Indignant soul,
> Blessed is the womb that bare thee!" [2]

Almost every commentator exclaims that Dante is here displaying a cruel and unchristian spirit, and that it is highly unbecoming in Virgil to hail him with words that were originally used to Christ. But this kind of criticism comes of forgetting that Dante's pilgrimage through Hell is a pilgrimage made inside Dante. The soul that rises from the

[1] *Inf.* vii. 100–108.   [2] *Inf.* viii. 33–45.

mud is only *literally* the spirit of the Florentine Filippo Argenti; *allegorically* it is the image of Dante's sin. In the marsh of Styx, sin for the first time consciously recognises its own ugliness and, for the first time, consciously repudiates itself. However feebly, however ungraciously, and for whatever inadequate motives,[1] the sinner sees himself as he is and, for the first time, sides with God's judgment against himself. Dante, who had honoured the pagans, swooned for pity of Francesca, been sorry for Ciacco the Glutton and felt himself vaguely distressed by the Hoarders and Spendthrifts, turns on Filippo Argenti in horror and invokes the justice of God against him. It is the first faint stirring of the birth of Christ in the heart. "Blessed is the womb that bare thee." And if the civilisation which Dante (at that level of interpretation) represents first recoils from its own corruption only when war has made that corruption unmistakeable, then, however ill-phrased and ill-directed its expressions of horror, nevertheless, so far as it goes, blessed is that recoil and blessed that self-recognition.

Yet to know and hate one's own sin is not necessarily to repent and amend it. There may be other consequences. Across the waters of Styx the iron ramparts of Dis appear, glowing red-hot, as though they burned in a furnace. The demon-guardians slam the gates in Virgil's face: Virgil is human wisdom—he is science, poetry, statesmanship; but none of these things will of themselves carry us any further along the path of self-knowledge. Above the gate-tower appear the Furies; they call for Medusa to turn Dante to stone. Here Virgil can intervene, and he does. "Turn away—shut your eyes tight; if once you look on the Gorgon, there is no returning to the light of day."[2] The Furies are remorse; the Gorgon is despair; if self-hatred and self-horror lead only to remorse and despair, the heart turns to stone and no amendment is possible. Dante covers his eyes, and Virgil lays his hands on Dante's, interposing between him and despair the accumulated wisdom of all ages—all beauty, all art, all decency, all reason, all the great tradition of the natural order. He cannot open the gates or quell the demons, but he can at least do that. They wait. Then, with a sound like thunder, the supernatural order breaks through. The great and terrible Angel comes striding dry-shod over Styx and the gates open at the touch of his wand. We enter Nether Hell and are within the City.

From this point on, the images are those of souls who have looked

[1] "It is something to be sure of the deed; our courteous Lord will deign to redeem the motive". Charles Williams, *op. cit.*, p. 104.

[2] *Inf.* ix. 55-57.

on the face of the Gorgon. The will is set in obduracy; it no longer drifts at the service of the appetite but drives and uses it.

The first circle of Nether Hell is that of the Heretics, for Heresy is the first effect of obduracy. The Heretic, taken literally, is one who at the same time accepts the Church and defies it; for when he departs from the doctrine he justifies his departure. The incontinent sinner is the man who says: "I know I am breaking the Law, but I can't help myself." The heretic says: "I know I am breaking the Law, but I am justified. The Law did not provide for my special case. I propose to amend it. I accept it only so far as I choose and no farther." The heretics are enclosed in burning tombs. Among them is Farinata degli Uberti—ruthless, magnanimous after his fashion, bearing his torment defiantly, "seeming to hold all Hell in deep despite".[1] He is Dante's first great image of Pride—the first image of the dark, Satanic façade of nobility that almost persuades us to be of the devil's party. People have asked where, in the *Inferno*, is the punishment of the proud? The answer is: in Upper Hell, nowhere; in Nether Hell, everywhere. All sins that justify themselves are proud sins. But, as Hell deepens, we shall see the progressive degeneration of pride.

Below the Circle of the Heretics there comes a cliff with a great drop. We descend from the sins of the Leopard to the sins of the Lion. The will that is bent on destruction, justifying its choice, breaks out into open violence. The first consequence of saying "I am right, Law or no Law" is violence against one's fellow-man and the tyrannical imposition of one's naked will on others. Rapine, murder, oppression —these are the corruptions of absolute power; here the tyrants stand, plunged in the river of boiling blood which is called Phlegethon. Violence heated their blood; they shed blood; the blood that was their argument is their torment. We cross the river on the back of one of the Centaurs—half-beast, half-man—who guard these human beasts, and come into a wood full of withered trees. We pluck a branch, and it bleeds and speaks. The trees are the souls of Suicides, in whom self-disgust has bred despair. Through the barren wood rush the shades of men, pursued and mangled by black hounds. They are the Profligates who madly gambled away their substance. These are not the comparatively harmless spendthrifts of the Fourth Circle—they are those who flung away their goods in a desperate thirst for sensation; they squandered, not for any pleasure bought with spending, but for the morbid thrill of ruining themselves. Why are they classed with the

[1] *Inf.* x. 36.

Suicides as the "Violent against Self"? Because their sin too was a sin of desperation; they "turned to weeping what was meant for joy".[1] When an acquisitive and tyrannical society has despoiled others, it cannot stop. It goes on to despoil itself. It flings away the possessions it holds in trust and begins to prey upon its own vitals.

We pass to the Third Ring of the Circle of Violence; here are the Violent against God, Nature, and Art. It is a huge, sterile desert of burning sand, over which falls a perpetual fiery rain. Hatred of self now turns outward and embraces the whole of creation. Its types are the Blasphemers, the Sodomites and the Usurers. The Blasphemers lie supine, spitting their hatred in the face of Heaven. Here is Capaneus, one of the Seven who fought against Thebes. He is the second image of Pride. Where Farinata suffered in silence he is loud and voluble:

"That which in life I was, in death I am.

Though Jove tire out his armourer, who supplied
His wrathful hand with the sharp thunder-stone
That in my last day smote me through the side;

Though he tire all the rest out, one by one,
In Mangibel's black stithy, and break them quite,
Crying, 'To aid! Vulcan, lay on, lay on!'

As once before he cried at Phlegra's fight;
Yea, though he crush me with his omnipotence,
No merry vengeance shall his heart delight!" [2]

Hell, says Dante, is the dwelling of those who have "lost the good of the intellect". Pride here has so far parted company with intellect that it issues in an impotent spite. We look and pass to the Sodomites, who run upon the burning sand and may not rest. They blaspheme against Nature and so blaspheme against God. Violence has taken a fresh twist: it no longer merely beats and brutalises: it perverts. Sitting upon the sand in the same circle are the Usurers—they are violent, not only against Nature, the child of God, but also against Art, which is the child of Nature. How so? Because, says Dante, in effect, there are only two sources of real prosperity: the produce of the earth and the labour of men's hands (that is what he means by "Nature" and "Art"); but the Usurer has found a third way which does violence to both Art and Nature. Here the old commentator Gelli has written the brilliant gloss: "The Sodomite makes sterile that which was meant for

---

[1] *Inf.* xi. 44. [2] *Inf.* xiv. 51–60.

11

fertility; the usurer makes breed that which was meant to be sterile." Money breeds money—but in so doing makes sterile everything else. The nineteenth-century commentators, brought up in the tradition of financial autonomy and the sacro-sanctity of banking, were aghast at this astonishing listing in one doom of unmentionable vice and irreproachable finance; they could only suppose that Dante's genius had been entangled, willy-nilly, in a net of mediaeval nonsense. To us, pondering upon the "End of Economic Man", and looking at a world full of dust-bowls, unemployment, strikes, and starvation, yawing hideously between over- and under-production, the connection between usury and the barren and burning sand does not, perhaps, seem altogether too far-fetched.

The Circle of Violence, the Circle of the Sins of the Lion, ends here. The Leopard is a beast of the jungle, where uncontrolled passions sprawl and proliferate. The Lion is a beast of the desert; and Violence makes a desert of the world. The river, the wood, the sand are all barren. We are left with a society that has exhausted all pleasure, stripped the earth bare, and no longer cares either to live or to propagate itself.

We are now half-way down Hell, looking over the iron-grey precipice of the Great Barrier, stretching beneath us to an unfathomable depth. Close beside us, the cataract of Phlegethon plunges downwards with a noise so loud that we can scarcely hear ourselves speak. What further profundities of misery wait to be plumbed? The mystery of iniquity has, we may say, only begun to unveil itself. We have still to see what Dante calls the Grand Woes—the Sins of the Wolf. Up through the thick air comes swimming the monster Geryon—triformed, with the face of a just man, the forepaws of a beast, the body of a serpent,

> Painted with ring-knots and whorled tracery.
>
> No Turk nor Tartar ever wrought coloured stuff
> So rainbow-trammed and broidered; never wore
> Arachne's web such dyes in warp and woof.[1]

We mount the glittering back of that "unclean image of Fraud", and are carried in slow spirals down the black funnel of the Abyss. At the bottom are fire and stink, and the ten circular pits of Malebolge, carved in the eternal rock, and bridged by radiating spurs of stone. Far below

---

[1] *Inf.* xvii. 15–18.

the circles of appetite indulged and appetite self-justified lie the circles where appetite is exploited.

At the upper confine of Malebolge, as at the upper confine of the Circles of Incontinence, we again encounter a sexual image. Here the Panders and Seducers run continually, driven—not by an impersonal wind, but by the whips of devils. The perverted intellect makes gain of what it destroys. From now on, all relationships begin to be falsified. That which simple Lust gave and simple Tyranny violated has now become the subject of a traffic. The lost mutuality again appears, distorted into the relationship of buyer and seller. A demon cracks the lash about the loin of the man who sold his own sister to the lust of Ezzelino, crying: "Away, pander! there are no women here to coin."[1] In the opposite direction run those who were their own middle-men, and purchased love with gold, only to betray it.

In the next ditch are the Flatterers,

> plunged in dung, the which appeared
> Like human ordure, running from a jakes;[2]

and here we are called upon to look at

> . . . that uncleanly and dishevelled trull
> Scratching with filthy nails, alternately
> Standing upright and crouching in the pool.

> That is the harlot Thaïs. "To what degree,"
> Her leman asked, "have I earned thanks, my love?"
> "O, to a very miracle," said she.[3]

Is that all? Certainly, as Terence says, from whom the episode is taken, "Great thanks" would have been sufficient. But is an extravagance of speech culpable to this extent, that it leaves Thaïs so far below the harlots of the First Circle, and even below the Panders and Seducers, who traffic in flesh? Thaïs shows us how Dante understood Flattery; it is the prostitution of language—of the means of intellectual intercourse. Words are falsified for gain. Flattery—wheedling (for the word *lusingare* means that too)—shall we go on to say advertisement, journalism, propaganda?—this is the filth and ordure of the falsifying intellect, steeped in its own slime. It is inaccuracy—"Hell", says Charles Williams, "is inaccurate . . . Flattery is precisely the unfruitful excrement of mankind; its evil is that it asserts falsely what can be asserted truly . . . Meaning is lost, accuracy is lost, and accuracy is

---

[1] *Inf.* xviii. 65–66.   [2] *Inf.* xviii. 113–114.   [3] *Inf.* xviii. 130–135.

fruitfulness—it is the first law of the spiritual life."[1] Is there an image here that we recognise? Could we perhaps have supplied Dante with examples more striking than that of Thaïs? Are we tempted to wonder whether the Second Ditch of Malebolge is not now filled to overflowing? No matter: "Look and pass". "*E quinci sien le nostre viste sazie*— Having seen this, we have seen enough." [2]

In the Third Ditch are the Simoniacs, who trafficked in sacraments and spiritual offices: panders, Dante calls them, who prostitute the bride of God. The image is in form ecclesiastical; the phrase conflates it with a sexual image. It is true that there are more kinds of sacrament than one. Marriage is a sacrament, and art may be. Where such things are used for gain, the body of God is bartered. The Simoniacs are thrust head downwards into holes in the rock: the flame runs, licking, upon the soles of their feet, like a descent in judgment of those cloven tongues which were the sign of the outpouring of the Holy Ghost— for, if the Spirit can be known to such as these, it can be known only as judgment.

Here again, that which could be used truly is used falsely. The consecration of these Simoniac priests is a true consecration; the sacraments they administer are valid. But they are fraudulently exploited by the lean Wolf whose maw is never filled. So, too, in the next ditch, where the Sorcerers walk backwards, with their heads so twisted that their tears

> Spilled down to bathe the buttocks at the cleft.[3]

Prophecy is a true gift. But it may be aped by charlatans, or, worse still, exploited by those who truly possess it, and used as an instrument of domination. Here are the fortune-tellers, here are the witch-wives. The image is of the twisted magical art, which deforms knowledge to an end outside the order and unity of creation; it is the image of the abuse of all psychic power and of all scientific knowledge—it includes the "conditioning" of other people to selfish ends by the manipulation of their psyches, as well as the vulgarer forms of spirit-rapping, and the more disgusting excesses of Satanism. Magic, even when it uses the legitimate technique of the scientist, is distinguished from true science by the "twisted sight", which looks to the ego of the practitioner: the truer the gift, the greater the power, and the more dangerous and criminal its abuse. Whatever form it takes, magic thrives upon credulity,

---

[1] *The Figure of Beatrice*, p. 133.   [2] *Inf.* xviii. 136.
[3] *Inf.* xx. 23.

and it is therefore not difficult to see why, in the time-sequence of the City's deterioration, it should follow upon the prostitution of language, and the loss of integrity in the Church. When religion is discredited, men turn to the wizards who peep and mutter; and if they have been put at the mercy of words, and so have lost the gift of tongues, they will not easily retain the gift of the discerning of spirits.

So far, there is disorder in the State, but the State itself may still function after a fashion. The next stage is the beginning of the rot within the organism of the State. Below the Sorcerers come the Barrators. They are to the State what the Simoniacs are to the Church: they traffic in the offices of the State. One is at first, perhaps, surprised to find the circles in this order: is it worse to sell the things of Caesar than to sell the things of God? We remember, indeed, that for Dante the State, like the Church, derives its authority directly from God. But whether or not we agree with Dante about this, it is not difficult, I think, to see his point. There is a sense in which the State, which is of the natural order, lies at a deeper level of man's being than Religion, which is of the spiritual order. This the Lord Christ recognised: "If you cannot be honest about worldly riches, who shall trust you with the true?" "If a man love not his brother whom he hath seen, how shall he love God whom he hath not seen?" When Dante was lost in the Dark Wood, he had gone beyond the reach of Beatrice, who is Divine Grace; she had to make Virgil her messenger, to reach him upon the natural level. The Simoniacs sell Beatrice; the Barrators sell Virgil himself.

Out of the stream of boiling pitch in which the Barrators are immersed, an attendant devil forks up Ciampolo the traitor. Ciampolo is a great fellow. Ciampolo is a regular card. He is one too many, even for the devils. The canto which tells how he tricked and foiled his tormentors bubbles, like the boiling pitch itself, with an ugly and oily chuckle. We rather like Ciampolo—indeed, we always do. He is a smart chap and there are no flies on him. Graft and the pulling of strings, the little bit off-the-ration and under-the-counter—who does not to some extent practise and admire these things? Unless, of course, we are personally inconvenienced; and unless, by some accident, the thing should happen to boil up on a big scale in a Marconi case or a Stavisky scandal. Then we are naturally indignant and talk about corruption. Between our admiration and our indignation, between our recognition that Barratry is worse than Simony and our strong disposition to countenance and practise it so far as is reasonable, there might appear to be some contradiction. Is it possible that we are hypocritical in these matters?

It is possible, at least, that Dante thought so; for in escaping from the devils of the Fifth Ditch, he and Virgil fall promptly into the Ditch of the Hypocrites, who walk in leaden cloaks, gilded and glittering.

The next ditch is the Ditch of the Thieves. The "orderly devolution of property" is disintegrated. No man can say what is his own; and in Hell the Thieves lose even their own bodies, being changed from man to serpent and from serpent to man, or blended hideously, two bodies welded into one. That which a man possesses, he holds in trust for God and his fellows: but if that which he has is not his own, where is the trust? Here, in the place where no personal rights are respected, appears Vanni Fucci, the third great image of Pride. He respects nothing, not even himself; his pride is in his own beastliness, and out of that beastliness he screams his blasphemies and makes the figs in God's face. The façade is being stripped from Pride: Farinata was silent; Capaneus, defiant; Vanni Fucci is vulgar.

From the Thieves of Property we pass to the Thieves of Personality. In the next ditch walk the Counsellors of Fraud, who filched away the integrity of those they counselled and now walk for ever wrapped in living flame. They used other men's tongues to deceive; and now the flame is the only tongue they have. The "thievish flame", Dante calls it; for the substitution of personality that was adumbrated in the circle above is here accomplished at the level of the intellect. Mutuality and exchange discover a fresh perversion. The 26th canto itself is the noblest in the whole *Inferno*, but we cannot pause to examine its beauties. We must pass on to the Ninth Ditch, where the Sowers of Dissension are continually mutilated by a demon with a sword.

Religious schism, political sedition, family dissension: the fomenters of discord split the State at every sensitive point. Their will is to disintegrate; by this means they achieve their personal power. Divide and rule; we are familiar with the principle. All groupings, all centres of union, must be split up, because they are centres of resistance, in which justice and truth and other positive and divine things may find a refuge and a rallying-point. Exchange is driven out of yet another stronghold: the coinherence of the community takes one more step down the way of incoherence.

In the Tenth Ditch the last—or almost the last—step is taken. In this ghastly place are the Falsifiers—they falsify their persons, they falsify speech, they coin false money. Is this an anti-climax? Why is money so important? It is important precisely because it is the means of exchange. In the other circles everything is bought and sold—sex and religion and government, and art and speech and intellect and power: now the very coin for which they were sold is itself corrupted. That no state can hold together when its currency is hopelessly debased is a practical fact with which we are only too familiar; but that fact is itself only a symbol of the greater truth which it symbolises.

Of this last Ditch of Malebolge, Dante says:

> Could all disease, all dog-day plagues that stew
> In Valdichiana's spitals, all fever-drench
> Drained from Maremma and Sardinia, spew
>
> Their horrors all together in one trench—
> Like that, so this: suffering and running sore
> Of gangrened limbs and putrefying stench.[1]

The diseased lie heaped on one another—leprous, dropsical, fevered, rabid; the place crawls: it is the image of a society in the last stages of its mortal sickness and already necrosing. Every value it has is false; it alternates between a deadly lethargy and a raving insanity. All intercourse is corrupted, every affirmation has become perjury, and every identity a lie. No medium of exchange remains to it, and the "general bond of love and nature" is utterly dissolved.

Can there be a lower deep than this? Yes; there is a lower deep. In the dissolution of the natural tie, some special trust, some lingering personal loyalty might yet remain. We cross the grey plain. In the distance we see the towering forms of the Giants, who stand about the rim of the Well which leads to the core of Hell and throne of Dis. When the intellect is wholly perverted, what can remain? Blind forces —great blocks of primitive mass-emotion, the more dangerous because they are not just mindless, like "elephants and whales", but stupid like imbeciles, like crowds, like cunning and half-witted children—a pinpoint human brain in a body of superhuman strength. These are fitting "executives of Mars"; at once the victims and the tools of that which lurks behind and beneath them.

We pass Nimrod: he is a braggart idiocy—the doom of nonsense. We pass Ephialtes: he is a senseless rage—the doom of nihilism, or smashing-for-smashing's-sake. We come to Antaeus: he is a brainless vanity and the doom of triviality. He is persuaded to lower us "into the bottom of sin".

[1] *Inf.* xxix. 46–51.

> Then I turned round, and saw before my face
> And 'neath my feet a lake, so bound with ice
> It did not seem like water, but like glass.[1]

This is the end of all things; this is treachery—"the freezing of every conception".[2] Here the final ties which bind man to man are broken: the tie of kindred goes first, and then the tie of country: into these we are born—we did not choose them, though we are bound to them. Here, there is still room for a little remorse—tears may flow, if the shade, frozen to the neck in ice, keeps his face down. We pass Caïna, we pass Antenora, where Count Ugolino gnaws forever upon the scalp of Ruggieri. This is the last appearance of mutuality: the disorder which began in mutual indulgence ends in a mutual hatred and betrayal. The phrases with which Ugolino begins his story are a close parallel of those in which Francesca begins hers, and they share between them the echoes of the same passage of the *Aeneid*. There is no mistaking Dante's intention here. We pass to Ptolomaea: here lie those who betrayed their invited guests. Is that a worse thing than to betray kindred or country? It is worse: the special obligation is of the traitor's own choice and making. Chosen guests, chosen friends—they who betray these "go down quick into Hell". They come there before their death, and that which walks the earth in their bodies is but a devil in their shape. These shades cannot weep, for they lie on their backs, and the bitter wind that blows across the ice of Cocytus freezes the tears into a mask of ice. They can, however, still speak.

In the last region of the thick-ribbed ice they cannot even speak. They are wholly immersed, unable to communicate. The last semblance of community, the last vestige of humanity is withdrawn from the "social animal", man. This is Giudecca, the circle of Judas, the circle of those who betray the ultimate bond of deliberately sworn allegiance.

One thing only remains; the miserific vision, the confrontation with the head and source of evil.

> The Emperor of the dolorous realm was there,
> Out of the girding ice he stood breast-high . . .[3]

It is the final image of Pride. It is he that was fairest of the sons of light. He is still an angel ruined, but the ruin here is total. The Satanic façade is wholly shattered: he is not noble; he is horrible; he is grotesque. His face is threefold, in a hideous Trinitarian parody; he retains the

---

[1] *Inf.* xxxii. 22–24.   [2] Charles Williams: *The Figure of Beatrice*, p. 144.
[3] *Inf.* xxxiv. 28–29.

six wings of his primal cherubhood, but they have become the wings
of a bat—

> . . . and as they flapped and whipped
> Three winds went rushing over the icy flat
> And froze up all Cocytus; and he wept
> From his six eyes, and down his triple chin
> Runnels of tears and bloody slaver dripped.[1]

In the jaws of Dis are three shades: the shade of Judas who betrayed
God; the shades of Brutus and Cassius who betrayed Caesar. This is
the end: treachery to God and treachery to the City—to God and to
Man. Here, in the heart of cold, in the place that knows neither obligation nor community nor coherence nor exchange, treachery devours
treachery for ever.

That is Dante's vision of a corrupted society. Whether it is borrowed
or original matters little. The question is rather: is it rational? is it
true? Can we recognise the steps of that inexorable progression? Have
we ever seen anything at all like it?

We cannot, mercifully, see anything *exactly* like it in this world,
for here the City of Dis contains always some admixture of the City
of God. Dante's vision is of the City in Hell—of the City as it would
be if the good were, through the gaps, as it were, in time or space,
wholly drawn away. It is the *absolute* negation whereof we can have
no experience while time and space endure. But it is necessary, perhaps,
for us to contemplate the City of Dis in its essential possibility in order
to recognise clearly its approximations in a living society. The road to
restoration and the Earthly Paradise lies—not through Hell, for from
Hell itself there is no issue, but—through the understanding of Hell.

We pass the centre, we enter the hemisphere of the Antipodes, we
leave Beelzebub behind us; we see him, now, upside-down, impotent,
ridiculous. It is not he that has moved; it is we that have passed through
the ultimate self-knowledge and look upon things from a new view-
point. On that yonder side of experience, from the Mount of Purgation,
the stream of Lethe, the stream of forgetfulness, runs down into the
Abyss. We follow its course—upward—towards recollection and
renewal:

> There is a place low down there underground
> As far from Satan as his tomb is deep,
> Not known to sight, but only by the sound

---

[1] *Inf.* xxxiv. 50–54.

Of a small stream, which trickles down the steep,
Hollowing its channel, where with gentle fall
And devious course its wandering waters creep.

By that hid way my guide and I withal
Back to the lit world from the darkened dens
Toiled upward, caring for no rest at all,

He first, I following; till my straining sense
Glimpsed the bright burden of the heavenly cars
Through a round hole; by this we climbed, and thence

Came forth, to look once more upon the stars.[1]

[1] *Inf.* xxxiv. 127–139.

THE COMEDY OF THE *COMEDY*

I HAVE sometimes played with the idea of writing a story, and dropping into it, casually and without comment, the following sentence:

George was curled up comfortably in the big arm-chair, chuckling over *The Divine Comedy*.

The game would be to see how many reviewers and correspondents could be lured into accusing me of gross illiteracy, and solemnly pointing out that the work in question, so far from being a humorous piece, was a Great Religious Poem, permeated from end to end by Awful Sublimity and unmitigated Grimth. I fear, however, that it is now too late; my interest in Dante has been advertised and even the reviewers would probably smell a rat. Nevertheless, it is surprising how many people do contrive to read Dante—apparently with interest and attention—without ever discovering the comedy of the *Comedy*. There are, indeed, some honourable exceptions. Canon Lonsdale Ragg and Dr. Barbara Reynolds have each ventured to write an article devoted to the subject of Dante's humour; Benedetto Croce admits that there is laughter, not only in Heaven, but also in Hell, though he seems rather to have missed its significance. Charles Roden Buxton hazards the opinion that Dante and Goethe display "more humour" than Virgil and Milton—though this does not perhaps commit him to very much. But we are more accustomed to sweeping assertions in the other sense. "The poet was without humour", says H. A. L. Fisher, in the course of an otherwise sensitive and judicious appreciation. Ernest Newman somewhere refers to "the tight-lipped Dante, who probably never saw a joke in his life"—but possibly he has not read him, and is only going by the appearance of the not very authoritative sixteenth-century bust. Bishop Boyd-Carpenter, in his preface to Warren Vernon's *Readings on the Paradiso* excuses Dante's failings in this respect: "He may be said with justice to be lacking in humour; but amid the stern and sublime regions through which he takes us, the lack of a quality which would be incongruous is little missed." John Jay Chapman—a modern American writer who has translated some select passages of

the *Comedy* into dislocated *terza rima*—lets himself go at length upon
the subject:

> Dante's attempts at humour are lamentable. The demons who fight in the
> air above the pitchy sea—and who are introduced as a sort of black *scherzo*
> —raise no smile in us, but remind us of Dante the traveller who left the ice
> on the face of a culprit after he had promised to remove it, and who describes
> with gusto the sewn-up eyelids of the gentry in Purgatory. Dante's cruelty
> ruins his humour. There are a few kindly greetings during the journey, but
> I can remember only one jovial note in the *Comedy*. It is where the poet
> seems almost to slap Judge Nin on the shoulder as he cries, "Ah, Judge Nin,
> how glad I am not to find you among the cast-aways." [1]

This last outburst is interesting, because it shows how a man may
read Dante with enough appreciation to wish to translate him, and yet
so carelessly as to fall into the grossest inaccuracy. That the "pitchy
sea" is in fact not a sea but a moat is a trifle; and one may pardon a
reader whose interests are more literary than theological for not understanding the profound allegorical significance of Dante's betrayal of
the traitor in the ice. But what is one to say about the "gusto" with
which Dante is accused of describing the sewn-up eyes of the Envious
on the Second Cornice? Here is the passage:

> I looked attentively and, further on,
>   Beheld some shades wrapped up in cloaks, whose grey
>   Could scarcely be distinguished from the stone,
>
> And when we had advanced a little way
>   I heard them crying: "Mary, pray for us,"
>   And, "Michael, Peter, and All Hallows, pray!"
>
> I think there's no man so dispiteous
>   Walking the earth, whose heart would not be stung
>   By what I saw, could he but see them thus;
>
> For when I'd travelled far enough along
>   To make their features plainly visible
>   The heavy sorrow from my eyes was wrung.
>
> It seemed coarse hair-cloth clothed them one and all
>   And each one's shoulder propped his neighbour's head,
>   And all of them were propped against the wall.
>
> In just that way the blind who lack for bread
>   Sit at the pardons, begging for their need,
>   Pillowing each other, all their suffering spread

---

[1] John Jay Chapman: *Dante* (Houghton Mifflin Company, Boston and New
York, 1927), p. 94.

> Before the passer-by, that he may heed
> More quickly, moved not only by their speech
> But by their piteous looks, which likewise plead.
>
> And as no profit of the sun can reach
> Blind men, so with the aforesaid shades; the fire
> Of heaven is niggard of his light to each;
>
> For all their eyelids with an iron wire
> Are stitched and sealed, as to a wild young hawk
> That won't be still, men do to quiet her.
>
> It seemed a kind of outrage thus to walk
> Looking at them, when they could not see me . . .[1]

"Gusto" hardly seems the right word for that long, pitiful exordium, leading up to the stanza about the wild hawk, in which the tenderness for the suffering souls seems somehow to overflow upon the bird, and followed as it is by that oddly moving touch of sensitive and instinctive courtesy:

> *A me pareva andando fare oltraggio,*
> *Veggendo altrui, non essendo veduto.*

Virgil gives Dante permission to make his presence known by speaking, and he proceeds:

> My other side, the praying shadows kept
> Their places still, and through the ghastly seam
> Squeezing slow drops to bathe their cheeks, they wept.
>
> "O people," I began, being turned to them,
> "Assured of looking on that one great good
> Your hearts desire, the heavenly light supreme . . ."[2]

Observe the delicacy of this greeting. Dante does not, in the modern manner, affect to notice no difference between the shades and himself; neither does he thrust upon them any of that condescending pity by which sighted people so frequently make themselves offensive to the blind. Not crudely, but allusively and with infinite tact, he conveys to them that he has observed their affliction and recognises it for what it is—the sign that their penitence is accepted, the certain promise of the

---

[1] *Purg.* xiii. 49–74.   [2] *Purg.* xiii. 85–90.

great vision to come. His words may indeed be an encouragement, if the spirits deign to accept them so—yet who is he to encourage those who are already beyond him on the road to Heaven? *They* are *assured* of a blessed eternity—*he* is not; privileged as he is to behold the Last Things while yet in the flesh, he remains mortal and fallible. He must not presume openly to pity or encourage; modestly, as to his superiors, he congratulates them and bids them god-speed; let them receive it as celestial courtesy may dictate.

So subtle is Dante; such is the lovely precision of line with which he expresses and defines the contours of a feeling thought. It seems on the face of it unlikely that a poet capable of this should portray himself elsewhere as crying with back-slapping familiarity to another "elect spirit": "O good man! How glad I am to see you're not damned!" Nor, of course, does he. As the use of the past tense (*quanto mi piacque* —how glad I was) should have shown the slap-dash Mr. Jay Chapman, that cry of relief is addressed, not to Judge Nino, but to the reader. If it strikes us as funny that the pilgrim Dante should confess to any doubts about his friend's salvation, we must remember he had seen the obduracy in damnation of many people whom he had loved, reverenced or admired—Aldobrandi, Rusticucci, Francesca, Farinata, Brunetto Latini, Virgil himself—and had not found it funny at all. He is rejoiced to know that Nino at any rate is saved, and he candidly says so—but not to Nino. With him he exchanges *"bel salutar"* and we may be sure that the salutation was a courteous one.

I have dealt with Mr. Jay Chapman at more length than, perhaps, he deserves, because his observations illustrate very clearly three errors which will prevent us from discovering the true quality of Dante's humour, or indeed of anything else about him. The first is sheer careless reading—Dante, the compact and exact, is more intolerant even than most poets of the impressionistic and the *à peu près*. The second is irrelevant period prejudice—in this case, the early twentieth-century feeling that anything to do with religion should be very soothing and spiritual, and that it is not quite kind or nice to say bluntly that suffering really hurts. The third is a sort of mental short-windedness, which prevents many people—especially modern people, brought up on headlines, snappy paragraphs, and digests—from reading a long poem as a connected whole. What the average reader looks for is comic lines and episodes—and these are rare in Dante. What the reader will find, if he looks for it, is rather a comic attitude, a diffused spirit of high comedy permeating the whole poem, and springing from two main

roots: the characterisation (particularly where Dante's own self-por-
traiture is concerned) and the satiric intention. This means that comedy
often lurks in innocent-looking lines which in themselves are not funny
at all. They are funny only in the whole context, as the delicate touches
by which a comic character or situation is built up; and their effect is
cumulative. They are not likely to evoke a loud guffaw—an appreci-
ative smile or a soft chuckle of inward delight at most will greet them,
and only from the reader who follows the story with attention and
remembers what he reads.

The very passage from which we have just quoted about the Cornice
of the Envious, contains an example of this. On the previous page, I
omitted a couple of stanzas, which I will now restore to their context:

> It seemed a kind of outrage thus to walk
>   Looking at them, when they could not see me:
>   I turned to my wise mentor, but of talk
>
> There was no need, for he right easily
>   Guessed what the dumb would say, nor stayed for it:
>   "Speak—to the point and briefly, please," said he.
>
> Virgil was now abreast of me, to wit
>   That side the cornice whence, if you mis-stept
>   You'd fall, since there's no girding parapet.[1]

From these matter-of-fact and seemingly innocent lines, little threads
of laughter run back to the Dark Forest and forward into the sublim-
ities of Paradise. Dante, aware of himself from within as poet and
prophet (and no man was ever more candidly aware of his own greatness) is able simultaneously to look upon himself from without and
see himself with the eyes of Virgil and of Beatrice as an inquisitive
child, a gauche adolescent, an absent-minded potterer, a nervous ass,
a burden, a bore, and a nuisance. He is under no delusions about
himself—the whole fabric of the *Comedy* is tremulous with his self-
mockery. That he has qualities for which he can be loved and valued
he admits by implication, but it is only gradually that he shows us
Virgil's faint irritation turning to a tender paternal affection, neither
does he ever allow Beatrice's heavenly charity to obscure for her that
sense of his absurdity which keeps her so humanly and characteristically feminine.

[1] *Purg.* xiii. 73–81.

Consider that opening scene on the edge of the Forest. Virgil is there, not because he particularly wants to meet Dante, but because he is eager to oblige Beatrice. His first impression of his new pupil is scarcely prepossessing, and his own attitude remains rather cold. Dante is running away in a fright; to his frenzied appeal for assistance Virgil replies by disclosing his own identity, and adds, rather sternly: "But you? Why are you running the wrong way? Why aren't you climbing the Blissful Mountain?" This unlooses a torrent of speech: "What! you are Virgil? the great Virgil? What a marvellous writer you are! May I ask a favour, because you are my favourite author and I know your books by heart and have modelled my style on yours. I have been greatly complimented on my style. Do please get me out of this—I am terrified of the Wolf." [1] Stripped of its poetic dress, this kind of mixture of *Schwärmerei* and egotism reaches established writers, even to-day, by every post, and exasperates them almost beyond endurance. Ignoring the compliments, Virgil looks at Dante, now reduced to tears and hysteria, and says firmly: "This won't do. You'll never get past the Wolf. You'll have to come the other way with me." Dante accepts with enthusiasm, but in the next Canto gets cold feet, and offers a whole string of ingenious excuses—nine jumbled and breathless stanzas long. Virgil brushes them all aside: "If," he begins, with a suave and deadly irony, "if I have rightly grasped what you are saying—*se io ho ben la tua parola intesa*—you are overcome with cowardice. Listen now, and get rid of this fear." And having explained his errand and Beatrice's part in it, he concludes: "What on earth is the matter with you? Why can't you have courage when three such blessed Ladies are looking after your interests in the court of Heaven, and when I have assured you of such a happy result?" "You and Beatrice have made a new man of me," says Dante, in effect: "let's go. I have no will but yours—you are my master, leader and lord." [2]

On these terms they at length set forward—and one does not get the impression that Dante has exactly distinguished himself, or that Virgil's feelings about the matter can be anything much more cordial than a strong sense of duty, and an impatient contempt held in polite control by the Four Cardinal Virtues.

As master and pupil proceed upon their journey, we are aware of certain misunderstandings and maladjustments. Sometimes, as on approaching Acheron, Dante asks too many questions or asks at the

---

[1] *Inf.* i. 67 *sqq.*   [2] *Inf.* ii. 10 *sqq.*

wrong moment. (Here we must allow for the poet's short-hand method of writing. A passage like:

> . . . *Maestro, or mi concedi*
> *ch'io sappia quali sono, e qual costume*
> *le fa parer di trapassar si pronte*
> *com'io discerno per lo fòco lume* . . .[1]

with its rove-over endings, its cramming of two or three questions within as many lines, and its final confession that that talker can't really see the people he is talking about, stands for a whole spate of excited chatter that would do credit to a Miss Bates, and which a realistic prose-writer would-expand into a long paragraph).[2] Sometimes, abashed by Virgil's rebuke, he fails to ask a question when a question would have been appropriate. (I am never quite certain whether Virgil's *"tu non dimandi che spiriti son questi"* [3] in Canto iv. 31–32 is a reproach or an encouragement—whether he means: "Why don't you ask?" or "I see that you are politely restraining your curiosity, and so I will tell you.") Sometimes he asks silly questions—"What is this Luck, who seems to get her claws on all the good things of life?" [4] or thoughtless ones to which he might have found the answer himself, so that he lets himself in for a scolding:

> "What error has seduced thy reason, pray,"
> Said he: "thou art not wont to be so dull—
> Or are thy wits wool-gathering miles away?
>
> Hast thou forgot the doctrine of thy school . . .? " [5]

And on more than one occasion he refrains from asking the question and only thinks it—whereupon Virgil disconcerts him by a little thought-reading, as he does among the Tombs of the Heretics, or in the matter of Geryon. But always Dante asks questions, incessantly he talks, repeatedly he dallies, in spite of repeated admonitions to be brief, to be precise, to remember that the allotted time is short. He

---

[1]   "Sir", said I, "pray tell
Who these are, what their custom, why they seem
   So eager to pass over and be gone—
If I may trust my sight in this pale gleam".
                         Inf. iii. 72–75.

[2] The passage is imitated, of course, from *Aen.* vi. 318–320, where the question is not asked until Aeneas and his guide have reached the river's bank.

[3] thou dost not ask what spirits these are?
                         Inf. iv. 31–32.

[4] *Inf.* vii. 68–69.   [5] *Inf.* xi. 76–79.

dallies with Farinata, expatiating, arguing, asking questions which it would take weeks to answer; he implores to be allowed to wait and speak to the Thievish Flame which holds Ulysses; in the Bolgia of the Schismatics he dawdles until Virgil asks him sharply whether he intends to count all the souls in it—

> "Consider, the place is twenty-two miles round,
> And already the moon is underneath our feet"—[1]

and in the Bolgia of the Falsifiers he lingers so eagerly listening to the disagreeable dispute of Sinon with Master Adam that he earns a reproof not merely for idle curiosity but for downright vulgarity.

Moreover, he is heedless. Forever timid where courage is called for, he is also forever reckless where commonsense would dictate caution. He forgets his heavy body, and goes "bemused", while the stones roll away under his clumsy human feet; or he hangs out perilously from lofty bridges at imminent risk to his neck, or we hear Virgil's anxious voice as he pushes him up the crag between the Fifth Bolgia and the Sixth: "Try this stone, now that—be sure before you move that it will bear your weight".[2] He is a trying companion. Before the gates of Dis, when the Angelic Messenger passes them, with his terrible still face, Virgil exhorts him to "be still, and bow to him".[3] Be still—this is no moment for fidgeting or twittering, still less for an outburst of volubility beginning with that familiar bleat *"Ma dimmi . . ."* [4] which punctuates all Dante's conversation. But it is hard to repress Dante. You may squash him, silence him, reduce him to blushes and confusion, but he bobs up again like a cork, eager to see all that there is to be seen and to learn all that there is to be learnt. Terrified one moment, rash the next, but always inquisitive and talkative, he prattles his way through Hell and Purgatory; and as he goes, his real charm and child-like impulsiveness get the better of Virgil, whose manner to him grows more and more indulgent and fatherly as the journey proceeds. Sweetly and subtly the tone of their exchanges alters: "*Virgilio*", "*dolce padre mio*", take the place of "*maestro*" and "*signore*", and a tenderer accent creeps into Virgil's "*figliol*". We see Dante gradually learning his lesson, finding his feet, establishing a happier and more elastic relationship with the great Pagan who is so wholly his superior in virtue and knowledge, and his inferior only in the gifts of Grace. Already by the time the centre of the Universe is reached, Dante has gained sufficient self-assurance to dig his toes in.

[1] *Inf.* xxix. 8–10.   [2] *Inf.* xxiv. 28–29.   [3] *Inf.* ix. 87.   [4] but tell me.

> "Up on thy legs!" the master said; "the way
> Is long, the road rough going for the feet,
> And at mid-terce already stands the day." [1]

But Dante has a whole host of questions to ask, and he will not budge
until he gets an answer:

> "One moment, sir," said I, when I had risen;
> "Before I pluck myself from the Abyss,
> Lighten my darkness with a word in season.
>
> Kindly explain: What's happened to the ice?
> What's turned him upside-down? or in an hour
> Thus whirled the sun from dusk to dawning skies?" [2]

This time he is not rebuked—only rallied upon his weak grasp of
cosmography; and the questions are answered fully and at once.

It is tiresome, ineffective, and above all unfair to the poet, to under-
score with heavy-handed emphasis the dainty touches by which the
comedy of the *Comedy* is brushed in; humour so reticent and of such
masterly economy ought not to be mauled about and pinned on the
dissecting table. Only, when we read such passages as the one I began
by quoting, we must have our ears open for the echoes of other lines,
other situations. We must feel the whimsical resignation with which
Virgil silently moves over to that side of his feckless charge "from
which one might fall, since there is no parapet"; we must smile at the
recollection of Dante's prolonged parleying with Farinata, and be
pleased to notice how far his style and manners have improved since
then:

> "*O gente sicura*,"
> *Incominciai*, "*di veder l'alto lume . . .*" [3]

The smile of amusement melts into a smile of pure pleasure and by
the end of the stanza we have perhaps forgotten why we began to
smile.

But we shall smile at Dante again. We shall smile appreciatively
when, on the steps leading up to the Cornice of Sloth, Dante has been
listening to Virgil's great discourse on Love:

> Thus the great teacher closed his argument,
> And earnestly perused my face to see
> Whether I now appeared to be content;

---

[1] *Inf.* xxxiv. 94–96. [2] *Inf.* xxxiv. 100–105.
[3] "O people", I began, "assured of beholding the light above".
Purg. xii. 85–86.

> While I, though a new thirst tormented me,
> Kept outward silence, and within me said:
> "My endless questions weary him, maybe."

> But he, true father that he was, had read
> My timid, unvoiced wish, and now by speech
> Nerved me to speech, and so I went ahead . . .[1]

It is the scene by Acheron over again—but with a difference. The verbal echo is unmistakable:

> *Allor con gli occhi vergognosi e bassi,*
> *temendo no l'mio dir gli fussi grave,*
> *infino al fiume dal parlar mi trassi . . .*[2]

> *Di fuor taceva e dentro dicea, "Forse*
> *lo troppo domandar, ch'io fo, gli grave"* . . .[3]

Such echoes abound in Dante, and are never without significance. He spins his verse as a spider spins her thread—the least vibration at any point makes the whole web quiver.

So we shall smile again when Dante, following Virgil and Statius along the ledge, and not liking to interrupt their conversation, compares himself to a little stork, flapping its wings with eagerness to fly, and then dropping back, afraid to leave the nest:

> *Tal era io con voglia accesa e spenta*
> *di domandar, venendo infino all'atto*
> *che fa colui ch'a dicer s'argomenta.*[4]

We smile again when, in Paradise, he asks a foolish question and Beatrice, "after a sigh of pity" turns her eyes towards him "with that

---

[1] *Purg.* xviii. 1–9.

[2] Abashed I dropped my eyes; and, lest unmeet
   Chatter should vex him, held my tongue, and so
   Paced on with him, in silence and discreet,

   To the riverside . . .
                              Inf. iii. 79–81.

[3] *Purg.* xviii. 5–6.

[4]   just so was I—

   On fire to ask, but quenched as soon as lit;
   I got as far as making sounds like one
   About to speak, and then thought better of it.
                              Purg. xxv. 13–15.

look a mother casts on her delirious child."[1] We know that not only does Dante know his own absurdity, but that he also knows (a rare thing in the male) exactly how absurd all men appear in the eyes of the women who are fond of them—admirable, adorable, maybe, but always delirious children. We smile when we find him hesitating between two eager questions "like a man between two foods equally distant and appetising; like a lamb between two wolves or a dog between two hinds",[2] till Beatrice comes to his rescue. We smile when, abashed by the knowledge that in Heaven all his thoughts are known, he has to be urged by Cacciaguida to speak aloud, for the pleasure of hearing his voice ring out "secure and bold and joyous".[3] We smile when at last Beatrice, that heavenly schoolmistress, proudly presents him to be examined in the Faith by SS. Peter and James and John, and he steps forward to say his piece: "Even as the baccalaureate arms himself, but does not speak until the master sets forth the question . . . so did I arm myself while she was saying this, so that I might be ready for so distinguished an examiner and so important a profession."[4]

Sometimes the comedy, while equally delicate and allusive, is more concentrated and elaborated than the examples we have so far quoted, and builds up into a tiny comic scene. Almost the whole of the Fourth Canto of the *Purgatory* is steeped in comedy, whose scattered elements at length combine to produce the enchanting little dialogue with Belacqua. Dante and Virgil begin by negotiating the steep and narrow fissure that leads from the first to the second Terrace—a task so breathless that the very verse jolts and rattles with the strain:

> *Vassi in San Leo e discendesi in Noli . . .*

> You can mount up to San Leo or to Noli scramble down,
> You can tackle tall Bismantova and clamber to the top
> On your two flat feet; but this way has to be flown . . .[5]

and having duly "flown" on the wings of desire, they are confronted by a further ascent up the grassy slopes of the Mountain, which soars up out of sight with a gradient of 45°.

> Soon I grew weary and began to bleat:
> "Stop, stop, dear father! See, I shall get stuck
> All by myself here, if thou wilt not wait."[6]

Encouraged by Virgil, however, he hauls himself up, and they both sit

[1] *Para.* i. 100–102.   [2] *Para.* iv. 1–6.   [3] *Para.* xv. 67.
[4] *Para.* xxiv. 46–51.   [5] *Purg.* iv. 25–27.   [6] *Purg.* iv. 43–45.

down to measure the distance they have climbed, "for", says Dante, "it's grand thus to look back, and gives all travellers pleasure." The unexpected appearance of the sun in the north-east leaves Dante dumb-founded, and offers Virgil the occasion for a little astronomy lesson— in which, I may say, his pupil shows himself a good deal more intelli-gent than most of the modern people on whom I have tried the passage —and their conversation ends with a beautiful assurance:

> "This mount is such," he answered, "that to those
> Starting at the foot it's hard in the extreme;
> The more they climb, the easier it grows;
>
> Therefore, when the ascent of it shall seem
> Right pleasant to thee, and the going smooth
> As when a boat floats downward with the stream,
>
> That will be journey's end, and then in sooth
> After long toil, look thou for ease at last;
> More I can't say, but this I know for truth."
>
> He'd hardly spoken when, from somewhere fast
> Beside us, came a voice which said, "Maybe
> Thou'lt need to sit ere all that road is passed."
>
> At this we both glanced round inquiringly,
> And on our left observed a massive boulder,
> Which up till then we had not chanced to see.
>
> This, when explored, revealed to the beholder
> A group of persons lounging in the shade,
> As lazy people lounge, behind its shoulder.
>
> And one of them, whose attitude displayed
> Extreme fatigue, sat there and clasped his knees,
> Drooping between them his exhausted head.[1]

This is too much for Dante, who either has forgotten how much prodding he needed on the way up and how glad he was to sit down or—with some justice—feels that this particular shade is not exactly in a position to jeer at him.

> "O good my lord," said I, "pray look at this
> Bone-lazy lad, content to sit and settle
> Like sloth's own brother, taking of his ease."

---

[1] *Purg.* iv. 91–108.

Then he gave heed, and turning just a little
Only his face upon his thigh, he grunted:
"Go up then thou, thou mighty man of mettle!"

I knew him then; and proved that, though I panted
Still from the climb, I was not so bereft
Of breath, I could not reach him if I wanted.

When I drew near him, he would scarcely shift
His head to say, "Nay, hast thou—really, though—
Grasped why the sun's car drives upon thy left?"

My lips twitched at the grudging speech and slow
Gestures . . .[1]

Dante smiles, because Belacqua is lazy Belacqua still, and because it
is pleasant to be reminded of old times, and because he is glad to know
that he need feel no further anxiety about his friend's salvation; but
if *we* smile, it is because Belacqua has so shrewdly touched off Dante's
little foibles—his self-approval, his eagerness in undertaking and his
readiness to be discouraged half-way (we have not forgotten his haver-
ings in the Dark Forest), his "'satiable curiosity" and passion for
scientific explanations; and also because it is pleasant to see Dante the
poet—that sour, grim, tight-lipped, acrimonious, and self-conceited
person—taking this humorous and depreciatory view of himself. It
is immediately after this scene that Dante stops climbing and turns
back, tickled in his vanity to hear the shades cry out with surprise on
realising that he casts a shadow and is a living man.

> *E vidile guarder per maraviglia*
> *pur me, pur me, e il lume ch'era rotto.*[2]

Whereat Virgil is down upon him like a ton of bricks:

> *che ti fa ciò che quivi si pispiglia?* [3]

Then there is, of course, the entrancing scene, much higher up the
mountain, when Statius says that to have lived when Virgil was alive

---

[1] *Purg.* iv. 109–122.

[2]   and saw them stand and stare
At me, me only, and the broken light.
                    Purg. v. 8–9.

[3]   what does it matter
To thee what they are whispering over there?
                    Purg. v. 11.

he would gladly consent to undergo another year of Purgatory, and Virgil makes Dante a sign to be silent, but Dante gives the show away by grinning.[1] I remember how this passage delighted me when I first read it and how I wrote to the late Charles Williams about it. "Dante", I said, "*would* of course be simply bursting with his exciting secret, and *would* smile mysteriously, and *would* get himself into a small, preposterous social jam half-way up Purgatory Hill between a gentleman who wished to avoid publicity and a redeemed but still dignified gentleman who thought he was being made game of. That *happened* somewhere—probably in Florence, when one was very young, and found one's self trapped between two grown-ups, one of them making admonitory faces, and the other saying, Speak up, boy! And it's such *delicate* fun, moving in and out from the great style into laughter and back again as smoothly as a snake crossing a stream. '*Frate, non far, chè tu se'*, *ombra ed ombra vedi*' [2]—style, *style*, STYLE! It looks so easy, and how does he manage it?"

It pleases me to quote that letter now, because it expresses an immediate and untutored reaction to Dante; that is the way the comedy of the *Comedy* hits one if it is given a chance to make its own impact, and if one has never read any of the solemn books which assert that "the poet is without humour".

And here is another passage—to my mind the supreme instance of Dante's comedy—that very highest kind of comedy which is shot through with human pathos, and which, as Goethe said of Molière: "*côtoie sans cesse le comique et n'y tombe jamais*."[3] The great journey of self-knowledge and purgation is well-nigh finished; there remains only one more river to cross—and that is the river of fire which runs round the Cornice of the Lovers. Here, if ever, is the chance for Dante to represent himself as the perfect lover, daring all things for the love of his lady. Throughout, the name of Beatrice has been a spur to revive his lagging courage and exhausted limbs, and here is the final test. "He is", says one commentator,[4] "perfectly frank about his cowardice, and no argument can persuade him to go on until Virgil says: But Beatrice is on the other side! and immediately the terrified pilgrim

---

[1] *Purg.* xxi. 100 *sqq.*
[2]   "Brother, do not so,
For shade thou art, and look'st upon a shade".
           Purg. xxi. 131–132.
[3] "Continually skirts the brink of the comical without ever falling into it"—*cit.* Emile Faguet: *Dix-Septième Siècle* (Paris), p. 276.
[4] Alice Curteyne: *A Recall to Dante* (Sheed & Ward, 1932), p. 146.

plunges into the fire." But the whole pitiful, charming absurdity of the thing is that he does nothing of the sort. Even after the mention of Beatrice he continues to hesitate, and the final manner of his going is discreetly veiled. How can any reader so miss the point—so romantically simplify and sentimentalise Dante's unflinching analysis of his own weakness? Once again I look back to my own impressions, jotted down hot-and-hot at the first reading:

"Does he leap into the wall of fire with a resounding cry, 'For God and Beatrice!'? Not a bit of it. He comes over as limp as a corpse— *quale è colui che nella fosse è messo* [1]—bending forward over his clasped hands (one knows that queasy clutch at the pit of the stomach,) he 'powerfully imagines—*immaginando forte*—burnt bodies he has seen': just the nasty trick a strong visual imagination plays on you in the middle of an air-raid, the penalty of being sensitive and poetic and all that. Some nasty, charred thing that has been lurking at the back of your eyeballs for years comes horribly up at you, and you imagine *hard*. Not helpful, of course, but that is what you do. So Virgil coaxes him like a child—'*Ricordati, ricordati e, se io Sopr'esso Gerion ti guidai salvo, Che farò ora . . .?*' [2] Can't you trust Nanny? (Can you hell!); promises him, 'It won't hurt you—if you don't believe me, try it on something that doesn't matter—*fatti far credenza con le tue mani al lembo de' tuoi panni*'.[3] No response—he stands, toes dug in, mute and miserable. Then Virgil holds out the big bribe: '*Or vedi, figlio, Tra Beatrice e te è questo muro.*' [4] Then indeed he turns, not to the fire but to Virgil—only the eyes turn, large and frightened, as the eyes of the dying Pyramus turned to Thisbe. And Virgil shakes his head, rallying him '*Come? Volemci star di qua?*—Are we to stay here after all?', and smiles, 'as though to a child that is won over by an apple,' then finally: 'Statius, if you will go behind him . . .' There is a certain reticence about the crucial moment—*did he go, or was he pushed?* I *think* there is

---

[1] even as one that's carried to the tomb.
[2] "Remember, O remember! and if clear
    From harm I brought thee, even on Geryon's back,
    What shall I now . . .?"
                     Purg. xxvii. 23–24.
[3] "Prove it—go close, hold out a little bit
    Of thy skirt's hem in thine own hand, and try".
                     Purg. xxvii. 29–30.
[4]   "Look, my son", he said,
   "Twixt Beatrice and thee there is this wall".
         Purg. xxvii. 35–36.

a convulsive start—better to go *before* one is pushed—and the humiliating consciousness that it's no good trying to bolt, because one will
be caught and stopped. It is not heroic, but how one sympathises!
Divine Comedy?—divine, no doubt, but certainly comedy even in the
narrower sense of the word." [1]

Such was my first, immediate, innocent and prejudiced judgment.
And yet—"the poet was without humour": and it is possible to read
whole volumes of erudite commentary without ever learning from
them that there is comedy in the *Comedy*. It seems to be one of those
things which are hidden from the wise and learned and revealed unto
babes. One must leave it at that. Nobody can be argued into laughter.
Some people find Jane Austen tedious, while splitting their sides
over American comic strips which bore Miss Austen's admirers to
tears.

There is, it is true, another kind of laughter in Dante—a laughter
which shocks and scarifies; the laughter which people like John Jay
Chapman have in mind when they say that Dante's "attempts at
humour are lamentable". But this kind is not humour at all, nor meant
to be—it is the terrible satiric laughter, the laughter of a Dean Swift,
bitter and coarse and cruel. Dante can wield that great lash—but, true
enough, it does not make us smile. It is intended to make us wince, and
it does. Only a very few poets, and those the greatest, have both kinds
of laughter at command. The same hand that wrote *Timon of Athens*
wrote *The Tempest*, but Swift cannot write like Jane Austen, nor Jane
Austen like Swift. Dante, who outgoes the one in strength and the
other in tenderness, is one of the great ones; and it is only when one
has understood his mocking gentleness that one can admire, or even
abide, his ruthless mockery.

The whip—as is fitting—cracks loudest in Hell; that is why it is
often supposed to be more characteristic of Dante than the other
laughter, since twenty people have skimmed through the *Inferno* for
one who has read the *Purgatorio* or the *Paradiso*. It makes an ugly
noise—but Hell is full of ugly noises: that is its nature. We are all still
unconsciously influenced by Byron, and disposed to believe that the
Prince of Darkness is a gentleman. Dante knew better. He knew that
for all his façade of dark beauty, proud defiance, and stoicism in suffering, the Devil is a fool, and a vulgar fool at that. With a kind of ghastly
buffoonery, he strips away the exterior show and displays the disgusting and ridiculous fact of evil. The demons of the Fifth Bolgia are

[1] See also Note at the end of this paper.

grotesque and detestable—rat-catchers in a sewer; and the rats themselves are no better. All are tarred with the same pitch.

> Down bobbed the swimmer, and up in a writhing knot,
>   But the fiends beneath the archway yelled as he rose up,
>   "No sacred Face will help thee here! it's not
>
> A Serchio bathing-party! Now then toes up
>   And dive! 'Ware hooks! To save thyself a jabbing
>   Stay in the pitch, nor dare to poke thy nose up!"
>
> Then, with a hundred prongs clawing and stabbing:
>   "Go cut thy capers! Try down there to do
>   Sub-surface deals and secret money-grabbing!" [1]

The devils fork up Ciampolo—streaming, shining, sleeked head to
heel in the black pitch, "looking like an otter". He whines and jeers;
they pull bits off him, like nasty children tormenting flies; he offers to
betray his fellow-sinners; the devils fall for the trick; he escapes and
they turn tooth and nail on one another; they tumble into the pitch
and are left squabbling and scalding. "*O tu che leggi, udirai nuovo ludo*".[2]
But there is nothing here for smiles, or for the thing called a "sense
of humour". What laughter there is, when Hell thus preys on Hell, is
of a dreadful sort: "He that dwelleth in the Heavens shall laugh them
to scorn; the Lord shall have them in derision."

Hell preys on Hell—Hell gibes at Hell: in the "bottom of sin" there
is neither humanity nor sympathy nor decency. The traitors hasten
to denounce one another, and their brutal witticisms echo under the
stone vault and over the unyielding ice.

> "Thou shalt not find, search all Caina through,
>   Two shades more fit to stand here fixt in jelly . . ."
>
>   "Hey, Bocca, what's to do?
>   Don't thy jaws make enough infernal chatter
>   But, what the devil? must thou start barking too?" . . .
>
> "He wails the Frenchmen's *argent*, treason's price;
>   'Him of Duera,' thou shalt say, 'right clear
>   I saw, where sinners are preserved in ice' " . . .
>
> "He is Ser Branca d'Oria; in this pit's
>   Cold storage he has lain this many a year . . ."[3]

---

[1] *Inf.* xxi. 46–54.
[2] New sport, good Reader! Hear this merry prank.
                    Inf. xxii. 118.
[3] *Inf.* xxxii. 106–108; 115–117; xxxiii. 137–138.

If we want to know whether we are expected to find these sour japes humorous, or even agreeable, we may turn back to the end of the 30th Canto, where Dante stands, all agog, listening to Sinon and Master Adam, "between whom" (in the words of Dante's nineteenth-century translator, the Rev. Ichabod Wright, a respectable Oxford don, who should have known better), "takes place a most comical dialogue." Neither Dante's absorption, nor (one may imagine) Mr. Wright's idea of fun, wins any approval from Virgil: "*chè voler ciò udire è basso voglio*—It's vulgar to enjoy that kind of thing." [1]

What hampers the Anglo-Saxon in his judgment of satiric poetry is his fixed idea that all laughter ought to be kindly and all humour good-humoured. If he combines with this the notion that all religion ought to be sweetly consolatory and perfectly refined and "nice", and the humanistic delusion that wickedness is more a misfortune than a fault, he will find himself in a position where he is hopelessly out of key—not only with Dante, but also with both the Old Testament and the New. If his critical judgment is not to be seriously impaired, he must, while reading the *Commedia*, accept the central Christian affirmations —that holiness is a joy to those that love it and a horror to those that hate it; that sin is a hideous illusion and Hell the wilful persistence in that illusion; that Redemption is bought with blood and tears; that Love is most truly a "lord of terrible aspect".[2] He must not take evil lightly, but know it as the proper object—indeed the only proper object—of the emotions of wrath and scorn.

Between this satiric laughter and the laughter that arises from the sense of the comic there is a great gulf fixed. Both, indeed, arise from an apprehension of Man's inadequacy: his pretensions are so vast and his nature so limited; his immortal destiny so high and his mortal achievements so petty. But there the likeness ends. The comic spirit can afford to be indulgent to man, because, when all is said and done, it rates him but as a poor creature from whom little is to be expected. It looks on him and all his works as Dr. Johnson looked on learned women or dogs walking on their hind legs—the thing is not well done but it is a marvel that it is done at all. Indeed, without God's grace, it never can be done. But satire looks upon man in his noblest potentiality, and rages that he should fall so short of his divine self. It is aware of the profound tragedy of the human situation, and its harsh laughter bears witness to an agony of the spirit. One might say of satire that it is the exact inverse of the spirit of high comedy: that it is

[1] *Inf.* xxx. 148.   [2] *Vita Nuova*, iii.

a form of tragedy, "*qui côtoie sans cesse le tragique et n'y tombe jamais*".

Let us look once again, more closely, at those 21st and 22nd Cantos of the *Inferno*, through which the ugly satiric laughter blares and brays as harshly as that *diversa cennamella* [1] which sets the demons marching along the bank of the Fifth Bolgia. If our critical ears are not deafened by the clamour, we shall hear the soft undercurrent of the more heavenly mirth run chuckling all the way along, like wood-wind among the brass. Virgil, serene in the consciousness of his innate virtue and the protection of the celestial powers, strides down to confront the devils at the bridge-head, bidding his companion to hide his terrified and shrinking person behind the crags. He reassures him with what, if it were not Virgil speaking, would sound almost a boast:

> "And whatsoever outrage or displeasure
> They do to me, fear nothing; I have faced
> Frays of this sort before, and have their measure." [2]

We have heard this note in Virgil's voice before: it was conspicuous before the gates of Dis, where the results of a similar encounter were not, when one comes to think of it, wholly satisfactory. No matter. For the moment all goes well. Virgil defies Malacoda and his merry men; he speaks his word of power, which quells all opposition; he calls up to Dante:

> "*O tu, che siedi*
> *tra gli scheggion del ponte quatto quatto*
> *sicuramente omai a me ti riedi.*" [3]

And Dante slithers down—*ratto*;[4] one sees him slipping across, nimble as a mouse when the cat is on the prowl; the demons press forward, and he slinks for safety close to his master's side. He has good reason to fear—or he has at least good satiric reasons for painting his fear in the liveliest colours; for this is the Bolgia of the Barrators, and was not Dante Alighieri to be actually accused of the crime of Barratry, and sentenced to perpetual exile under pain of burning alive? The alleged date of the vision is 1300—the accusation and sentence were to be

---

[1] strange trumpeting.
[2] *Inf.* xxi. 61–63.
[3]   "Thou, cowering there discreet,
Hid mousey-mouse among the splintery, cracked
Crags of the bridge, come down! all's safe for it."
            Inf. xxi. 88–90.
[4] quickly.

promulgated in 1301; in 1300, therefore, at the very moment of this infernal encounter, he may be presumed to be in the very thick of his nefarious practices. If all his enemies said were true, would he not have every cause to shudder at the sight of the boiling pitch? So Dante the politician and poet makes capital out of the alarm of Dante the pilgrim. He chooses this moment to remind his readers, and his accusers, that he was once a soldier; he fought for the Republic and indeed was on the winning side: "Even so did I see the footmen who marched out under treaty from Caprona alarmed at being so closely surrounded by the enemy." [1] But this time it is he who marches out—if you can call it marching—he who is surrounded by enemies who may or may not observe the treaty terms; and the terror is all his—

> *e non torceva gli occhi*
> *dalla sembianza lor ch'era non buona.*[2]

(The Anglo-Saxon ought at any rate to appreciate that meiosis—their looks were "not amiable".)

> They lowered their hooks to the ready, and, "Just for fun,"
> Says one, "shall I tickle his rump for him?" "Yes, try it,"
> Says another, "nick him and prick him, boy—go on!" [3]

But Malacoda is suave. He proposes that a picked band of demons shall escort the travellers and see them safe as far as the next bridge, which is unbroken:

> "I'm sending a squad your way to fork and fix
> Any rash soul who may be taking the air;
> Why not go with them? They will play no tricks." [4]

This kindly offer might inspire confidence, if it were not delivered with such an air of genial ferocity, and if, perhaps, the speaker had waited for an answer, and had not taken so wholly for granted the poets' acquiescence in the *fait accompli*. Without the formality of a pause, the escort are selected; neither their aspect nor their names add any new charm to the prospect—"Ciriatto with the Tusks", "Raving Rubicante", and the rest of the gang—"*ahi! fiera compagnia!*" [5]

---

[1] *Inf.* xxi. 94–96.
[2]   keeping a sharp eye upon
[ɨ] Their looks, which were by no means amiable.
[3] *Inf.* xxi. 100–103.
[4] *Inf.* xxi. 115–117.
[5] Queer company—but there!

Whether or not the names are modelled upon those of the actual Dante's Florentine accusers, the jest is double-edged. The situation is not a pleasant one, and the unhappy pilgrim's nerves go back on him.

> "*O me, maestro, che è quel ch'io veggio?*"
> *diss'io; "deh! senza scorta andiamci soli*
> *se tu sai ir, ch'io per me non la chieggio.*
>
> *Se tu sei si accorto come suoli,*
> *non vedi tu ch'ei digrignan li denti,*
> *e con le ciglia ne minaccian duoli?*"[1]

Virgil rather pooh-poohs all this agitation:

> "I'd have thee firmer-minded—No!
> Let them go grind and gnash their teeth to suit
> Their mood—'tis the broiled souls they glare at so."[2]

The demons, being a vulgar lot, exchange derisive signals—the squad put out their tongues, Malacoda "makes a bugle of his breech", and away they go, Dante (in whom desperation has now reached that point, familiar to the British Tommy, where one can but resign one's self, shrug one's shoulders and take refuge in a proverbial cynicism) merely observing drily: "Queer company! but there! 'With saints to church and with roisterers to the tavern'."[3]

Here, we may say, is just the old, persistent self-mockery. But the thing is a little more complex than that. For poor, foolish Dante, that quivering ready-to-halt Christian, is perfectly right, and Virgil's complacent superiority turns out in the sequel to be as unjustified and as inadequate to the real situation as that of any well-intentioned liberal statesman assuring a nervous House that he "believes Herr Hitler to be an honest man and sincerely eager for peace". It is not at the "broiled souls" that the demons are making faces; they have been gleefully baiting a malicious trap, and Virgil—where, indeed, is his "wonted caution"?—has swallowed the bait, hook, line and sinker. He with

---

[1] "Sir, I don't like the looks of this one bit",
   Said I; "no escort, please; let's go alone,
   If thou know'st how—for I've no stomach to it!

   Where is thy wonted caution? Ugh! they frown,
   They grind their teeth—dost thou not see them? Lo,
   How they threat mischief, with their brows drawn down!"
                                Inf. xxi. 127–132.

[2] *Inf.* xxi. 133–135.
[3] *Inf.* xxii. 14–15.

his high-minded pagan rationalism has no means of understanding this irrational and meaningless malignity. But Dante has. The abyss of Hell opens upon the profundities of the human heart, and it is perhaps a measure of his progress into self-knowledge that he is quick to recognise and tremble at the fathomless mystery of iniquity.

It will not do to excuse Virgil, and to say that, though he has well grasped the evil intentions of the demons, he thinks it best to assume a bold front in face of an inevitable situation. Virgil is not putting on an act for Dante's benefit; he is actually deceived, and is undeceived only when, in the Bolgia of the Hypocrites, Fra Catalano explains that there is not in fact any unbroken bridge, so that Malacoda's safe-conduct as far as that totally apocryphal point is not worth the snap of a finger.

> Lo duca stette un poco a testa china,
> poi disse: "Mal contava la bisogna
> colui che i peccator di là uncina." [1]

One sees him, standing in thought, turning the insult over in his mind. And the Hypocrite slily rallies him:

> "I heard the Devil's iniquities
> Much canvassed at Bologna; among the rest
> 'Twas said he was a liar, and father of lies." [2]

And Virgil is angry, as he had been angry before, when the gates of Dis were shut in his face, and he shows it:

> With raking steps my guide strode off in haste
> [s'en gì—note the abrupt vigour of the masculine rhyme]

> Troubled in looks, and showing some small heat
> Of anger . . . [3]

The laugh, in fact, is on Virgil. He has been properly fooled. And it is probably not by accident that Fra Catalano is made to quote the saying that the Devil is the father of lies. He heard it "at Bologna", in the School of Theology—but it was not originally spoken at Bologna:

---

[1] My guide stood with bent head and downward look
    Awhile; then said: "He gave us bad advice,
    Who spears the sinners yonder with his hook."
                    Inf. xxiii. 139–141.

[2] *Inf.* xxiii. 142–144.

[3] *Inf.* xxiii. 145–147.

it was spoken by Christ.[1] The timid Christian, and even—perhaps even especially—the corrupt Christian, knows more about the intimate processes of pure evil than any professor of humanism can ever do. The trembling of the individual sinner may be laughable, but the security of the ethical systems to which he flees for shelter are, in a sense, more laughable still. Sooner or later, Morality finds itself fleeing (with that *fretta* which "robs all actions of their dignity")[2] before a naked menace which its calm arguments in favour of the Good Life never contemplated—fleeing as Virgil fled clutching his pupil in his arms:

> And over the flinty edge of the great rift
> He slithered and slid with his back to the hanging spill
> Of the rock that walls one side of the next cleft:
>
> Never yet did water run to the mill
> So swift and sure, where the head-race rushes on
> Through the narrow sluice to hit the floats of the wheel,
>
> As down that bank my master went at a run
> Carrying me off, hugged closely to his breast,
> Truly not like a comrade, but a son.[3]

The rush and speed of the verse, the noble simile that precedes it about the mother with her child, Virgil's devotion, and the general excitement of the story, cannot altogether efface from our minds the humiliating truth that Virgil has been caught on the wrong foot, and that he has to negotiate that cliff with an unseemly rapidity and, not to put too fine a point upon it, on his backside. That is the best that man's philosophy can do for him; "so foolish was I and ignorant, even as it were a beast before Thee".

The gentle laughter makes mock of proud man, of his strength as well as of his weakness. Yet Dante knows that it scarcely becomes Man to sneer at human nature. Tenderness is never absent, nor does the pupil dream of reproaching his master. Virgil strides away, angry with the devils, and angry with himself:

> *ond'io dagl' incarcati mi partì,*
> *dietro alle poste delle care piante.*[4]

---

[1] *Joh.* viii. 44.   [2] *Purg.* iii. 11.

[3] *Inf.* xxiii. 43–51.

[4]   So I left those spirits oppressed,
  Following in the prints of the belovèd feet.
        Inf. xxiii. 147–148.

If we look for a parallel passage to this, we shall find it, in a higher and sweeter key, on the shores of Mount Purgatory, where Virgil is betrayed into lingering with the rest to listen to the song of Casella.[1] If we want to hear the last silver ripple of heavenly laughter at the mild follies of humanity, we shall find it accompanying Beatrice's little smile, when Dante in the Fifth Heaven remains a little too conscious of the "glories of our blood and state".[2]

Dante, his outlook upon humanity firmly controlled from its Christian and Catholic centre, can see Man in both of his contrasted and paradoxical aspects. He sees him as a vessel "frail, though full of God's light"—a creature feeble, foolish, infantile, absurd, yet a child of Grace, coaxed with an infinite Divine tenderness along the path to glory; stumbling, penitent, "transhumanised" and at last "ingodded" amid a celestial paean which is like *"un riso dell 'universo"*.[3] He sees him, in that other aspect, as a thing lower and worse than the brutes or brute-matter, a traitor to God and self, obstinate in the will to destruction, the child of the Devil, the scorn and outcast of creation. The twin laughters pursue him down to the seat of Dis and up to the very steps of the Throne. The damned think highly of themselves; fixed in a ghastly self-sufficiency and rooted in pride, they caper grotesquely to the whips and prongs of an insatiable and demonic appetite; the laughter is terrible and tragic. The redeemed think humbly of themselves and recognise their own folly; for them is the song, the shouting, the celestial dance, revolving like a mill-wheel, spinning like a top— *"e letizia era ferza del paleo"*[4]—for them the laughter of the rejoicing universe, for them the Divine Comedy.

NOTE

It should not be necessary to say—though in fact I find it is—that I do not think there is anything in itself comic about pain and fear. The question is a purely literary one—whether the passage on the Cornice of Fire is written in the "sublime" or "heroic" style appropriate to Tragedy and Epic, or in the style of High Comedy. It

---

[1] *Purg.* iii. 7–9.
[2] *Para.* xvi. 13–15.
[3] a smile of all the universe.
     Para. xxvii. 4–5.
[4] and joy was the whip to the top.
     Para. xviii. 42.

appears to me to admit of but one answer: the repeated assurances that the fire can only hurt and not destroy; the coaxing smiles of Virgil; and, above all, the poet's determined refusal to allow his "hero" to assume any kind of heroic attitude, all belong to Comedy—though to Comedy of the most moving and poignant kind. The distinction is best seen by a comparison with other passages which—differing among themselves in their degree—are yet all authentically "heroic" in their treatment of pain and peril. I have carefully avoided examples in which the hero is facing the *certainty* of death.

Here is the so-called "primitive" epic, with the hero's characteristic air of self-assertion and defiance. The River-god Scamander has been rebuking Achilles for his slaughter of the Trojans:

"Scamander, son of Zeus," replied Achilles the great runner, "your will shall be done. But I am not going to stop killing these arrogant Trojans till I have penned them in their town, tried conclusions with Hector, and found out which of us two is to be the conqueror and which the killed."

With that he fell upon the Trojans once more like a fiend. But now Scamander of the Deep Eddies appealed to Phoebus Apollo. "For shame," he cried, "god of the Silver Bow and Son of Zeus! Is this how you obey your Father? Did he not tell you many times that you were to stand by the Trojans and protect them till the evening dusk should throw its shadows over the fruitful fields?"

When he heard this, the great spearman Achilles leapt from the bank and plunged into the middle of the stream. Scamander rushed on him in spate.

Homer's *Iliad* xxi (trans. E. V. Rieu).

And here Roland, confronted with overwhelming enemy forces, refuses to summon Charlemagne to his aid at the Pass of Roncevaux.

> Dist Oliver: "*Paien unt grant esforz;*
> *De noz Franceis, m'i semblet aveir mult poil.*
> *Cumpaign Rollant, kar sunez vostre corn,*
> *Si l'orrat Carles, si returnerat l'ost.*"
> *Respunt Rollant: "Jo fereie que fols!*
> *En dulce France en perdreie mun los.*
> *Sempres ferreie de Durandal granz colps;*
> *Sanglant en ert li branz entresque l'or.*
> *Felum païen mar i vindrent as porz:*
> *Jo vos plevis, tuz sunt jugez a mort.*"
>
> Chanson de Roland: Laisse lxxxiii.

[Quoth Oliver: "Huge are the paynim hordes,
And of our Frenchmen the number seems but small!

Companion Roland, I pray you sound your horn,
That Charles may hear, and fetch back all his force."
Roland replies: "Madman were I and more,
And in fair France my fame would suffer scorn!
I'll smite great strokes with Durendal my sword,
Bathing the brand high as the hilt with gore.
This pass the paynims reached on a luckless morn;
I swear to you, death is their doom therefor!"]

Here, from "secondary" epic, is an example in which boasting in the
face of unknown perils is replaced by a stoic and silent dignity; Aeneas
is following the Sibyl into Hades. Compare this passage with Dante's
imitation of it at the beginning of *Inf.* iii. and contrast the tone:

ecee autem, primi sub lumina solis et ortus,
sub pedibus mugire solum, et juga coepta moveri
silvarum, visaeque canes ululare per umbram,
adventante dea. "Procul o, procul este, profani,"
conclamat vates, "totoque absistite luco:
tuque invade viam, vaginaque eripe ferrum.
nunc animis opus, Aenea, nunc pectore firmo."
tantum effata, furens antro se inmisit aperto:
ille ducem haud timidis vadentem passibus aequat.
Aen. vi. 255–263.

[But now, when sunrise is at hand and dawning of the day,
The earth falls moaning 'neath their feet, the wooded ridges sway,
And dogs seem howling through the dusk as now she drew anear
The Goddess. "O be far away, ye unclean!" cries the seer.
"Be far away: ah, get ye gone from all the holy wood!
But thou, Aeneas, draw thy steel and take thee to the road;
Now needeth all thy hardihood and steadfast heart and brave."
She spake, and wildly cast herself amidst the hollow cave,
But close upon her fearless feet Aeneas followeth.
Trans. William Morris.]

Here is an example from the Heroic ballad, with the recollection and
invocation of a beloved object:

Round turned he, as not deigning
Those craven ranks to see;
Nought spake he to Lars Porsena,
To Sextus nought spake he;

But he saw on Palatinus
The white porch of his home;
And he spake to the noble river
That rolls by the towers of Rome.

"O Tiber! father Tiber!
To whom the Romans pray,
A Roman's life, a Roman's arms
Take thou in charge this day!"
So he spake, and speaking sheathed
The good sword by his side,
And with his harness on his back
Plunged headlong in the tide.
                    Macaulay: *Lays of Ancient Rome: Horatius.*

Here is a very close parallel from heroic drama. Siegfried is preparing
to leap through the ring of fire to Brunnhilde:

"*Ha! wonnige Gluth! leuchtender Glanʒ!*
Strahlend nun offen steht mir die Strasse.
In Feuer mich baden! im Feuer ʒu finden die Braut!
Ho-ho! Ha-hei!
Jetʒt lock'ich ein liebes Gesell!"
                    (*Horn call*)
                    (*Er stürʒt sich in das wogende Feuer*)
                    Richard Wagner: *Siegfried*, Act III, end of Sc. 2.

[Ha! rapturous glow! glory of light!
Radiant before me now opens the roadway!
To bathe me in fire! in fire to find me a bride!
Ho-ho! ha-hey!
Now I win me a mate to my mind!
(*He plunges into the surging fire*)]

And with lyric tragedy, we come perhaps closer still. Here, in the
scene where Juliet takes the sleeping-potion, are the hesitations, the
fears, the "strong imaginings", the reaction to the thought of the
beloved. Note that the speaker is not a grown man, but a girl of
fourteen, and that she is quite alone.

I have a faint cold fear thrills through my veins,
That almost freezes up the heat of life . . .
Come, vial.
What if this mixture do not work at all?

What if it be a poison, which the friar
Subtly hath minister'd to have me dead? . . .
I will not entertain so bad a thought.
How if, when I am laid into the tomb,
I wake before the time that Romeo
Come to redeem me? There's a fearful point!
Shall I not then be stifled in the vault,
To whose foul mouth no healthsome air breathes in,
And there die strangled ere my Romeo comes?
Or, if I live, is it not very like,
The horrible conceit of death and night,
Together with the terror of the place,
As in a vault, an ancient receptacle,
Where, for these many hundred years, the bones
Of all my buried ancestors are pack'd;
Where bloody Tybalt, yet but green in earth,
Lies festering in his shroud; where, as they say,
At some hours in the night spirits resort;
Alack, alack! is it not like that I,
So early waking, what with loathsome smells,
And shrieks like mandrakes torn out of the earth,
That living mortals, hearing them, run mad:
O! if I wake, shall I not be distraught,
Environed with all these hideous fears,
And madly play with my forefathers' joints,
And pluck the mangled Tybalt from his shroud?
And, in this rage, with some great kinsman's bone,
As with a club, dash out my desperate brains?
O, look! methinks I see my cousin's ghost
Seeking out Romeo, that did spit his body
Upon a rapier's point. Stay, Tybalt, stay!
Romeo, I come! this do I drink to thee.

Shakespeare: *Romeo and Juliet*, IV. iii. 15-59.

The reaction here is immediate, and the scene tragical—particularly
for us who know that the play ends tragically. If the scene were
re-written, introducing the Apothecary and the Nurse, who by
reiterated soothing, coaxing, rallying and scolding should at length
persuade the reluctant girl to swallow the draught, it could scarcely
escape turning into comedy, though comedy of a very poignant kind.

(1949)

THE PARADOXES OF THE *COMEDY*

THE Christian revelation is centred about a paradox—a paradox of identity. This, from the beginning, Dante obscurely knew. Theoretically, he knew it because he was an instructed Catholic; empirically, also, he experienced it, because he loved Beatrice. But in his early life knowledge and experience had not yet been brought into focus so as to produce that duple and stereoscopic vision which is perhaps best called "understanding". After Beatrice had refused him her salutation, his Love appeared to him, no longer as the "Lord of terrible aspect", but as a weeping youth; and he said to him, "Lord of all nobleness, why dost thou weep?" And Love answered: "I am as the centre of the circle to which all parts of the circumference bear a like relation; but with thee it is not so."[1] In the final vision at the end of the *Paradiso*, understanding comes to Dante in a flash, and thereupon

> *volgeva il mio disio e 'l velle,*
> *si come rota ch'igualmente è mossa,*
> *l'amor che muove il sol e l'altre stelle.*[2]

He had come into the centre and was identified with Love. In the most literal sense of the words he was *in* Love, and desire and will moved in perfect stability about that central point. And that which had come to him in that flash of understanding was precisely the quiddity of the revealed paradox—the inner mystery of duality within the mystery of the tri-unity:

> *Veder volea come si convenne*
> *l'imago al cerchio e come vi s'indova.*

"I sought to see how the image (that is to say the Humanity) is conjoined with the circle (that is to say the Godhead) and there has its dwelling"—more literally, its "whereabouts", or its "whereness".[3] The word must, I think, be taken absolutely, in the sense that its

---

[1] *Vita Nuova*, xii.

[2]   Yet, as a wheel moves equal, free from jars,
Already my will and desire were wheeled by love,
The love that moves the sun and the other stars.
                    Para. xxxiii. 143–145.

[3] More literally still: "How it *in-whered* itself there": cf. such similar phrases as "s'india", "s'inluia", "s'io m'intuassi, come tu t'immii", etc. (See above, pp. 53–54)

"where" is "there" unconditionally and not elsewhere. The Humanity and the Godhead of Christ are inseparably conjoined in a single Identity of Person; and, as a corollary, all humanity and every identity made in that Image are in reality centred there and have no other "where".

This truth is, of course, in one sense, a Christian commonplace. Dante did not need to take the long and arduous road through Hell and Purgatory and mount into the Tenth Heaven to be assured that it was so. He had only to read it in the New Testament and to assent to it day by day in the Liturgy and in the Creeds. But to believe, however firmly, *that* a thing is, is not the same thing as to understand it by immediate intuition; it is to know only the *quia* and not the *quid*. The difference is, one may say, like that between reading up the pathology of sex and being actually in love. Virgil, knowing, too late to participate in salvation, the verities of the Gospel, had warned his pupil from the attempt to overpass the limits of human intellect:

> Madness! that reason, lodged in human heads,
>   Should hope to traverse backward and unweave
>   The infinite path Three-personed Godhead treads;
>
> Content you with the *quia*, sons of Eve,
>   For could you have perceived the whole truth plain
>   No need had been for Mary to conceive.[1]

But the pupil of Beatrice, having grasped the *quia* by reason or by faith, is admitted to the vision of the *quid*. Not in his own power, nor in Virgil's power, but by supernatural Grace of which Beatrice and Mary are the vehicles.

Dante is clear about this distinction. The vision of the whole, without diversity or contradiction, is a divine gift. It does not belong to human nature—not even to human nature in its original perfection —but is something superadded. Nature must not indeed be lost in order to attain vision, but it must be "transhumanised". When Dante has finished his purgation, he is restored to the primal perfection of the First Paradise. It is then that he beholds the pageant of the Church, and the Car drawn by the Gryphon, the "single-personed ambiguity",[2] the portent of two natures in one identity. Mr. John D. Sinclair has drawn attention to the sacramental significance of the symbolism here. The attendant spirits cry *Benedictus qui venis*, the hymn that is sung at the

[1] *Purg.* iii. 34–39.
[2] Charles Williams: *The Region of the Summer Stars* (O.U.P., 1950), *Prelude*.

sacring of the Mass; and that which descends upon the car is Beatrice. I say "descends" because that is the word which many commentators use, and because we must suppose that if Beatrice arrives from any "where" in especial, she arrives out of Heaven. But "descends" is not Dante's word. The "ministers and messengers of life eternal" rise upon the car, and through the clouds of their strewn roses and lilies, like the sun at dawn breaking through the mists, *"donna m'apparve"*. Beatrice appears; she is, in the words of the sacramental hymn, "here, we know not how", and the ministers and messengers cry, not *"Benedicta"*, but *"Benedictus qui venis"*. Something or someone, to whom that salutation is not inappropriate, is displayed upon the car, lifted upon it, it would seem, as the Holy Host is lifted and displayed above the ciborium. Whether that identity descends or rises is, perhaps, all one; that which came down from Heaven is that which is also mysteriously raised up. And that which so appears and is so saluted is no stranger to us; it is that which we have loved from the beginning, clothed in a terrible yet familiar beauty so that the blood pounds in our natural veins:

> men che dramma
> di sangue m'è rimaso, che non tremi;
> conosco i segni dell'antica fiamma.[1]

In the presence of this manifestation, Dante confesses his sins and is cleansed in the absolving waters of Lethe. The Virtues and the Graces lead him to Beatrice, praying her to unveil: "Look that thou spare not thine eyes," they say to Dante, "we have set thee before those emeralds whence Love once shot his shafts at thee." [2] And when Dante gazes into the eyes of Beatrice, he sees in them, as in a mirror, "the twy-formed beast beaming within them, now with the one, now with the other nature".[3] Not, however, with both at once. The ambiguity remains ambiguous; it is only that, when it is seen mirrored in the familiar symbol and sacrament of love, it can be known wholly in the one or wholly in the other nature: perfect eagle and perfect lion, perfect God and perfect Man, perfectly whole and perfectly diverse, perfectly infinite and perfectly finite—successively but not in the

---

[1]   there is scarce a dram
That does not hammer and throb in all my blood;
I know the embers of the ancient flame.
Purg. xxx. 46–48.

[2] *Purg.* xxxi. 115–117.
[3] *Purg.* xxxi. 122–123.

eternal instant and simultaneously. In the Earthly Paradise and in the perfection of original innocence we may perceive the paradox perfectly, but not the unifying simplicity which is hidden within the paradox.

Now, whether or not we accept the Christian revelation, it is important when reading a poem like the *Divina Commedia* to remember that this paradox is held by Christian people to be integral to the structure of all that is—to be indeed the ultimate and central fact about the nature of things. It is the centre from which all knowledge radiates and about which all phenomena revolve. It follows from this, as a quite plain and practical formula of literary criticism, that problems and ambiguities in the interpretation of the allegorical symbolism can seldom be settled by an "either-or", but on the contrary usually demand an answer involving "both-and". The significance of characters and situations and of the images generally is likely to be ambivalent; and to dismiss the one sense in order to concentrate upon the other will usually turn out to be one of those false simplifications which lead us into a morass of misunderstanding and eventually bog us down in exaggerations, distortions and absurdities. A ruthless and one-eyed logic will force us to draw wilder and wilder conclusions from our truncated and lopsided premises, till we find ourselves in the Vestibule of the Futile, in full cry after some whirling banner with a very strange device indeed. We shall prove to our own satisfaction that the *Divine Comedy* is an anti-papal tract, a political programme for the Ghibelline party, a Thomist (or anti-Thomist) manifesto, an anagram, a code of ciphers, an incitement to Protestantism, heresy, or atheism; that Beatrice is a myth, an abstraction, a religious vocation, Dante's Muse, or his spiritual self; that Dante was a Dominican, a Franciscan, a Catharist, a black magician, a homosexual—or, for all I know, the pseudonym under which all his works were written by somebody else. Of such perversities there is no end.

I cannot hope to do more here than to indicate a few of the so-called "Dante-problems" which involve ambivalence, and which can be most readily resolved by reference to the paradoxical nature of Christian truth. And before we begin on these, let us look once more at the great image of the wheel and its centre. It is, of course, a favourite one with Dante. He sees the heavenly hierarchies and the whole visible universe held to their centre by the cords of love and spinning about it in that celestial dance of which the spinning of the planets is the symbol and material image. At the centre of that mighty wheeling, at the hub of the *magne rote*,[1] lies the paradox of the double nature. If we liked to modify Dante's Ptolemaic image slightly under the influence of a more modern astronomy, we might say that these planetary orbits are ellipses, of which the foci are the positive and negative poles of the same paradox. The negative pole lies in the Old Testament: it presents us with the paradox of contradiction in identity, and we know it as the myth of the Fall. This is the split in knowledge, by which the sole Reality, which is all God and all good, is known in a double identity: as God and not-God, as reality and illusion, as good and evil, as heaven and hell. The positive pole lies in the New Testament: it presents us with the paradox of identity in contradiction, and we know it as the history of God incarnate. This is the atonement, the making-one: God with Man, Infinite with finite, Eternal with temporal, the Unmoved Mover with the Lamb slain from the foundations of the world, the Basis with the Image, the Reality with the material symbol. It is also, in the strangest paradox of all, the identity of the Sinless with the sinful, so that St. Paul can say boldly of Him who is the "express image of the Father's person" that "He was made sin for us".

You will remember Beatrice's explanation of the "just vengeance" in the Seventh Canto of the *Paradiso*:

> As for the penalty, therefore, inflicted by the cross—if it be measured by the Nature assumed, never did any other bite so justly; and likewise, never was any so outrageous if we look to the Person who assumed it, in whom this Nature was conjoined. So from one act there issued things diverse: God and the Jews rejoiced in the same death; thereat the earth was rent and the heavens opened.[2]

It is matter for profound astonishment that this magnificent statement of Atonement theology should have been accused of Nestorianism— of the heresy, that is, which separates the two Natures in the one Christ. In the contrary, it asserts with almost Apollinarian emphasis that the two Natures are so inextricably united in a single indivisible Person as to make the sentence of the law at the same time wholly just and wholly unjust. In so far as it represents God's judgment of Man it is absolute justice; in so far as it represents Man's judgment of God it is absolute injustice; and it is not possible to qualify either of those pronouncements in any way whatever.

I do not intend to delve any deeper than this into the intricacies of Atonement theology. I draw attention to the passage because it is a

---

[1] the great wheels (i.e. the courses of the heavens).   [2] *Para.* vii. 40–48.

key-passage, and a superb example of Dante's firm and explicit handling of the central Christian paradox. It also represents the moment in which the two foci of the ellipse draw closer together till they merge into that single point "upon which heaven and all nature hang", and the orbits traced by the *magne rote* become perfect circles.

Let us now turn to some of our specific problems. We may begin with Dante himself. He is often said to be arrogant and to have an overwhelming opinion of himself, his virtues and his poetic gifts. He presumes to sit in judgment on his fellow-men, and promote them to bliss or condemn them to torment according to his own taste and fancy. He delivers a lengthy rebuke to Pope Nicholas III, and self-righteously pretends that Virgil heard it with great approval. He represents himself as the privileged favourite of the celestial powers— not only Beatrice but Our Lady herself, Saint Lucy, St. Bernard and innumerable other beatified personages, interrupt their blissful contemplation to rush about and look after him; the souls in Hell and Purgatory are transfixed with astonishment at this preferential treatment. Moreover, he is much too fond of quoting his own poems, and of paying himself compliments about them, through the mouths of Casella, Bonagiunta, Guido Guinicelli and so on; and he makes Homer, Ovid, Lucan and Horace admit him to the company of Virgil and themselves. He speaks (and this not as a character in the poem, but in his own person) of the destined fame of his *Commedia*, to which (he claims) both heaven and earth have set hand, and which ought to win him a crown in this world, at any rate, if not in the next. And so forth and so on. All this is exceedingly true. And yet, as we saw in discussing the comedy of the *Comedy*, one can put together other and more numerous passages from the poem to make the self-portrait of a very different Dante—cowardly, childish, foolish, garrulous and absurd.

What are we to do with these two pictures? It is easy to ignore one of them and put forward the other as "the real Dante"—easy, but also dishonest. It is equally possible to admit them both, and to say that the poet put in the self-depreciatory bits out of hypocrisy, because he thought it was the conventional and Christian thing to do, and that the self-righteous bits are his "real" opinion of his own character, cropping up spontaneously in spite of himself. But that would make Dante the poet out to be a bigger ass than is really believable; self-betraying remarks do often slip out in conversation and even in written auto-biographies, but seldom with quite that emphasis and blatancy. Where a man betrays his vanity is, as a rule, in his very pretence at humility;

but that does not happen with Dante. The two pictures stand, as it were, side by side; they bear an equal stamp of sincerity; he makes no attempt to reconcile them or explain them away. He does not seem to think they need any explanation. I think he is right.

No explanation is needed, if only we will abandon the effort to over-simplify, to find a "real" Dante without any interior contradictions. The Dante of the poem is, considered allegorically, a symbol of all mankind. And human nature is, as we have seen, paradoxical: an animal glorified with a rational soul, the image of God perverted and debased. Man is, in the words of another great Catholic poet:

> A being darkly wise and rudely great . . .
> In doubt to deem himself a god, or beast;
> In doubt his mind or body to prefer;
> Born but to die and reasoning but to err . . .
> Chaos of thought and passion, all confused;
> Still by himself abused, or disabused;
> Created half to rise and half to fall;
> Great lord of all things, yet a prey to all;
> Sole judge of truth, in endless error hurled,
> The glory, jest, and riddle of the world.[1]

The paradox which Pope displays in balanced antitheses is displayed by Dante in violently juxtaposed images. "Judge not" says the Gospel, "that ye be not judged." Nevertheless, "till heaven and earth pass, one jot or one tittle shall in no wise pass from the Law." The Law is for sin, and so long as there is sin, we must judge: we cannot help ourselves, for unless we judge there is no earthly justice. Judge we must, remembering that we ourselves are under judgment. Pope Nicholas is in Hell—but who is Pope Nicholas and where is Hell? Hell is in Dante's heart and Nicholas is something that lurks there, greedy and treacherous. The truth in the soul stands there to rebuke the lie in the soul: it looks down and knows itself in its opposite identity of evil. The dilemma is universal; the judge on the bench and the criminal at the bar are one in the bonds of nature; whenever a man condemns his neighbour, he condemns something that is latent or overt in himself. In the end of all things, judgment belongs to the "Man born sinless and who did no sin",[2] and who yet, being "made sin", knew in His flesh what it felt like to be forsaken of God; that is why He is the only fit judge.

---

[1] Alexander Pope: *Essay on Man*, Epistle ii.   [2] *Inf.* xxxiv. 115.

And so with all the other contrarieties of his nature: Man knows himself, at one pole of the paradox, as a schizophrenic, with a double self constantly at war with itself; at the other pole with a double self reunited and atoned: but always a "twy-formed ambiguity".

Dante is, so far, everyman. But he is also the individual Dante, a man who, as I believe, knew himself very well, both in his strength and his weakness. He says that he was greatly favoured by God's grace, and privileged with a vision which was for his own salvation and that of other men. We may believe that to be true; and if so, he is right to say it and to give gratitude where gratitude is due. But at the same time he does not in the least disguise the fact that he received these favours very dubiously and unwillingly. He is not alone in that. The mystical gift appears, in fact, to be bestowed purely at God's good pleasure, as capriciously (to our minds) as the gift of genius.[1] Great saints have admitted as much—St. Theresa of Jesus is one of the most famous examples. It is with difficulty, and against the violent opposition of the unregenerate will, that they are brought to accept beatitude.

> come degnasti d'accedere al monte?
> non sapei tu che qui è l'uom felice? [2]

Dante had indeed to be pushed, dragged, threatened, cajoled, laughed into submitting himself to felicity.[3] The spirits might well wonder at him. "They stared at me, only at me, and my shadow breaking the light." [4] "Pur me"—why, indeed, should it be he and not another? Dante asks a similar question of Peter Damian in the Eighth Heaven:

> "Perchè predestinata fosti sola
> a questo uffizio tra le tue consorte?"

The answer is that it is a mystery.

> ". . . quell'alma nel ciel che piu si schiara,
> quel serafin che in Dio più l'occhio ha fisso
> alla domanda tua non satisfara;

---

[1] cf. Victor White: God and the Unconscious (Harvill Press, 1952), pp. 108 sqq. Fr. White shows this arbitrary distribution of mystical and prophetic gifts to have been perfectly well known to St. Thomas Aquinas.

[2]   ". . . how didst thou deign to climb the hill?
Didst thou not know that man is happy here?"
                                    Purg. xxx. 74–75.

[3] cf. Charles Williams, Figure of Beatrice, p. 43.

[4] Purg. v. 8–9.

però che si s'inoltra nell'abisso
dell eterno statuto quel che chiedi
che da ogni creata vista è scisso." [1]

The mystery of personality, that "scandal of particularity" so offensive to the mind which is wedded to "chains of causation", is rooted in the fathomless abyss of free will. The only thing that a creature can say, when the choice has fallen upon it, is that it is in no way conscious of having deserved any such thing.

So, too, with the gift of genius. If we have it, it is an ungracious hypocrisy to pretend that we do not. Dante is right to admit it. When he is asked to account for it, he can only reply that he writes as love dictates. The genius is, that is to say, connected somehow with that Lord who sits at the centre of the wheel, and who came in upon him to bear rule over him. But he knows well enough that he ought not to take a personal pride in it. He puts his own pride and its rebuke in the mouth of Oderisi of Gubbio:

"Once, Cimabue thought to hold the field
 In painting; Giotto's all the rage to-day;
 The other's fame lies in the dust concealed.

Guido from Guido wrests our native bay,
 And born, belike, already is that same
 Shall chase both songsters from the nest away.

A breath of wind, no more, is earthly fame,
 And now this way it blows and that way now,
 And as it changes quarter, changes name.

Ten centuries hence, what greater fame hast thou,
 Stripping the flesh off late, than if thou'dst died
 Ere thou wast done with *gee-gee* and *bow-bow?*

Ten centuries hence—and that's a briefer tide,
 Matched with eternity, than one eye-wink
 To that wheeled course Heaven's tardiest sphere must ride." [2]

We may note that Dante probably under-rated the duration of his own

---

[1] "Why wast thou alone among thy companions predestined to this office?"...
"The most illumined soul in Heaven, the seraph who has his eye most fixed on God, will not satisfy thy asking; for that which thou askest lies so deep-hidden ('in-furthered') in the abyss of eternal law that it is sundered from the sight of every creature."

Para. xxi. 77–78; 91–96.

[2] *Purg.* xi. 94–108.

fame, and perhaps in his heart he knew better. However, he accepts the rebuke and walks on, bent double, beside the shade, as though he did indeed already "feel that load [of pride] weigh upon his shoulders".

In addition to this fairly obvious ambivalence between Dante the poet and Dante the man, there is, I think, yet another. The Dante of the *Commedia* is an affirmation of the identity in diversity of his own youth and maturity. We know from outside testimony that Dante Alighieri was reserved in manner, sparing of speech, and mordant to the point of bitterness, and that he conveyed an impression of being an arrogant man who did not suffer fools gladly. This impression is supported on the whole by the internal evidence of the *Convivio*, but not by the *Vita Nuova*, which contradicts it at every turn. *There*, we have the self-portrait of a young man gauche, emotional, enthusiastic, struck speechless by self-consciousness in the presence of the divine creature whom he so abjectly worshipped, but ready on all occasions to babble of himself and his feelings to any sympathetic friend, particularly of the female sex. Nor does he hide from us that he made a conspicuous ass of himself by these antics, and was heartily laughed at on more than one occasion. In the *Convivio* he appears to be a little embarrassed by the *Vita Nuova*: "If in the present work . . . the handling is more virile than in the *New Life*, I do not thereby intend in any way to cast a slight upon the latter but rather to strengthen that by this: seeing that it stands to reason that the one book should be fervid and impassioned, and this other temperate and virile. For a different sort of thing is proper to say and do at one age than at another . . . and in that book I spoke before entrance on the prime of manhood, and in this when I had already passed it." [1] Which, being stripped of its formalities, might be paraphrased: "I know very well that I am publicly labelled as the author of the *Vita Nuova*, but confound it! a man doesn't want to be perpetually confronted with his *juvenilia*. I rather let myself go in that book: of course I stand by the substance of what I said—I was quite sincere at the time and I don't admit to any inconsistency. But I am growing up now and my style I hope, has improved. Please do not gush over my youthful rhapsodies, or expect me to go on handing out the same stuff that I worked out of my system ten years ago." There is no serious writer who will not heartily sympathise with Dante; nothing is so maddening as to be told: "Of course, I admire what you are doing now. But that first book of yours is still my *favourite*." What with his defence-mechanism against

[1] *Conv.* I. i.

this kind of thing, and the uneasy touchiness that always troubles political exiles and other people who have lost their money and feel themselves in a false position, it is little wonder that the author of the *Convivio* displays from time to time an exaggerated prickliness and a rather schoolmasterish condescension, as of one making the mysteries of scholarship comprehensible to the fifth form.

But in the *Commedia*, side by side with great poet and arrogant prophet, there stands the young Dante of the *Vita Nuova*, staring in dumb rapture upon his incomparable lady—

> *perchè la faccia mia sì t'innamora*
> *che tu non ti rivolgi . . .*
>
> *. . . volgiti ed ascolta,*
> *che non pur nei miei occhi è paradiso!*—[1]

a shy young man, too modest to interrupt the conversation of his elders and betters, and getting no further than a preliminary gasp; an emotional young man, given to bursting into tears and fainting away in agitating situations. There is also a schoolboy Dante, bubbling over with adolescent enthusiasms, as panting to meet Ulysses as though he were collecting his and Don Bradman's autographs, and grinning irrepressibly into the face of Statius for sheer inability to keep a delicious secret. And there is a younger Dante still, a nervous and over-imaginative child, perpetually asking "Why?", passing from one mood to another as quickly as an April day, clinging to his *dolce padre*, running at one moment for comfort to Beatrice

> *come parvol che ricorre*
> *sempre cola dove più si confida* [2]

and at another hanging his head before her

> *quali i fanciulli vergognando muti*
> *con gli occhi a terra . . .*[3]

But it is no child that stands there, shaking and strangled with

---

[1] "Why does my face so enamour thee that thou wilt not turn? . . . Turn and listen, for not only in my eyes is paradise."
Para. xxiii. 70; xviii. 21.

[2] like a little child always having recourse there where he has most confidence.
Para. xxii. 2–3.

[3] like children, ashamed and dumb, with eyes cast down.
Purg. xxxi. 64–65.

14

humiliation, neither will Beatrice permit any escapism, or retreat into the womb. "Be your age," she says tartly, "*alza la barba*"—

> *e quando per la barba il viso chiese*
> *ben conobbi il velen dell argomento.*[1]

He is not a child, nor a schoolboy, nor the dreaming youth of eighteen; he is a grown man: that is why the prolonged and relentless breaking down of his defences is almost unbearable. The Dante of the *Comedy* is the whole Dante, with the marks of all his lifetime upon him, a bundle of contradictories in one identity: a shy man and a arrogant man, a man arrogant because he was shy, a man generous and disillusioned, responsive and reserved—the same man who, after years of eating other men's bread and being mortified by the patronage of his intellectual inferiors, could be touched by the clumsy enthusiasm of a Giovanni del Virgilio and take the trouble to laugh him off kindly in a Latin Eclogue.

From the image of Dante, it is natural to pass to that of Beatrice. So much has already been said and written on this subject that I will not dwell on it further than to say briefly that any attempt to make a disjunction between the living and the symbolical Beatrice lands those who make it immediately in the nemesis of nonsense. Beatrice is Salvation, Grace, and Theology and all the rest of it precisely *because* she is the Florentine girl in the love of whom he experienced the truth and the power of these things. The "problem" of Beatrice belongs to that Centre about which the *magne rote* turn; and when we have understood the one we understand the other.

A more intriguing, because a more doubtful problem and one about which nearly as much ink has been shed, is the problem of the "Lady of the Window". Let us add a few more Sibylline leaves to those with which the cave of controversy is already so liberally strewn. We will begin, I think, by consecrating a few minutes to that exercise which is so often neglected in the heat of argument—the contemplation of the obvious.

Now, to me—I speak, very likely as a fool, but I do speak also as one who read not only the *Commedia* but also the *Vita* and the *Convivio* before I read up the controversy, and almost before I knew that any controversy existed—to me, two things are and remain obvious to the

---

[1] And when, meaning my face, she said my "beard"
  I felt the venom the allusion hid.
  Purg. xxxi. 74–75.

point of blatancy. The first is that nobody who read the *Vita* as it was first published (that is, by itself and for itself as a complete work, without reference to anything written subsequently) would imagine for one moment that the "Lady of the Window" was anything but a woman of flesh and blood. In that book she is treated exactly on the same terms as Beatrice, and as all the other ladies whom Dante mentions: the "Screen Lady", Cavalcanti's Giovanna, the lady who was Beatrice's friend and who died, the close relation of Dante's who looked after him when he was ill, the ladies who were at the wedding-party and who made fun of Dante, and the other ladies who rallied Dante about his devotion to Beatrice and told him that he should make his poetry rather less egotistical. There is nothing whatever to suggest that any of these *donne* were mere allegories, or personifications, or that they did not go about their business in Florence and "eat and drink and sleep and wear their clothes" like anybody else. Beatrice, it is true, has acquired a mystical significance for Dante, because he is in love with her; and that significance spills over a little upon Giovanna; but at no point does Dante stop to explain that they, or any of the other ladies in the stories, have not an earthly existence of the most physical and literal kind. And this is important, because it is in the *Vita Nuova* that Dante takes pains to explain the distinction between allegory and fact. He has been telling us how, one day in the street, he saw Beatrice and Giovanna walking together, and that it was to him as though he beheld Love coming towards him in person. He also writes out for us a poem which he composed at the time. This is the poem:

I felt a spirit of Love, that slept, awaken in my heart; and then I beheld Love coming from afar, so joyous that I scarcely knew him. And he said: Now think of nothing but how thou shalt do me honour, and with every word of his, he laughed.

I saw Monna Vanna and Monna Bice coming towards the place where I was, one marvel following another; and even as memory retells the tale, Love said to me: This one is Primavera, and that other hath Love for name, so like is she to me.[1]

At this point, Dante breaks off to explain elaborately, for the benefit of persons "worthy of having all their perplexities cleared up", that when he says that Love came from afar, and laughed, and spoke and so on, he does not intend to imply that Love is an intelligent, still less a corporeal being. "Love is not a being in itself, but is a quality of a being."

[1] *Vita Nuova*, xxiv.

He then invokes at some length the authority of the classical poets for thus personifying an abstraction; and adds: "Neither did the poets speak thus without reason, nor should they who versify speak in this way without having in their own minds some interpretation of what they say; for great shame it were to a man if he should versify under cover of a figure or a rhetorical colour, and could not afterwards, if called upon, strip such vesture from his words, so as to give them a real meaning." [1]

Nothing, surely, could be more straightforward than this. Dante has made a poem which describes how two ladies were walking along the street and how Love also came walking along and laughed happily and talked to Dante about the ladies, saying that one of them was named after him. It then occurs to him that worthy persons like you and me might be perplexed and wonder how many people were, in fact, walking and talking in the street. He therefore considerately makes it clear that *one* of these personages is only an abstraction—a "quality in a substance". The others, we are left to infer, are real people, since the exception proves the rule. Having cleared up this little difficulty, he picks up the thread of his story.

The story goes on: Beatrice dies; sometime after her death, Dante is indulging in grief, when he sees a lady looking at him compassionately from a window. He is touched by this; the lady is young and beautiful and her complexion reminds him of Beatrice; he gets into a habit of frequenting this lady's company because when he looks at her his grief for Beatrice is the more readily relieved by tears. Then, to his horror, he discovers that he is beginning to take pleasure in the lady's attractions for their own sake. Can it be that he is actually in a fair way to recovery? He gets in a stew about it: "I was angry in my heart and held myself exceeding base, and many times did I curse the inconstancy of my eyes"; so he concentrates very hard on Beatrice and works himself up into crying fits, but his heart, it seems, is set on mending, and he thinks: "Perhaps Love has sent me this new lady on purpose to console me"; and writes a sonnet to this effect, beginning "A Gentle Thought"—"and I say *gentle* in so far as it discoursed of a gentle lady, for otherwise it was most base". And then, he had a new vision of Beatrice, and "my heart began to repent grievously of the desire whereby it had so basely allowed itself to be possessed for certain days, counter to the constancy of reason; and this evil desire being cast forth all my thoughts turned again to this *gentilissima Beatrice*." [2] And that,

[1] *Vita Nuova*, xxv.   [2] *Vita Nuova*, xxxvi–xl.

one feels, is that; and highly characteristic it is of romantic love in young people—except that, in ninety-nine cases out of a hundred the love that is so disconcertingly cured stays cured.

But there is no warning here that Dante was cured, even temporarily, by an abstraction. The Lady of the Window is introduced to us in exactly the same kind of terms as all the other ladies. Surely, if, without Dante's helpful explanation, we were liable to mistake Love for a "corporeal being", an explanation is still more urgently needed here; otherwise we can hardly fail to accept this beautiful and compassionate lady with the pale complexion as a being most attractively corporeal. But Dante, so assiduous and even officious with his explanations where, even unaided, we could scarcely have gone wrong, here leaves us uninstructed. Obviously, all intelligent readers are bound to conclude that the lady is a flesh-and-blood lady, since otherwise Dante would have warned us; equally obviously, all readers of the *Vita Nuova* did so conclude, since in the *Convivio*, Dante irritably and unreasonably complains that they did.

The second obvious thing is this: that by no means whatever is it possible honestly to reconcile the account of this episode given in the *Convivio* with that given in the *Vita Nuova*. Dante himself could not do it; neither have any of his interpreters had any better success. He expends a great deal of labour and ingenuity on this impracticable task. He goes at it very gamely, like a horseman negotiating a big black bullfinch. He sets his teeth and flogs and digs in his heels, and manages to scramble over somehow with twigs flying in all directions and a nasty peck and flounder on landing. But jump it clean he cannot. The more closely and critically one examines the shifty evasions of this remarkable piece of exegesis the less one is convinced. At the end of it, Dante emerges, rather breathless and scratched, proclaiming defiantly: "I declare and affirm that the lady of whom I was enamoured after my first love was the most fair and noble daughter of the Emperor of the universe, to whom Pythagoras gave the name of Philosophy." [1] Dutiful Dantists reply in a meek chorus: "We know this, because Dante says so himself": but the more sceptical, while not exactly calling Dante a liar, continue to murmur: "So what?"

And with very good reason. For in the passage just quoted, Dante "declares and affirms" nothing, one way or the other about the actual existence of any flesh-and-blood lady. Those who rely upon it to dismiss her into the realms of fancy ought in honesty to point out (though

[1] *Convivio*, II. xvi.

in fact they never do) that it occurs, not in the first portion of the treatise, which expounds the *literal* meaning of the canzone, but in the second portion, which expounds its *allegorical* meaning.[1] It is not in dispute that, at whatever point a figurative signification was imposed upon the poem, the figure of the Lady is, allegorically, the image of Philosophy. The real question is whether, in the *literal* signification, the Lady is a real person (like Virgil) or a *bella menzogna* (like the Three Beasts). If Dante had wished to say plainly that in the *literal* sense there "never was no sich a person" as the Lady of the Window, he could and should have said so in the course of his first exposition *per literam*: "Continuing, I show the power of this new thought by its effects, say-ing that it causes me to gaze upon *a lady*, and speaks to me flattering words—that is, discourses before the eyes of my intellectual affections; the better to draw me over, promising me that the sight of her eyes is my well-being (*salute*)." [2] The phrase "intellectual affections" is, to be sure, a little ambiguous; but to remove all ambiguity, nothing was needed but the unequivocal statement: "This lady is a poetic fiction." But this is precisely what Dante does not say. And a few pages further on, he uses a phrase which is clearly inapplicable to a poetic fiction. He says: "The effect of these intelligences [of the Third Heaven] . . . is indeed love . . . and inasmuch as they cannot preserve (*salvare*) it except in those subjects which are under the sway of (*sottoposti a*) their circulation, they transfer (*transmutano*) it from that region which is beyond their power to that which is within it, *that is to say, from the soul which has departed this life to that which is in it (cioè de l'anima partita d'esta via in quella ch'è in essa).*[3] From the dead Beatrice, that is, to the living Lady. But in what sense can a fictitious Lady be said to be "in this life" as contrasted with a real woman who has departed it?

And if, finding that Dante has evaded the direct statement in the very place where he could have made himself clear beyond all possibility of

---

[1] cf. Michele Barbi: *Razionalismo e misticismo in Dante* (*Stud. Dant.* Vol. xvii, p. 40, note 1), "*Bisogna tener ben distinta la parte del terzo trattato del* Convivio *dove Dante spiega il senso letterale della canzone (ii–x) da quella ove ci dà l'inter-pretazione allegorica (xi–xv): nell'una considera la donna gentile come* donna reale . . .; *nell'altra parte invece alla donna subentra la filosofia, &c.* It is necessary to distinguish very clearly that part of the third treatise of the *Convivio* in which Dante expounds the literal sense of the Canzone (ii–x) from that in which he gives us the allegorical interpretation (xi–xv): in the one he considers the 'gentle lady' as a *real lady* . . .; in the other part, philosophy takes the lady's place." The caution applies as cogently to the Second Treatise, or even more so.

[2] *Convivio*, II. viii.   [3] *Convivio*, II. viii.

misunderstanding, we turn to the opening paragraphs of the treatise, in which he distinguishes between the literal and the allegorical senses as such, we are again faced with a riddle. "Writings (*scritture*) may be understood and ought to be expounded chiefly in four senses. The first is called literal [and this is the one that extends no further than the letter of the fictitious words (*parole fittizie*) such as are the fables of the poets. The other is called allegorical,] and this is the one which hides itself under the mantle of these fables,[1] and is a truth hidden under agreeable fiction (*bella menzogna*); as when Ovid makes Orpheus, etc., etc."[2] Maddeningly enough, at this crucial point, the passage enclosed in square brackets is lacking in all the codices, and has to be supplied conjecturally in various different versions. Did Dante mean that by an *allegorical* interpretation one *always* means the interpretation of a fiction? He adds: "It is true that the theologians take this sense otherwise than the poets do, but since it is my purpose here to follow the method of the poets I shall take the allegorical sense after the use of the poets."[3] The theologians would indeed take exception to having the whole literal sense of the Scriptures dismissed as a poetic fiction or *bella menzogna*, and in explaining the *moral* and *anagogical* meanings Dante himself uses for his examples the Transfiguration of Christ, and the Exodus from Egypt, which he certainly did not regard as fictitious fables. Still, let us agree that when the interpretation is *allegorical*, the *literal* sense is fiction; or at least that, for the purpose of interpreting the canzone *Voi che intendendo*, Dante purposes to take it so. We shall then find ourselves faced with the very remarkable consequence that not only is the *Donna Gentile* a fiction, and Beatrice also a fiction (as indeed many people would have us believe), but that so are the seven planets and the physical heavens, allegorically representing as they do the seven sciences of the Trivium and Quadrivium.

I do not think Dante can have quite meant that. But I think that by his mention of poetic fictions he was trying to put it across the reader, without definitely saying so or telling a flat lie, that his "second love" was, in the literal sense, a *bella menzogna*. And a curious doubt arises whether that lacuna in the codices is after all really the result of a scribe's carelessness. Is it just possible that in the master-manuscript a repentant hand ran a pen through the disingenuous phrasing, with the half-formed intention of correcting it, and then, somehow, never carried the intention out?

[1] *favole:* the word means "tales", but not necessarily "fictitious".
[2] *Convivio*, II. i.
[3] *Convivio*, II. i.

The problem of the canzone and its interpretation presents us with no fewer than seven possibilities: (1) It was originally a perfectly straightforward poem about a man turning from love for a real dead woman to the consolations of love for a real living woman; and later it was made out to be an allegory about a man turning from love for a real dead woman to the consolations of Philosophy, imaged under the figure of a real living woman, or, (2) of a fictitious woman. (3) It was originally a straightforward poem about a real dead and a real living woman; and later it was made out to be an allegory about two fictitious women, the second of whom [1] represented Philosophy. (4) It was, from the start, conceived as an allegory about the transference of love from a real dead woman to Philosophy imaged under the figure of a fictitious woman; and it is thus explained in the *Convivio*. (5) It was originally conceived as an allegory about two real women, each representing an abstraction; and it is thus explained in the *Convivio*. (6) It was originally conceived as an allegory about two real women, each representing an abstraction; and subsequently the real existence of the second woman was veiled or denied in the *Convivio*. (7) It never was anything but an allegory about two fictitious women, each representing an abstraction, and is so explained in the *Convivio*.[2]

I will now hazard my own opinion. To me, this problem is extremely interesting, because I believe it is occasioned by Dante's first and last attempt to put asunder the two halves of a paradox. He was steeped in pagan rationalism at the time of writing the *Convivio*, and very possibly he felt it incumbent upon him to substitute an "either-or" where the whole truth called for a "both-and". His first mystical identification of Image with Reality, of Beatrice with Salvation, had been dictated to him by Love, and he set down candidly what he intuitively knew to be the truth about it. But he had not yet worked out any universal application for what was later to become his great system of symbolical imagery. Moreover, he had probably been exasperated by rather stupid and unimaginative jokes about his infidelity to his ideal—and if certain sonnets he wrote to his friend Forese, and the passage about Forese in the *Commedia*, are anything to go by, he possibly deserved the jests.

[1] The first may, of course, have represented Carnal Love, Romantic Love, Salvation, Faith, Grace, Theology, a Religious Vocation, the Joachimite Third Kingdom, or any other fancy of the commentators. In the absence of a real Beatrice there is nothing that need fetter the imagination.

[2] For the convenience of anybody who may find this as bewildering to read as it was to write, I have set the seven possibilities forth in a Table at the end of this paper.

And, as we have seen, he had reached an age and a situation in which, more than ever, he disliked being made to look ridiculous. So he made one of those sweeping simplifications of which his commentators are so fond, and by implication, if not in so many words, denied the corporeal Lady altogether. " 'He denies it,' said the King; 'leave out that part.' "

What actually happened is anybody's guess, and mine is this. I think the account in the *Vita Nuova* can be taken at its face-value: it wears an air of candour which is convincing. I think there was a real lady, that for a time he was attracted to her and desired her as a man desires a woman, and that he eventually conquered that desire, exactly as he says he did. But I think he went on seeing the lady, and that he came somehow in his mind to identify her calm and soothing personality with the philosophy that he was studying at the time, and in particular with that Lady Philosophy who appears in the *Consolations* of Boethius. He told himself—and perhaps told her—that she was a kind of Muse or Egeria to him; possibly, God help him! he sat in her parlour and explained to her with much eloquence how beautiful this kind of Platonic friendship was, with no foolish nonsense about sex. Young men do say these things. What the lady's reactions may have been is matter for illimitable fancy. She may have been secretly disappointed, she may have been what a later generation would have called a blue-stocking and thought it all very spiritual and uplifting. At any rate, in the end he doubtless succeeded in persuading himself that there never had been anything (as people say) "of that sort" about the affair; it had been a devotion to Philosophy first, last, and all the time. Unfortunately, there was the witness of his own hand against him in the *Vita Nuova*. He was frightened, he was irritated, and he lost his head: he said, "Rubbish! it was nothing but an allegory."

There is, I believe, no way out of the dilemma but to join together again these two halves of the paradox which he, in his fretful haste, illegitimately put asunder. The Lady of the Window was a fact, she was also a symbol; she was all the more truly a symbol because she was a living fact. For Dante, she was a woman and Philosophy in a single indivisible identity, as, for him, Beatrice was a woman and Salvation in a single indivisible identity; as, for all men, if we may venture the analogy, Christ is Man and God in a single indivisible identity. The Dante of the *Commedia* would have seen the matter so; but by the time he got to the *Commedia* the Lady's place had been filled—by Virgil. Dante never again made the mistake of burking one half of a truth, nor of watering down a natural symbol into an allegorical personification.

One could wish that he had not done it in this case, if it were not that the error is so interesting. He is groping for his means of expression; he hit the gold the first time almost, as it were, by accident; the second shaft went wide and did some damage; after that, every shot was true.

We now come to a set of paradoxes of a slightly different kind. A very simple example, which may serve as an introduction to the rest, is the case of Julius Caesar. In the 4th Canto of the *Inferno*, Caesar appears in his own person among the heroes of the Trojan race, in virtue of his alleged descent from Aeneas; and Aeneas, as we know from Canto II, ranks for Dante's purpose as the founder of the Roman Empire. The Caesar—*armato con gli occhi grifagni* [1]—is Julius, not Augustus: the Dictator, not the Emperor. The Middle Ages, with a sure political instinct, recognised in Julius the root of Imperial power, however many times he may have refused the Imperial Crown. Scholarship on the whole agrees that Julius here represents the sacred Empire —though we might, perhaps, fall back upon saying that he stands here simply for Rome. Yet, in the Ninth Pit of Malebolge, we find, mutilated among the Schismatics, Curio who counselled Julius to march upon Rome. The act of Caesar counts here as an act of political sedition —Rome is split by Caesar; not the Empire, but the Republic. Yet, once again, ground in the jaws of Lucifer in the deep of the Pit, hang Brutus and Cassius, who in the name of the Republic murdered Julius Caesar. The crime in either case is clear and the accusation definite; but the attitude to Caesar himself is ambivalent: he is Rome; he is the wound in the body of Rome; he is the body of Rome wounded. Is this a kind of carelessness? Does the poet juggle with names and personalities as the immediate need of his poem suggests, heedless of inconsistencies?

We may set beside this a still more startling ambiguity. If there is one person more than another for whom, one would say, Dante felt neither reverence nor pity, it is Pope Boniface VIII. He is the arch-Simoniac, the defiler of the Spouse of God:

> "Already standing there?
> Thou standing there already, Boniface?
> Why then the writ has lied by many a year.
>
> What! so soon sated with the gilded brass
> That nerved thee to betray and then to rape
> The Fairest among Women that ever was?" [2]

He is the "prince of modern Pharisees", making use of his sacred Office

---

[1] armed and eagle-eyed.   [2] *Inf.* xix. 52–58.

to pursue his private vendettas, and blasphemously exploiting the power of the High Keys themselves to cheat Guido da Montefeltro into damning his soul, and to extort from him the fraudulent counsel which put Penestrino in his power.[1] He has no right to sit in the Holy See from which he ousted Celestine V; St. Peter denounces him in The Tenth Heaven with a bitterness and violence unsurpassed even in Dante's bitterest moments; the whole Host of Heaven blushes red with wrath at his crimes, and the Emperor of the Dolorous Realm is glad of them:

> He that on earth has dared usurp that place
> Of mine, that place of mine, that place of mine
> - Which now stands vacant before God's Son's face,
>
> Has made my sepulchre a running rhine
> Of filth and blood, which to the renegade
> Down there, who fell from here, is anodyne.[2]

More terrible still, perhaps, in its implications is the mere fact that Beatrice's last word before returning to gaze upon the eternal fount of wisdom is an implacable reference to the doom of "him of Alagna".[3]

Yet, sandwiched between the former and the latter denunciations, there comes the agonised cry of Hugh Capet, prophetically looking upon the crime of Philip the Fair:

> To put crimes past and future in the shade
> I see the Lily storm Alagna's paling,
> And in Christ's Vicar, Christ a captive made.
>
> I see once more the mockery and the railing,
> I see renewed the vinegar and gall,
> 'Twixt living thieves I see His deadly nailing.[4]

Perjured, venal, corrupt, bloodstained, treacherous, and damned, Christ's Vicar is Christ's Vicar still, inseparably identified with Him in the mystery and sacrament of the chrism. The throne usurped stands vacant before God, but before men it is Christ's self that sits in Peter's seat; the sacrament profaned is available to damnation. The image is asserted in the very act of rejecting it; the identity is simultaneously denied and affirmed.

The paradox goes deeper than a plain distinction between the function and the man, nor can it be wholly summed up in the general statement that whoever wrongs his neighbour wrongs Christ. The

[1] *Inf.* xxvii. 85 *sqq.*   [2] *Para.* xxvii. 22–27.   [3] *Para.* xxx. 148.
[4] *Purg.* xx. 85–90.

manner of the writing here asserts vehemently that the seat of the identity is within the person, and that persons cannot be divided or generalised. For the passage is a double echo of Boniface's own words. When Sciarra Colonna and William de Nogaret broke into the Pope's palace at Alagna with their band of hired traitors, the old man, deserted by his cardinals and the greater part of his household, said magnificently: "Since I, like Jesus Christ, am to be taken by treachery and put to death, at least I will die as Pope"; and "immediately he caused himself to be clothed in the mantle of St. Peter with the crown of Constantine upon his head and the Keys and the Cross in his hand, and took his seat upon the papal throne".[1] Nor is this all: Dante's lines, with their four-times repeated "Veggio" echo Boniface's own Hymn to the Mater Dolorosa at the foot of the cross, with its four-fold repetition: "Vedera . . . vede . . . vede . . . vede . . ." "*Vede l'acete ch'era di fiel misto*,"[2] says Boniface, and Dante repeats: "*veggio rinnovellar l'acete e il fele*." No more noble tribute was ever paid by a man to his bitter enemy; never but in the mysterious phrase of St. Paul were the contradiction and the coinherence more solemnly affirmed in the identity of a single person.

We will pass now to another problem which has given some trouble to the critics. The Heaven of the Sun, which is the Heaven of the Doctors, is in an especial manner the heaven of reconciliation and exchange. The two great traditions of theology, the dogmatic and the mystical, represented by the two great Orders of St. Dominic and St. Francis, here tread their circling measure in harmony. St. Thomas Aquinas, speaking for the Dominicans, pronounces the eulogy of St. Francis; St. Bonaventure speaking for the Franciscans, pronounces the eulogy of St. Dominic; and each denounces the failings of his own order. The intention could scarcely be clearer: whatever the rivalries and disputes between the two Orders in this world, in the world of eternal things Francis and Dominic kiss one another as they do in the touching picture of Fra Angelico. The attempt to make Dante take sides in these theological controversies is singularly perverse: Dominic and Francis, he declares by the mouth of St. Thomas, are the two princes ordained by Providence to guide the Church:

> *L'un fu tutto serafico in ardore,*
> *l'altro per sapienza in terra fue*
> *di cherubica luce uno splendore.*

[1] Villani, *Chron.* viii. 63.   [2] she sees the vinegar mingled with gall.

Dell'un dirò, però che d'ambedue
si dice l'un pregiando, qual ch'uom prende,
perchè ad un finefur l'opere sue.[1]

He declares, by the mouth of St. Bonaventure, that these were the twin champions sent by Christ to succour His Church, the right and left wheel of her chariot. So far, so good; and nobody need find any difficulty about it, unless he has a Dominican or a Franciscan axe to grind. The real headaches begin when we examine the composition of the circles themselves. In each of them there stands, by the side of the spokesman, and occupying an emphatic last-but-not-least place in the enumeration when he introduces his companions, the spirit of a man whose opinions were not only strongly opposed by that spokesman when on earth, but also suspected of heresy. In the circle of the Mystical Theologians, next door to St. Bonaventure, is that queer prophetical visionary, Joachim of Flora; in the circle of the Dogmatic Theologians, next door to Thomas Aquinas, is Sigier of Brabant.

Why are they here? It is, of course, simple and spectacular to deduce that Dante was a crypto-heretic, and that he wrote all his eulogies of the orthodox with his tongue in his cheek, expending an infinity of pains upon them in order that he might have the gratification of popping in a couple of lines at the end to affront the pious and *épater le bourgeois*. But it is better on the whole to assume that he was not altogether unbalanced, and to find some explanation that will fit in with the whole argument of his poem. For this purpose it is advisable to begin by ascertaining the facts about Sigier and Joachim, and since the limits of one paper will scarcely accommodate both of them, we will concentrate upon Sigier of Brabant,

che, leggendo nel vico degli strami,
silogiʒʒò invidiosi veri.[2]

He lectured in Paris, in the *Vicus Stramineus* or *Rue du Fouarre* and

---

[1] The one [St. Francis] was wholly seraphic in his fervour [of love]; the other [St. Dominic] was for wisdom an earthly splendour (reflection) of the cherubic light [the seraphim being of the order of love, the cherubim, of knowledge]. I will speak of the one, because whatsoever praise is spoken of one—take which you will—is spoken of both, for both worked to one and the same end.
Para. xi. 37–42.

[2] who,
Lecturing there in Straw Street, argued home
Invidious truths, as logic taught him to.
Para. x. 137–138.

there "syllogised invidious truths"—truths, that is, which earned him hatred. The hatred is not disputed; the operative word is *veri*.

The name of Sigier of Brabant leads us straight into the great academic row which shook the universities of Europe in the thirteenth century and split their Faculties into opposing camps. The trouble began in the twelfth century, when the works of Aristotle, filtering into Christian Europe by way of Arabia and Spain, revolutionised the whole method of teaching and confronted the theologians with the challenge of pagan philosophy and metaphysics. The shock administered to the Divinity Schools was comparable to that which they sustained in the seventeenth century under the impact of Copernican physics and the inductive method, or in the nineteenth, under the impact of Darwinian biology and the theory of evolution.

The usual efforts were made to prohibit the reading of Aristotle, with the usual lack of success. A whole world of new knowledge had opened up before the astonished eyes of Christendom, and everybody was mad on Aristotle. Between 1160 and 1265, almost the whole of Aristotle had been translated into Latin, and the majority of the works had become set books in the Universities, despite papal prohibitions and exhortations to wait until the more dangerous portions had been vetted by experts and purged of their theological errors. It became abundantly clear that things could not go on like this. Albertus Magnus of Cologne, and after him his still greater pupil Thomas Aquinas, tackled in succession the colossal task of adapting the Aristotelian method to the exposition of Christian doctrine, and so bringing theology up to date. But in the meantime an uproar broke out and raged through the universities, the storm-centre being the University of Paris, at that time the leading seat of European learning.

It is not in the least surprising that there should have been trouble. Not only was Aristotle a heathen philosopher, but his principal translators and editors were Moslems, the most important among them being Averroës "*che il gran comento fece*",[1] and whom we meet in the *Inferno* among the great pagans in the Elysian Fields. Working upon the text of Aristotle, Averroës and his followers drew from it a number of conclusions which appeared to follow with impeccable logic from the premises, but which were and remained totally irreconcilable with the Christian revelation. In 1256, Albertus Magnus preached a sermon in Paris, "On the Unity of the Intellect, against Averroës." Between 1260

[1] who made the great commentary.
Inf. iv. 44.

and 1265 we find that Averroïsm has definitely emerged as an acknowledged, fashionable, and dangerous heresy.

In Paris, theology was taught by the Faculty of Theology; but philosophy by the Faculty of Arts. The Artsmen were for the most part seculars, who did their Arts course by way of preliminary to taking orders and passing into the Faculty of Theology. Consequently, the members of the Faculty of Arts, both lecturers and students, were, generally speaking, younger men than those in the Faculty of Theology, where the teaching consisted largely of exposition and commentary of the Scriptures along traditional lines. In 1266, Sigier of Brabant, then about thirty years old, was a well-known Master in the Faculty of Arts, but had not yet passed on to read Theology for the priesthood; he was an Averroïst, whatever that word may precisely signify.

In 1269, Thomas Aquinas was sent to Paris for two years with a special mission to preach against the Averroïst doctrine. The situation presents itself as a kind of three-cornered duel: the Faculty of Arts enthusiastic for Aristotle and vociferously asserting its right to study Averroës if it liked; the Faculty of Theology deeply suspicious of *all* Aristotelianism, including that of Aquinas; and Thomas himself resolutely upholding Christian Aristotelianism against the traditional theologians on the one hand and the Averroïsts on the other. The year 1270 produced a crisis; Aquinas and Sigier both published manifestoes about a particular point of Averroïst doctrine; the Bishop of Paris published a solemn condemnation of thirteen heretical propositions; and Thomas Aquinas preached a sermon in which the real point at issue makes itself very plainly manifest—more plainly perhaps to our eyes now than to those who were then involved in the conflict.

We find [he said] certain men who study philosophy and who say things which are not true according to the Faith; and when it is pointed out to them that this is repugnant to the Faith, they reply that this is what the Philosopher says; they themselves, they say, do not affirm it; they are merely repeating the words of the Philosopher.

Now, it should be evident, at any rate to us, that the situation described is one which involves a genuine case of conscience. Is it the duty of a commentator merely to expound what is in the text, representing fairly and correctly the opinion of the author, and leaving it to his audience to decide with open minds whether that opinion is right or wrong? Or is it his duty, having done all this, to bring his author to the bar of Christian truth, point out any discrepancies, and warn his audience against believing implicitly all the conclusions that may be drawn from the text? It is a dilemma that faces every lecturer and writer even to-day. The more detached and academic kind of scholarship inclines to the former view, which is that put forward by the Averroïsts; you expound the text, and take no moral responsibility whatever for the effect upon your students or readers. They—even if they are young, inexperienced, and susceptible—must accept the burden of forming their own judgment, and if they fall into error that is just too bad, but it is no affair of yours—even though (human nature being what it is) they are pretty certain to think that, since you have uttered no criticism, you are in agreement with the author, and are adding your own authority to his.

The other school of thought, convinced that it has a moral as well as an intellectual responsibility in the matter, inclines to the view which St. Thomas goes on to urge: that if the author's views are erroneous, wicked, or dangerous, you should say so and give your reasons.

Both these positions are perfectly consistent with honest scholarship; and it is pretty clear now that honest scholarship was the real matter in dispute. But it was not clear then. The orthodox party simply dismissed the whole contention of the Averroïsts as a quibble or a lie, and accused them of teaching heresy under the pretext of elucidating the text of Aristotle. The Averroïsts in their turn accused the orthodox party of falsifying the readings and distorting their arguments in order to drag out of Aristotle conclusions which could not be legitimately drawn from his text. Both sides may have been partly right; but in the uproar the real point at issue became very much obscured.

The Condemnation of 1270 was a crisis which shook the University to its foundations. Two rival rectors were elected at the 1271 election, and the Faculty of Arts was split into two portions for three years. In 1272, the Masters of the orthodox party, who were in the majority, promulgated a decree which forbade any Master of Arts to determine or dispute any theological question; which pronounced that anyone, concluding in Paris on any theological or philosophical question, in a manner contrary to the Faith, should be reputed a heretic and cut off from the society of the Masters; and which directed that if a Master or Bachelor of the Faculty had to handle any difficult text which might be subversive of the Faith he should confine himself to refuting the arguments or the texts and pronouncing them false or erroneous.

There followed this unfortunate clause: "He shall also refrain from lecturing on or discussing any difficulties arising from the texts or from other authors (i.e. commentaries) but shall omit them entirely as being alien from the truth."

It is evident that the Faculty had completely lost its head. To prescribe the complete burking of the issue was to put a premium upon dishonesty and make scholarship meaningless. An anonymous Averroïst treatise of this period contains the inevitable retort rather magnificently phrased:

> *Sciendum quod sententia Philosophi ab hiis qui ejus libros suscipiunt exponendos non est celanda, licet sit contraria veritati.*[1]

Be it known that the opinion of the Philosopher must not be concealed by those who undertake to expound his works, even though it may be contrary to the truth.

After three years of complete anarchy the University authorities appealed to the Papal Legate, who soundly trounced the fomenters of dissension and appointed a new Rector and officers; though, interestingly enough, he promulgated no doctrinal prohibitions and took no repressive action against Sigier and his party. The University made an effort to pull itself together, and made a number of new regulations (including one which forbade Masters to hold torchlight parades and lead choruses in the streets by night). The Averroïsts became for a time more prudent, abandoned public lecturing and took to giving private coachings, so that in 1276 the University had to prohibit the reading of the forbidden texts even in private. About this time, the Pope called for a report and Etienne Tempier, Bishop of Paris, instead of sending one, took it on himself to pronounce a sweeping condemnation of his own, which included in one and the same reprobation the doctrines of Thomas Aquinas and of Sigier of Brabant. This condemnation comprised 219 propositions, in which important errors were mixed up indiscriminately with others which were quite trifling and with some which were not errors at all; and he chose to promulgate it on 7th March 1277, the anniversary of the death of Thomas Aquinas.

In October 1277, Sigier of Brabant and a companion of his, who had fled before the storm, were cited to appear before the tribunal of the Inquisitor "to answer for their faith and tell the whole truth and

[1] *Cit.* P. Mandonnet: *Siger de Brabant et l'averroïsme latin au XIIIᵉ Siècle:* Louvain, Institute de Philosophie, 2nd ed. 1908, 1911, ch. IX.

15

nothing but the truth about themselves and others touching the crime of heresy". Instead of appearing, they betook themselves to Rome, and appealed to the Roman Curia. There Sigier, at any rate, seems to have been kept under guard, as it were, and under observation; and some time between 1281 and 1284, when the Curia was at Orvieto, he died —stabbed by his clerk in a fit of frenzy.

In the meantime, the Anti-Aristotelians had been busy elsewhere. In 1277, the year of the Paris condemnation, they succeeded in getting certain teachings of Thomas Aquinas condemned at Oxford as heretical and Averroïst in tendency, the condemnation being pronounced by the Archbishop of Canterbury, Robert Kilwardby, in a special congregation of all the Masters of the University. This, whether it was done in concert with him or not, exactly suited Etienne Tempier, who was just planning to get the condemnation endorsed in Paris, when Rome suddenly put its foot down and stopped all further proceedings. Kilwardby was a little later removed to Rome and given a Cardinalate, and thus prevented from hindering the Thomist movement in England; and punitive measures were enforced in Oxford against those who had been lacking in respect for the teachings of Aquinas.

The story, you see, is long and involved, and it is further complicated by a grievous history of rivalry and antagonism between the Dominican and the Franciscan Orders. But now, where does Dante stand in all this? Why did he give Sigier of Brabant so conspicuous a place in the *Paradiso*? It will scarcely do to say, with Mandonnet, that he was ignorant of Sigier's opinions and merely included him among the Doctors as a specimen of that rather rare mediaeval bird, the secular philosopher. Dante had studied in Paris, he may have met men there who had actually sat under Sigier in the *rue du Fouarre*; the row had been a resounding one and had taken place within Dante's own lifetime—how could he be ignorant of it? Besides, the parallel placing of Sigier and Joachim of Flora cannot be without significance. Nor will it do to say that Dante sympathised with the condemned doctrines— not only does he in places explicitly contradict them, but they run counter to the whole tenor of his work, destroying as they do that Christian concept of human personality which lies at the very basis of the *Comedy*. And although recent research into Sigier's later writings tends to show that his own opinions were orthodox,[1] and that when he

[1] Ferrand von Steenberghen: *Siger de Brabant d'après ses Oèuvres Inédites* (Louvain: Editions de l'Institut Supérieur de Philosophie, 2 vols., 1931–1942). The attribution of the writings is contested by Gilson and Nardi.

declared that he was speaking for Aristotle and not for himself he was speaking the truth, it will not do to say either that he owes his position in the *Paradiso* to his mere orthodoxy—the *invidiosi veri* on which Dante lays such stress were "syllogised" in the *rue du Fouarre*, the very lecture-rooms where he incurred the suspicion of heresy.

Let us clear up one possible misconception: Sigier was not a condemned heretic. He never appeared before the Inquisitor; he appealed over his head to the Curia, which seems to have detained him in a kind of honourable seclusion, attended by his clerk. There is no record of condemnation or excommunication pronounced against him personally, either by the Inquisitor or by the Curia. Etienne Tempier's general condemnation was irregular in form, confused and partly invalid in substance, and in any case had no validity outside the diocese of Paris; and Sigier was cited before the Inquisitor for enquiry and for no other purpose. On the facts as we know them, there is nothing to prevent Dante from placing Sigier in Paradise.

But there was something about Sigier that Dante thought important. It is not for nothing that he puts into the mouth of Thomas Aquinas, who wrote and preached against him, that line about the *invidiosi veri*. The rhyme and emphasis fall upon *veri*; Dante's intention has something to do with Truth. There is, I believe, only one explanation which fits the facts: Dante is occupied here with the paradox of the apparent conflict between two kinds of truth. The scholar must be true to his text and the philosopher to his natural reason; the theologian must be true to his faith and to the super-rational verities of revelation. But how if they seem to contradict one another? Can truth be divided? No. All truth is one, said the theologians; therefore if anything conflicts with the Scriptures it is not true. To which the Averroïsts in effect replied: All truth is one, therefore, if anything is demonstrably true, it cannot in the long run disagree with the Scriptures: but to reconcile the two truths is the business of Theology, not of scholarship; in the meantime, we must not shirk the issue, deny the natural reason, or distort or suppress the facts. Dante's tribute to Sigier is, then, his tribute to the honest scholar.[1] Thomas Aquinas, side by side with Sigier in Paradise, may well say to him, "Down there in Paris you were right to say what you did; down there in Paris I was right to oppose you; but here, where all truth is seen to be one, we are wholly and perfectly reconciled: truth to reason and truth to revelation are here only the two halves of the one

[1] cf. S. J. Curtis, *A Short History of Western Philosophy in the Middle Ages*, (Macdonald, 1950), p. 120.

paradox which is God's single truth." Therefore, he can turn to Dante and say:

> "That's the eternal light of Sigier, who,
> Lecturing there in Straw Street, argued home
> Invidious truths, as logic taught him to." [1]

I have dealt with only a few of the paradoxes of the *Comedy*. There are, of course, many more—notably that simultaneous rejection and affirmation of the visible world which runs all through the poem. If the world is not known as the vehicle and image of the Glory, then it is a substitute and an idol; it must be renounced as an idol before it can be received as an image; "after the affirmations we may have to discover the rejections, but we must still believe that after the rejections the greater affirmations are to return".[2]

All truth is one, all diversity is unified, all paradoxes are reconciled in a single meaning, there where the double nature sits within the Threefold Unity at the still centre of the turning world of all things visible and invisible:

> *Nel suo profondo vidi che s'interna*
> *legato con amore in un volume,*
> *ciò che per l'universo si squaderna;*

> *sustanzia ed accidenti, e lor custume,*
> *quasi conflati insieme per tal modo,*
> *che ciò ch'io dico è un semplice lume.*[3]

"I think I really saw it," says Dante, "because, as I say this, I feel that I rejoice."

[1] See Note at end of this paper.
[2] Charles Williams: *The Figure of Beatrice*, p. 10.
[3] In that abyss I saw how love held bound
  Into one volume all the leaves whose flight
  Is scattered through the universe around;

How substance, accident, and mode unite
  Fused so to speak together, in such wise
  That this I tell of is one simple light.
      Para. xxxiii. 85–90.

TABLE

The poem *Voi che intendendo* is about the transference of love

Literally	*Allegorically*	
1. from one real woman to another	1. from a real woman to an abstraction; literal existence of *both* ladies admitted in *Convivio*	
2. from one real woman to another	2. from a real woman to an abstraction; literal existence of second lady veiled or denied in *Convivio*	Allegorical signification added subsequently to time of composition
3. from one real woman to another	3. from one abstraction to another; literal existence of *neither* lady admitted in *Convivio*	
4. from a real woman to a fiction	4. from a real woman to an abstraction	
5. from one real woman to another	5. from one abstraction to another; literal existence of both ladies *admitted* in *Convivio*	Allegorical signification intended at time of composition
6. from one real woman to another	6. from one abstraction to another; literal existence of *second* lady subsequently veiled or denied in *Convivio*	
7. from one fiction to another	7. from one abstraction to another	

NOTE

Dante's apparent approval of Sigier's attitude, and hence of the Averroïst doctrine of the "two truths", has naturally been associated by Gilson and others with his own doctrine of the independence of the "two felicities". Both doctrines are, in fact, particular instances of a much wider theory, for which the Middle Ages had no generic name, but which we have since learned to call "the autonomy of techniques". Every art and science has its "proper truth", any violation of which, even upon the highest grounds, remains a violation of truth. Theological truth must, therefore, not be imposed upon art and science in such a manner as to falsify their proper truth.

The crisis that arose in the thirteenth century centred upon the question of how far it was consistent with the proper truth of philosophic method to elicit from the principles of Aristotle conclusions which could be arrived at only in the light of Judaeo-Christian revelation. The task of producing a "Christian philosophy" was undertaken by St. Thomas; and the brilliant ingenuity with which it was accomplished is set forth in Gilson's *Spirit of Mediaeval Philosophy*.[1] That without this fructifying Christian graft, the old Hellenic stock would have declined, and in Averroïst hands actually did decline, into sterility is true enough; nevertheless, the originality with which St. Thomas handled his material, and modified it in the handling, might perhaps warrant the complaint that what he was doing was "magnificent, but you must not call it Aristotle". *A fortiori*, there was every reason in the world for objecting to the dishonest and ostrich-like tactics of the University of Paris.

The political aspect of the matter loomed large in Dante's eyes, and still awaits solution. It is customary to dismiss the concluding paragraph of the *De Monarchia* as a clumsy and half-hearted attempt to appease authority, involving the virtual abandonment of the writer's whole position. But what Dante is saying is, *mutatis mutandis*, neither more nor less than what Maritain says of the relation between Art and Prudence: "[They] each claim dominion over every product of man's hands. From the point of view of poetic or, if you like, working values, Prudence is not competent. From the point of view of human values

---

[1] Etienne Gilson: *The Spirit of Mediaeval Philosophy* (Eng. trans., 2nd ed., Sheed & Ward, 1950). Note particularly the passages dealing with the concept of creation *ex nihilo*, and the distinction between essence and existence.

and the position of the free act, to which everything with regard to the subject is subordinate, there is no limitation upon its rights to govern."[1]

If, however, the *De Monarchia* were Dante's last word on the subject, there would be some truth in the contention that he envisaged a complete emancipation of philosophy from faith, and the establishment of a totally secularist monarchy—whether or not he fully realised the logical consequences of his own doctrine. In his recently published Cardinal Mercier Lectures, Professor Gilson (dealing only with the *De Monarchia*) convicts Dante of two errors. The first is to have supposed "that natural reason was capable, alone and in its own power, of bringing about a common agreement among men upon the truth of one and the same philosophy". As to this, M. Gilson asks: "Is it certain that the triumph of Aristotle in the middle ages was purely philosophical and rational, and that faith and theology had nothing to do with it? . . . It was the theologians who exhorted [candidates for monarchy] to govern the world according to the principles of the Stagirite. . . . With that ingratitude which men so often display towards the Faith, Dante's philosophy relied on what it owed to the Christian revelation to justify its intention of dispensing with revelation in future." The second error (he says) is graver: "St. Thomas had repeatedly said that the end of man was twofold (*finis duplex*); Dante repeatedly says that man has two ends (*fines duo*) . . . Dante [thus] ignored the fundamental principle that the hierarchic subordination of any inferior order, far from destroying its autonomy, establishes and perfects it, and, in short, ensures and maintains its integrity. Nature is all the more perfectly nature when it is informed by grace."[2]

It is precisely these two errors, already very much less evident in the *De Monarchia* than in the *Convivio*, that Dante has himself seen and rectified in the *Commedia*: that is why the Great Philosophers are relegated to Limbo; why Virgil is throughout "under orders" from Beatrice—an alien in Purgatory, and an exile from both Paradises; why the Earthly Paradise no longer represents "the felicity of this life", but the necessary point of departure in quest of any kind of felicity.[3]

---

[1] Jacques Maritain: *Art and Scholasticism* (Eng. trans., Sheed & Ward, 1939), p. 84.

[2] Etienne Gilson: *Les Métamorphoses de la Cité de Dieu* (Paris: Jean Vrin, 1952), pp. 150–152 (my translation).

[3] The development of Dante's thought in this connection, to which P. H. Wicksteed drew attention some thirty years ago (*From Vita Nuova to Paradiso*,

Nevertheless, when these errors have been eliminated, the problem of the "autonomy of techniques" remains, as Dante very well saw. The rise of Humanism in all its forms, with the consequent increasing secularisation of every branch of social and intellectual activity, leading to the disastrous dislocation and failure of communication from which we are suffering to-day, is sufficient proof that the mediaeval hierarchy of orders, however correct in theory, was imperfect in its practical working.

From the sixteenth to the nineteenth century, the problem became endemic throughout the West, not merely in politics, but even more acutely in connection with the autonomy of scientific techniques. Neither the condemnation of Galileo nor the theological polemic against the exponents of evolutionary theory argues very strongly in favour of ecclesiastical interference with the "proper truth" of scientific method; and the fact that, with the further development of experimental method, the alleged "quarrel" between science and faith has shown itself to be largely illusory suggests that in every case the apparent contradiction between the "two truths" will end by resolving itself, provided that the autonomy of both techniques is respected.

The cognate problem of the autonomy of art has never received the consideration which it merits. Collingwood [1] and Maritain are among the few modern philosophers who have given it serious attention; the latter's *Art and Scholasticism* (quoted above) should be carefully studied, in particular the chapters on "Christian Art" and "Art and Morality".[2]

The whole question is exceedingly intricate; its roots run deep and spread widely. Nothing is gained by lightly stigmatising as "quibbles" and "evasions" the disjunctive formulae proposed by those who, whether in the thirteenth or the twentieth century, have done their conscientious best to grapple with it.

Manchester, 1922), has been recently emphasised by A. P. d'Entrèves (*Dante as a Political Thinker*, Clarendon Press, 1952) and by Nancy Lenkeith (*Dante and the Legend of Rome*, Warburg Institute, London, 1952).

[1] R. G. Collingwood: *The Principles of Art* (Clarendon Press, 1938).

[2] See also his article "On Artistic Judgment" in *The Range of Reason* (Eng. trans., Geoffrey Bles, 1953).